Developing Web Components with Svelte

Building a Library of Reusable UI Components

Alex Libby

Apress®

Developing Web Components with Svelte: Building a Library of Reusable UI Components

Alex Libby
Belper, Derbyshire, UK

ISBN-13 (pbk): 978-1-4842-9038-5   ISBN-13 (electronic): 978-1-4842-9039-2
https://doi.org/10.1007/978-1-4842-9039-2

Managing Director, Apress Media LLC: Welmoed Spahr
Acquisitions Editor: James Robinson-Prior
Development Editor: James Markham
Coordinating Editor: Gryffin Winkler

Cover image designed by eStudioCalamar

Distributed to the book trade worldwide by Springer Science+Business Media New York, 1 New York Plaza, Suite 4600, New York, NY 10004-1562, USA. Phone 1-800-SPRINGER, fax (201) 348-4505, e-mail orders-ny@springer-sbm.com, or visit www.springeronline.com. Apress Media, LLC is a California LLC and the sole member (owner) is Springer Science + Business Media Finance Inc (SSBM Finance Inc). SSBM Finance Inc is a **Delaware** corporation.

For information on translations, please e-mail booktranslations@springernature.com; for reprint, paperback, or audio rights, please e-mail bookpermissions@springernature.com.

Apress titles may be purchased in bulk for academic, corporate, or promotional use. eBook versions and licenses are also available for most titles. For more information, reference our Print and eBook Bulk Sales web page at http://www.apress.com/bulk-sales.

Any source code or other supplementary material referenced by the author in this book is available to readers on GitHub via the book's product page, located at www.apress.com/. For more detailed information, please visit http://www.apress.com/source-code.

Printed on acid-free paper

This is dedicated to my family, with thanks for their love and support while writing this book.

Table of Contents

About the Author xi

Acknowledgments xiii

Introduction xv

Chapter 1: Getting Started 1

What Are Web Components? 2

Taking First Steps 4

  Breaking Apart the Code 5

Background to the Project 7

Our Approach and Strategy 8

Determining Our Needs 10

Setting Up the Project 11

  Understanding What Happened 13

Integrating a Playground 14

  Understanding What Happened 17

Summary 18

Chapter 2: Creating Basic Components 19

Creating the Input Field Component 20

  Breaking the Code Apart 22

  Hooking the Component into Storybook 23

  Understanding What Happened 27

  Adding Variants 29

Constructing the Checkbox Component...31

    Exploring the Code 34

    Adding Variations in Storybook...35

    Breaking the Code Apart...39

    Adapting for Radio Buttons...40

Constructing the Slider Component 43

    Adding the Component to Storybook...................................47

    Exploring the Code 50

Summary...51

Chapter 3: Building Action Components 53

Creating the SelectBox Component 53

    Understanding What Happened 56

    Adding the Component to Storybook...................................57

    Exploring the Code in Detail 60

Creating the Spinner Component..62

    Understanding What Happened 64

    Adding the Component to Storybook...................................65

    Breaking Apart the Code...68

    Creating Variants 68

Creating the Accordion Component 74

    Understanding What Happened 78

    Adding the Component to Storybook...................................79

    Reviewing the Code...82

Summary...83

Chapter 4: Building the Navigation Components 85

Creating the Breadcrumb Component 86

Understanding What Happened 89

Adding the Component to Storybook 90

Exploring the Code in Detail 95

Building a SideBar Component 95

Breaking Apart the Code 100

Adding the Component to Storybook 101

Understanding the Changes Made 106

Constructing the Tabs Component 107

Exploring the Code Changes 110

Accessibility – A Note 111

Hooking the Component into Storybook 111

Understanding the Changes Made 114

Creating a Variant 115

Summary 119

Chapter 5: Creating Notification Components 121

Creating the Alert Component 122

Sourcing the Icons 122

Building the Component 123

Adding the Component to Storybook 130

Creating a Variant 133

Creating the Dialog Component 136

Understanding What Happened 139

Adding to Storybook 139

Creating the Tooltip Component 143

Understanding What Happened 147

Adding the Component to Storybook...148

Creating a Variant 152

Summary...154

Chapter 6: Creating Grid Components 157

Determining the Approach 157

Building the Table Component 159

Understanding What Happened 160

Creating the Grid Component...161

Breaking Apart the Code...163

Creating the Cell Component 164

Understanding What Happened 166

Adding to Storybook 167

Adding a Variant..170

Understanding How It Works 172

Summary...173

Chapter 7: Writing Documentation 175

Setting the Scene...176

Adding Status Badges..178

Understanding What Happened 181

Updating Our Documentation – Our Approach 183

Writing Documentation for Basic Components 184

Breaking Apart the Changes...195

Updating Documentation for Action Components 196

Exploring the Changes Made..206

Summary...207

Chapter 8: Documenting More Components 209

Adding the Remaining Documentation 209

Adding Documentation for Notification Components.........................210

Exploring the Code Changes in Detail...219

Updating Documentation for Navigation Components.......................220

Breaking Apart the Code Changes...228

Updating Documentation for Grid Components................................230

Understanding What Changed 233

A Final Tidy-Up..234

Summary...235

Chapter 9: Testing Components...237

Setting Up the Testing Environment..237

Breaking Apart the Code Changes...240

Testing the Components 241

Writing Tests for Our Library..241

Exploring the Changes in Detail...249

Bundling the Components...250

Configuring the Build Process 250

Running the Build Process 255

Creating Demos in a Test Environment 261

Breaking Apart the Code...264

Testing with Other Frameworks 265

Understanding What Happened 267

Summary...268

Chapter 10: Deploying to Production 271

Performing Final Checks 271

Understanding the Deployment Process 273

Publishing to GitHub 274

    Setting Up a GitHub Pages Repository 275

    Uploading Components to GitHub 278

Releasing Components to npm 284

    Building a Demo 290

Publishing Storybook to Netlify 294

    Setting Up Netlify 296

Adding Polish to the Repository 300

    Adding a Custom Domain Name 300

    Breaking Apart the Code 307

Summary 308

Chapter 11: Taking Things Further 309

Reviewing the Site 309

Taking the Next Steps – Setting a Road Map 311

Converting Our Next Component 312

    Dissecting the Code 316

    Adding to Storybook 317

    Understanding the Changes Made 323

Remember That RadioButton Component? 325

    Adding to Storybook 329

    Breaking Apart the Code 332

Summary 334

Index 337

About the Author

Alex Libby is a front-end engineer and seasoned book author who hails from England. His passion for all things open source dates back to the days of his degree studies, where he first came across web development and has been hooked ever since. His daily work involves extensive use of React, Node.js, JavaScript, HTML, and CSS. Alex enjoys tinkering with different open source libraries to see how they work. He has spent a stint maintaining the jQuery Tools library and enjoys writing about open source technologies, principally for front-end UI development.

Acknowledgments

Writing a book can be a long but rewarding process; it is not possible to complete it without the help of other people. I would like to offer a huge vote of thanks to my editors – in particular, Shobana Srinivasan, Rami Morrar, Gryffin Winkler, and James Robinson-Prior; my thanks also to Tanner Dolby as my technical reviewer, James Markham for his help during the process, and others at Apress for getting this book into print. All have made writing this book a painless and enjoyable process, even with the edits!

My thanks also to my family for being understanding and supporting me while writing. I frequently spend a lot of late nights writing alone, or pass up times when I should be with them, so their words of encouragement and support have been a real help in getting past those bumps in the road and producing the finished book that you now hold in your hands.

Lastly, it is particularly poignant that the book was written at a time when the world is emerging from events of an unprecedented nature, where memories are still too raw. It was too easy to think about those who lost the greatest thing we as humans could ever have; life hasn't been easy for anyone. Having a project to work on, no matter how simple or complex it might be, has helped me get through those tough times and with the hope that we face a new, improved, and hopefully better future.

Introduction

Developing Web Components with Svelte is for people who want to learn how to quickly create web components that are efficient and fast using the upcoming Svelte framework and associated tools.

This project-oriented book simplifies the setting up of a Svelte component library as a starting point before beginning to explore the benefits of using Svelte to create components not only usable in this framework but equally reusable in others such as React, Vue, and Angular. We can use this as a basis for developing an offer that we can customize to our needs, across multiple frameworks. It will equip you with a starting toolset that you can use to create future component libraries, incorporate the processes into your workflow, and that will allow you to take your components to the next level.

Throughout this book, I'll take you on a journey through creating the base library, before adding a variety of components such as a select box, tabs, and the typical tooltip components. We will also touch on subjects such as writing documentation, testing components, and deploying into production – showing you how easy it is to develop simple components that we can augment later quickly. With the minimum of fuss and plenty of practical exercises, we'll focus on topics such as building the functionality, styling, testing in a self-contained environment, and more – right through to producing the final result viewable from any browser!

Developing Web Components with Svelte uses nothing more than standard JavaScript, CSS, and HTML, three of the most powerful tools available for developers: you can enhance, extend, and configure your components as requirements dictate. With Svelte, the art of possible is only limited by the extent of your imagination and the power of JavaScript, HTML, and Node.js.

CHAPTER 1

Getting Started

Let's suppose for a moment that you've spent any time developing with frameworks such as React. In that case, I'm sure you will have come across the principle of creating web components – these self-contained, reusable packages of code that we can drop into any number of projects, with only minor tweaks needed to configure the package for use in your project. Sound familiar?

What if you found yourself creating multiple components and were beginning to reuse them across multiple projects? We could use them individually, but that wouldn't be the most effective way – instead, why not create a component library?

Creating such a library opens up some real possibilities – we could build our library around standard components that everyone uses or focus on a select few that follow a theme, such as forms. At this point, you're probably assuming that we'd do something in React, right?

Wrong. Anyone who knows me knows that I like to keep things simple – while there is nothing technically wrong with React (it's a great framework), I want to do something different.

We're going to build such a component library for this book, but the framework I've elected to use is a relatively new kid on the block – Svelte.

There are many reasons for doing this, but performance is the most important one – Svelte's architecture is different from most frameworks, making it super-fast than many of its rivals. Throughout this book, we'll

© Alex Libby 2023
A. Libby, *Developing Web Components with Svelte*,
https://doi.org/10.1007/978-1-4842-9039-2_1

explore how to write web components using Svelte, learn how to bring them together in a unified library, and explore the steps required to release them to the world at large with minimal effort.

In time-honored tradition, we must start somewhere – there's no better place than to kick off with a look at what we will create through this book, set some boundaries, and get some of the tools and resources ready for use. Before we do so (and get anyone up to speed, who hasn't used web components), let's first answer this question.

What Are Web Components?

To answer this question, we have to go back ten years to Fronteers Conference in 2011, where web components were first introduced to developers.

There are many ways to describe what a web component is, but I like the definition given by Riccardo Canella in his article on the Medium website, where he states that

> *"...Web components are a set of web platform APIs that allow you to create new custom, reusable, encapsulated HTML tags to use in web pages and web apps."*

This definition is just a small part of what they are – in addition, it's essential to know that they

- Are based on web standards and will work across modern browsers

- Can be used with any JavaScript-based framework

Wow – that's powerful stuff! Gone are the days when we had to use a React component in a React-based site, or likewise for Angular. Just imagine: we could build a component in Svelte and then use it in different frameworks – as long as they are based on JavaScript.

There is one question, though, that I bet some of you are asking: Why choose Svelte? It's a valid question, as Svelte is not so well known as other frameworks such as React.

However, there are three reasons for choosing this framework:

- It's a fair bet that many of you use React in some capacity; we could develop a web component in React, but we would be missing out on one key factor: interoperability. We need to build the component in a different framework, such as Svelte.

- Svelte's architecture pushes the compilation into the build process, avoiding the need for a runtime library when operated in a browser (unlike its competitors such as React). It means the end code is super-fast – it doesn't have the overhead of that library, plus compiled code is as close as you will get to pure HTML, CSS, and JavaScript. It helps that Svelte's developers decided not to try to reinvent the wheel – if JavaScript already has a perfectly adequate solution, then Svelte uses this instead of trying to add a custom equivalent!

- This lightweight architecture also means that any core dependencies will be minimal compared to frameworks such as React. Any that we need will be just those required to operate the framework – it does not include any extra dependencies for operations such as manipulating date or time.

Okay – enough talk: let's crack on with something a little more practical! Before we get into the nuts and bolts of building our library, let's first have a quick peek at a small example I've put together to see how a Svelte-based web component works in more detail.

Taking First Steps

For the first demo, I've reworked an example by Simon O. available from GitHub – you can see the original version at `https://github.com/FroyoNom/Svelte-Weather-Forecast`. My version is cut down to only display the current weather, hardcodes the location to New York (Apress' office!), and uses the `luxon` date library instead to provide the current date.

RUNNING A DEMO COMPONENT

To run the weather component demo, follow these steps:

1. First, we need to get a key from OpenWeatherMap.org – head over to `https://home.openweathermap.org/users/sign_up`, and sign up with the correct details (it's a free service, although I would recommend a webmail address such as Gmail!). Make sure you store the key in a safe place, as we will need it later in this exercise.

2. Next, go ahead and download the archive file from the code download that accompanies this book – extract the contents to a new folder, **not your project folder**.

3. Once extracted, open the .env file at the root of the folder you created in step 2, then add your API key from step 1, as indicated in the file.

4. Fire up a Node.js terminal session, then change the working folder to that separate folder from the previous step.

5. At the prompt, enter `npm install` to install the demo, and press `Enter`.

6. Once done, enter npm run dev at the prompt, and press Enter to run the application. We should see a weather component displayed on the page if all is well, as shown in Figure 1-1.

Figure 1-1. *The OpenWeatherMap component demo*

I designed that demo to be a quick and easy start, although, in reality, it hides a lot of code under the covers. At face value, it would be difficult to tell if this had been written using Svelte – don't worry, it has!

To prove this is the case, crack open a copy of the weather-app folder from the code download, then look at the contents in your text editor. Don't worry if you don't understand it all – it's more important at this stage to get a feel for how a Svelte component is structured. We'll go through it in more detail when we start creating components in the next chapter.

Spend a few moments reviewing it, then let's dive into a more detailed breakdown of the code before continuing with the rest of this chapter.

Breaking Apart the Code

At first glance, you might be a little bewildered by some of the code in the example – what does it all do? There is quite a bit of code used, but we only need to be concerned with what's in the src folder at this stage.

We went through the usual steps of downloading, extracting, and firing up the demo in localhost, using standard Node commands to get the demo running.

What makes our demo tick, though, is the code within the `src` folder – there are other files and folders present, but we will come back to these later in the book. The `src` folder is where we store all of the core component code – ours has `lib` and `assets` folders, as well as `vite-env.d.ts` and `App.svelte`. The `lib` folder holds the code for each component – in this example, we have two, `Date.svelte` and `Current.svelte`.

Although Svelte comes with two files that act as a starting page for a Svelte site (`main.js, in the \src folder,` and the index.html file at root), it's only the former we will really need to use. The plan for our library is to display each component using Markdown files in a Storybook installation, but to also use the index.html file to demonstrate how we might reference each component outside of a Svelte environment. Don't worry too much about the specifics of how we will do this – we will go through everything in detail over the course of this book! For now, it's important to know where our components will be stored, and that we have two ways to display them in our environment.

There are other files and folders that we will use throughout this book – some you will recognize, such as `package.json`. Others may not be so familiar; we will go through examples throughout this book.

Okay – let's move on: now that we've created a demo component, it's time we got stuck into the star attraction for this book: our component library!

Throughout this book, we'll create the basis for our component and then flesh it out with a selection of components. There is plenty we could choose from – indeed, space constraints mean we can't add them all! The key is that we'll learn how to structure our library, add components, test them, and generally make sure we have something worthwhile toward the end of the book.

Let's start first with the background to this project, so we can set the scene and understand what's coming up later in the book.

Background to the Project

So – where do we begin? Let me introduce you to what we will be creating: the Cobalt UI library.

This UI library will contain a mix of components – all of these you will find in use on many websites, particularly e-commerce ones! The great thing about creating a component library is that you can pick and choose which components to add; if people don't like one or are not using it, we can always deprecate and remove it from the library.

Hopefully, that won't be the case with the ones I've chosen – I've listed them in Table 1-1.

Table 1-1. *List of components for our Cobalt UI library*

Category	Components
Basic Components	Input box and variations, such as email or password fields
	Checkbox
	Radio *(we'll cover this one as an adaptation of the Checkbox component)*
	Slider
Action Components	SelectBox
	Accordion
	Spinner
Navigation Components	Breadcrumbs
	SideBar (and Hamburger)
	Tabs
Notification Components	Dialog boxes (such as error, info, warn)
	Alert
	Tooltip
Grid Components	Grid (Row and Column)

If you're wondering about the name – it came from an interest I have in precious stones and a trip to a gemstone museum in Prague a few years ago. They had an incredible array of garnets on display (which is the national gemstone for the Czech Republic), but as a name, I'm not sure it works so well, hence using Cobalt instead!

Okay – let's crack on: now that we've decided what we will include in our library, let's turn our attention to strategy. What approach will we take? It's time to decide on some of the tools we will use and our approach for each component.

Our Approach and Strategy

As with any project, it's crucial to have a strategy – we need to decide where (and how) to take the project. Otherwise, it could quickly become a disorganized mess!

We could take this project in many different directions; for now, we will focus on simplicity (mainly as space constraints mean creating something feature rich and complex in the space of a book would be difficult). With this in mind, I've outlined the approach we will take for this project:

- We'll be creating a minimum viable product or MVP approach – this will be enough to get something started and published, but we can then add to it later.

- I've elected to use GitHub and GitHub Pages for hosting; this is primarily as I already have several repositories, so using GitHub will help keep things simple. Feel free to use an alternative such as Bitbucket or GitLab – both operate similarly to GitHub.

- An essential theme for this project will be to keep things simple, at least for now – I would love to create something complex and full of features, but I won't be able to do it justice in this book! For us, it's more important to get the groundwork in place and running first; it will mean that some features we might want are not present initially (such as using vanilla JavaScript rather than TypeScript or excluding some properties for a component). We can always develop and refine the library later, once the basis is operational.

- For each component, we'll work on developing code first. Once done, we'll then style it before hooking it into an instance of Storybook as our demonstration tool. Tests for each component will come later, once we have built all of the components, in Chapter 8.

- For this library, I've elected to use the Cypress testing suite as a personal choice – there are others out there, such as testing-library or Jest, which work equally well. You may have a testing tool you already use, so feel free to use that instead; the critical point is testing our new components, not which tool to use!

Okay – I think that's enough for now: let's move on! The next task is to determine what we need in terms of accounts, tools, and the like. As a developer, you may already have some of these tools installed; feel free to use them, or use alternatives if you prefer! That aside, let's take a look at the list in more detail.

Determining Our Needs

Before we can get stuck in setting up Svelte and begin building our library, we need to determine which tools we will use for our project. In a sense, we need to do a little housekeeping – I loathe housekeeping, but hey: needs must, as they say!

This list will cover everything needed: I will assume that you will use the tools outlined in the list for this book. If you already have something installed, feel free to skip the requirement or use an alternative solution.

Leaving that aside, let's cover which tools we need to have, alongside the usual requirements such as Internet access and a decent text editor:

- The first requirement is Node.js (and NPM) – we will use this to structure our Svelte project and turn code into components. Please download and install the version appropriate for your platform: default settings will suffice for this project.

- We also need an account at GitHub and a valid email address – we use the latter to validate your account. Once registered, we will use it to set up two repositories – one for the code and another for documentation.

- To publish the component on NPM, we will also need an account – you can sign up for one at `www.npmjs.com/signup` if you don't already have one.

- A project folder on your PC or laptop – for this book, I will assume you are using one called cobalt, and it is at the root of your C: drive. If you want to use something different, please adjust it to suit as you work through each exercise.

This list should be enough to get us started – anything else we can download, or I will give you directions at the appropriate time. Let's crack on now with the bit I know you're waiting for: installing Svelte and getting our library set up.

Setting Up the Project

The first task in building our library is to get Svelte installed – assuming you have Node.js installed, we can use NPM to download and install the framework. Let's look at the steps involved in more detail as part of the next exercise.

INSTALLING SVELTE

To get the basis for our library set up, follow these steps:

1. First, crack open a Node.js terminal session, then change to the root of your C: drive.

2. At the prompt, go ahead and enter `npm create vite@ latest cobalt -- --template svelte`, then press Enter.

3. You will first see this question – when prompted, press y to respond:

   ```
   Need to install the following packages:
     vite@latest
   Ok to proceed? (y)
   ```

4. Svelte will now install – after a few moments, it will prompt us to run these commands; go ahead and enter each in turn, pressing Enter after each:

```
cd cobalt
npm install
npm run dev
```

5. When prompted, fire up your browser and navigate to
    `http://localhost:5173` – if all is well, we should see the
    demo site running in our browser, as shown in Figure 1-2.

count is 0

Check out SvelteKit, the official Svelte app framework powered by Vite!

Click on the Vite and Svelte logos to learn more

Figure 1-2. *Our Svelte demo site running*

6. Browse to the `cobalt` folder in your file manager – if all is well,
    we should see something akin to the (partial) extract shown in
    Figure 1-3.

node_modules

public

src

.gitignore

index.html

jsconfig.json

package.json

package-lock.json

README.md

vite.config.js

Figure 1-3. *The initial file listing for our component library*

Excellent – we now have a basis for building our component library!

Although installing Svelte is pretty straightforward in itself, it's worth exploring what we achieved in the last demo. With that in mind, let's take a moment to review the changes we made in more detail.

Understanding What Happened

One of the great things about using Svelte is how easy it is to set up a starting site – everything is done using NPM, a tool many developers will have already used in their projects, so many commands will look familiar. The only oddity is that while we created a Svelte site, we downloaded Vite – what is all that about?

Vite is the bundling tool used by Svelte to package code ready for deployment – we ran the npm create command to create what is effectively a Vite site, but we use a template to format it as a Svelte site. It's worth noting that as part of running this command, we had to download Vite – this is a one-off; we won't be prompted if we create more Svelte sites.

Once the download had been completed, we then changed into the cobalt folder and ran a typical npm install command to set up dependencies. With that done, we then fired up the Svelte development server, before browsing the results in our browser. We still have a long way to go, but this last step helps confirm we at least have a solid basis in place, ready for building our project!

Okay – let's move on to our next task. We will, of course, be building components throughout this book, but – how are we going to display them? We need the means to show them off to potential users to see how they look and assess if they will suit their requirements.

The best way to do this is to use a tool called Storybook – it's available for download from `https://storybook.js.org/` and works with various frameworks, including Svelte. Let's set up an instance as part of our next demo.

Integrating a Playground

If you've spent any time developing code – particularly with frameworks such as React – you may well have come across Storybook.

For the uninitiated, it's an excellent tool for showcasing any components we developers write – the tool supports a wide range of frameworks, including Svelte. We'll be using it in our project to showcase the components we create for our library – let's dive in and explore how to set it up as part of our next exercise.

SETTING UP STORYBOOK

To set up Storybook for our Svelte project, follow these steps:

1. First, crack open a Node.js terminal session, then change the working folder to our project area.

2. At the prompt, enter `npx sb init --builder @storybook/builder-vite` and press Enter to install Storybook.

3. If prompted, press y to proceed (we're using npx to download and install, so it needs confirmation to proceed with the download).

4. Once installed, Storybook will preconfigure support automatically.

If Storybook fails to detect Svelte, choose yes and use the arrow keys to go down to svelte, then press Enter to select. Storybook will manually add support for Svelte.

---

5. Although we have installed Storybook, if we try to run it, it will fail with an ugly error:

    ```
    ERR! Error [ERR_REQUIRE_ESM]: require() of ES Module
    C:\cobalt\.storybook\main.js from
    C:\cobalt\node_modules\@storybook\core-common\dist\cjs\
    utils\interpret-require.js not supported.
    ```

To fix it, we have to make a change – first, change the line `"type": "module"`, to `"type": "commonjs"`, in `package.json`.

6. There are a couple more changes we have to make – the first is to tell Svelte that we're creating custom web components. Crack open `vite.config.js` at the root of our project folder, then update the code within as highlighted:

```
export default defineConfig({
  plugins: [svelte()],
  compilerOptions: {
    customElement: true
  }
}).
```

7. Next, we need to make one more change to the `main.js` file. Go ahead and rename it to `main.cjs` – this turns it into a CommonJS module, as Storybook has issues running the ESM modules used by Svelte.

8. With those updates out of the way, we can now execute `npm run storybook` to launch our instance of Storybook. If all is well, we should see it appear, as shown in the extract in Figure 1-4.

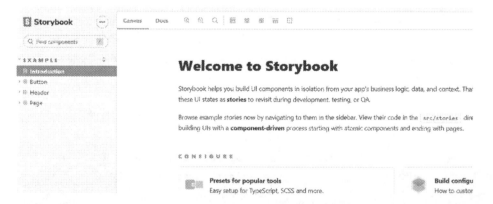

Figure 1-4. *Storybook successfully launched*

We have one last update to do: delete the `./stories` folder. This folder is the Storybook examples folder, which we don't need for our project.

Great – we now have Storybook in place, ready for us to start adding components! It is a perfect medium to show off the components we create throughout this book; while installing Storybook is effectively a one-liner, it's essential to make sure it installs the proper support for your project!

With that in mind, let's dive in and explore the changes we made in the last exercise in more detail to see how Storybook fits into the bigger picture of our component library.

Understanding What Happened

So – what did we achieve in the last demo?

We started by running the `npx sb init` command to download and set up Storybook; this set up both the application and support for Svelte automatically. While Storybook supports a wide range of frameworks, the developers have focused on automating detection for the chosen framework as part of the installation.

The key to making that automation work lies in detecting the presence of the correct configuration file – in our case, `vite.config.js`. To make sure it works, it's best to let Storybook install itself into a folder at the root level – if you browse the file structure, you will see it has created a folder called .storybook. If we hadn't, then the automated step could fail, and we might end up installing Storybook manually into the wrong folder, or not at all!

The next part was a little more complex – Svelte is still a relatively new framework, so we may encounter a hiccup or two. The error message we had back in step 5 was caused by Svelte set to use ESM-required syntax, which is not supported in Storybook.

In this instance, it was easy to fix the problem – we had to alter the property type in our `package.json` file. Once we fixed that incompatibility issue, we removed the demo stories that come with Storybook. We don't need these files for the final library, so removing them keeps the setup tidy. We then rounded out the demo by running the command to launch Storybook, so we could confirm it launched without issue.

17

Summary

We can see creating components and a library as something of a rollercoaster – there will be highs and lows, successes, and challenges to deal with, as we begin to develop what will become our final library. Over these last few pages, we've started to look at our project's background and get ourselves ready to create the component library – let's take a moment to review what we have learned before beginning the real development work.

We started with a quick demo of a Svelte component that I had adapted – this was to get a feel for typical code and how one would run. We then moved on to discussing the background of our project, before defining the approach and strategy we would take, along with what we would need.

We finished by setting up the initial framework ready for use, before finishing with integrating an instance of Storybook, ready for displaying our components.

Excellent – we have our initial structure in place, along with confirmed requirements: it's time we began the real development! We'll start with something simple first: creating the basic components, which we will do in the next chapter.

CHAPTER 2

Creating Basic Components

With our initial project set up, it's time to start creating and adding components!

For this (and the next few chapters), we will build some sample components ready for inclusion in our library. We could have chosen to include any one of dozens of different components, but to keep things simple, I've decided to pick three to start with: Input box, Checkbox, and Slider.

For each component, I've made a few assumptions in terms of how we will develop these components:

- Use HTML5 tags where possible.

- Aim to use an MVP approach: features will be missing, but that will come later.

- Take the approach of developing components, then adding styles, and finally linking into Storybook.

- Add variants where possible and start documentation (which we can improve over time).

Keeping this approach in mind, let's start with the first addition to our library, which is creating the Input field component.

© Alex Libby 2023
A. Libby, *Developing Web Components with Svelte*,
https://doi.org/10.1007/978-1-4842-9039-2_2

Creating the Input Field Component

We will start with something simple for our first component – the ubiquitous input field! You will, of course, see this versatile component anywhere: it might be as a text box on one website but configured to accept only email addresses or telephone numbers on other sites.

We'll keep things simple and start with implementing a plain text field for now but talk about more ideas later when we hook the component into Storybook.

BUILDING THE INPUT COMPONENT

To build our Input component, follow these steps:

1. First, go ahead and create a new folder called `lib` under the `src` folder.

2. Next, crack open a new file in your text editor, then add this code – there is a good chunk, so we'll add it section by section, starting with a Svelte directive to convert it into a web component:

   ```
   <svelte:options tag="cobalt-input" />
   ```

3. Leave the next line blank, then add this script block – this sets up some export declarations, along with an onInput event handler:

   ```
   <script>
       export let label = "Label:";
       export let placeholder = "";
       export let fieldType = "text";
       export let disabled = false;
       export let inputName = "";
       export let fieldID = "";
   ```

```
function onInput(event) {
  event.target.dispatchEvent(new CustomEvent("oninput",
  { composed: true }));
}
</script>
```

4. Once added, skip a line, then add in this markup – this will form the basis of our component:

```
<div class="cobalt">
  {#if label}
    <label for={fieldID}>{label}</label>
  {/if}
  <input type={fieldType}
     id={fieldID}
     name={inputName}
     placeholder={placeholder}
     disabled={disabled}
     on:input = {onInput}
     {...$$props}
  >
</div>
```

5. Miss a line after the closing `</div>` tag, then add this styling code:

```
<style>
  .cobalt { display: flex; flex-direction: row;
    font-family: Arial, Helvetica, sans-serif;
  }

  input[type="text"] { width: 200px; border-radius: 4px;
  border-color: #19247c; height: 30px; outline: none; }

  input[type="email"] { width: 200px; border-radius: 4px;
  border-color: #19247c; height: 30px; outline: none; }
```

```
    label { padding-right: 10px; display: flex; align-self:
    center; }
</style>
```

6. Save the file as `Input.svelte` in the Input folder.

We now have an Input component in place – most of it will look familiar as it is (in the main) standard HTML markup. However, there are a few exciting features in this code we should cover, so before we get stuck into testing our new component, let's look at the code in more detail.

Breaking the Code Apart

For this exercise, our first task was to create the initial folder structure – it might seem a little convoluted, but this is so we can take advantage of a feature unique to Svelte. We touched on this back in Chapter 1 – if we ever need to reference the `lib` folder, we can use a special `$lib` path alias, and Svelte will automatically find the folder.

Next up, we switched to creating the core component – we started with adding exports for various values such as `fieldType` or `onInput`. This export keyword makes each value available elsewhere, which will be ideal for when we test each component later in Storybook.

In the declarations at the top of `Input.svelte`, you will see that we've provided some values – Svelte will use these by default if no values are passed into the component when calling it in code.

The final task for this exercise was to add the markup that will form the basis for the Input component (plus the styles we will use for our component) – we based it on typical markup for a text input field but adapted it to reference each exported field. There are two exceptions: `on:input` and the `{...$$props}` spread operator.

The former (`on:input`) is Svelte's equivalent of a standard oninput change handler; it works in the same way as plain JavaScript, but the syntax looks slightly different!

It's worth noting that you don't always need to put the callback for the `on:input`; changing `on:input={on:input}` may also work just as well. If you use this route here, you should also remove the export declaration for `onInput` too. The same principle applies for other components we create later in the book, such as Checkbox.

We also have the {`...$$props`} operator – this tells Svelte to pass all remaining prop values into the component. If you've worked with the likes of React, then you will likely be familiar with {`...props`} – it works in the same manner.

Okay – let's move on: next up, we need to test our component. We will use the Storybook instance we set up in the previous chapter, and it's a perfect way to test the original component and add variants – let's dive in and take a look in more detail.

Hooking the Component into Storybook

As tools go, Storybook is an immensely versatile piece of kit. It supports various frameworks, such as React or Angular, and can also accept content in several formats (e.g., JavaScript or Markdown).

We should be aware of one thing, though, which is our use of Svelte. Although we are strictly speaking using SvelteKit (and not Svelte itself), Storybook support is not quite as mature as other frameworks! Therefore, it's important to note that although Svelte itself is supported, you may find documentation for SvelteKit to not be quite as complete. Some of the options available for the former don't work so well for SvelteKit.

Don't worry, though – Storybook is still perfectly stable and usable for our needs: we will use Svelte-formatted files to create the Storybook effect and Markdown content for documentation. It might seem a little confusing for now, but bear with me – it will all become apparent in the next exercise.

ADDING TO STORYBOOK

To set up the component in the Storybook instance, follow these steps:

1. First, crack open a new file in your text editor – save it as `Input.stories.mdx` in the Input folder from the previous exercise.

2. Next, go ahead and add this code – we'll break it into sections, starting with three `import` statements:

    ```
    import Input from "./Input.svelte";
    import InputDocs from "./InputDocs.mdx";
    import {
        Meta, Story } from '@storybook/addon-docs';
    ```

3. We can now add a page title, so Storybook knows how to display our component – for this, leave a line blank, then add this Meta tag:

    ```
    <Meta
        title = "Cobalt UI Library/Basic Components/Input"
        component={Input}
        parameters={{page: null}}
    />
    ```

The `parameters` entry here hides the **default** page that shows, ready for us to add a custom one later in this demo.

4. In order to render any component in Storybook, we need to specify a template. We could use different versions for each component, but for now, we'll use this one to keep things simple:

```
export const Template = (args) => ({
  Component: Input,
  props: args,
});
```

5. With a template in place, we can now display our component. Go ahead and add this Story block:

```
<Story name="Default"
  args = {{
    placeholder: "example text",
    label: "Text:",
  }}
  parameters={{
    docs: {
      page: InputDocs,
    },
  }}>
  {Template.bind({})}
</Story>
```

6. We have one more part to add before viewing the results – documentation. Go ahead and create a folder at the root of the lib folder – call this new folder storybook.

7. You will notice in the previous step, we call InputDocs, having imported it at the top of the file – extract a copy of InputDocs.mdx from the code download and drop it into the storybook folder.

25

It contains some rudimentary documentation in Markdown format –
we'll talk more about this when we review the code.

8. Save and close the file. Next, switch to your Node.js terminal
   session, then set the working folder to our `cobalt` project area.

9. At the prompt, enter `npm run storybook` and hit Enter – if
   all is well, we should see Storybook launch and display in our
   browser at `http://localhost:6006/`. Click on the Input
   link on the left to display the Default variant we just created, as
   shown in Figure 2-1.

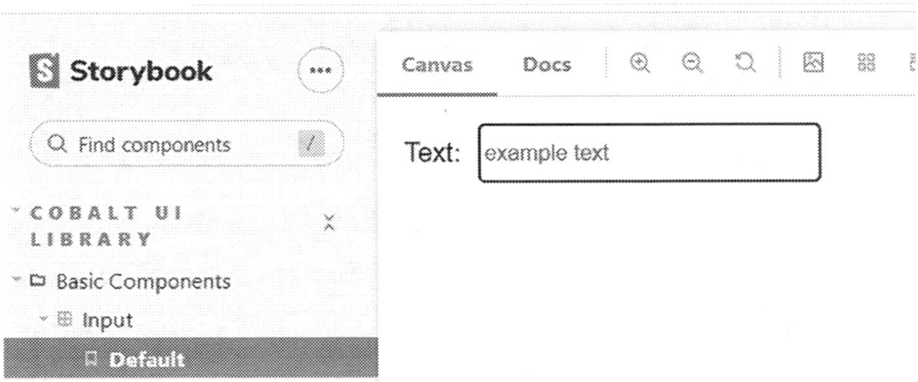

Figure 2-1. *Displaying the Input component in Storybook*

Just a heads-up – you will notice that although I've specified
`http://localhost:6006` as the URL, it does redirect on loading –
this is perfectly normal; it's easier to use the short form in text!

10. Now click on the Docs link at the top of the page, just above our component – if all is well, we should see an extract of the documentation appear, as in Figure 2-2.

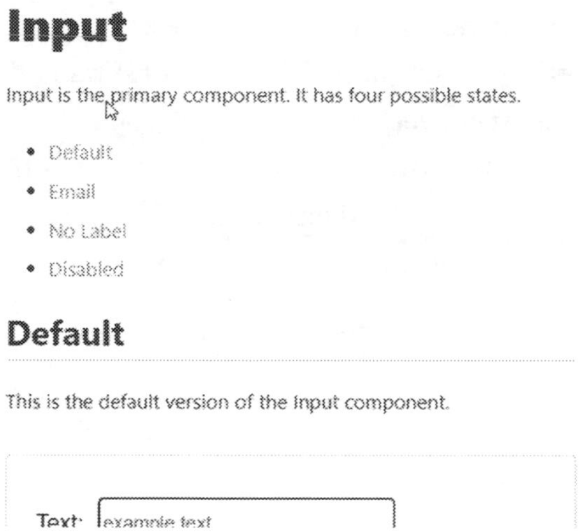

Input

Input is the primary component. It has four possible states.

- Default
- Email
- No Label
- Disabled

Default

This is the default version of the Input component.

Text: example text

Figure 2-2. An extract of documentation for the Input component

Excellent – things are starting to take shape now! We now have the first of many components set up in Storybook: it might be a simple one, but that doesn't matter! The critical point here is that we have a sound basis for building and developing our components.

In the meantime, now would be an excellent opportunity to review the code changes we have made so far. We've already talked about the core component, but we've covered some valuable features in the Storybook implementation, so let's take some time to review the code in more detail.

Understanding What Happened

Cast your mind back to the beginning of the previous exercise, where I mentioned that we would use Markdown for our documentation.

In that last exercise, we added a copy of the documentation file directly from the code download – you might be surprised to see that what we've used is not a strict Markdown syntax but more of a Storybook-flavored version. As we are using Svelte, this is the best way to get both documentation and code examples into the same document. We can use a JavaScript format, but it's a little more limiting since we can't show code samples in the documentation (at least not yet).

Leaving that aside, let's dive into the `InputDocs.mdx` file that we extracted from the code download and look at some of the contents. We start with a simple import from the Storybook package:

```
import { Story, Preview } from '@storybook/addon-docs/blocks';
```

We then have our title formatted by the use of a single # mark, as per standard Markdown syntax:

```
# Input
```

```
This file is a documentation-only "MDX" file to customize
Storybook's [DocsPage](https://storybook.js.org/docs/react/
writing-docs/docs-page#replacing-docspage).
```

We mainly use Markdown throughout the document, with entries such as the links and H2 tag in this block. For example:

```
## Input
```

```
Button is the primary component. It has four possible states.
```

```
- [Text](#text)
```

Things get a little more interesting in this next block, where we implement `<Preview>` tags. It tells Storybook to create a code extract using the ID of the Default example:

```
### Text

This is text for our text input field component

<!-- the IDs can be retrieved from the URL when opening a
story -->
<Preview>
  <Story id="cobalt-ui-library-basic-components-input--
  default" />
</Preview>
```

The simplest way to get the ID is to take the full URL of the Storybook page with the instance of our component – in our case, it was `http://localhost:6006/?path=/docs/`**`cobalt-ui-library-basic-components-input--default`**. Simply keep the part highlighted, and drop the rest – you now have the ID.

Hopefully, this now makes sense! In summary, we use the Svelte(Kit) format for rendering the component in the Canvas tab of our Storybook page and add any documentation in Markdown format, with an appropriate link to the file from the parameters block within each story.

Okay – we've almost finished with this component, but there is one more task we should take a look at: How can we add a variant for our component?

Adding Variants

It is something you will hear about when creating component libraries such as ours and which highlights the importance of good planning: variants. So what are they?

They are just variations on a theme – we can use elements such as Input fields for plain text, email addresses, or even choosing colors! The trick here is to understand what each element can support and make sure we have sufficient properties to support that variation. For example, if we wanted to add email support to our component, we might create something like this in Storybook:

```
<Story name="Email"
  args={{
    placeholder: 'email@example.com',
    label: 'Email:',
    fieldType: 'email',
    onInput: () => alert('this is an email field')
  }}
  parameters={{
    docs: {
      page: InputDocs
    },
  }}>
{Template.bind({})} />
```

Notice that I've highlighted several fields which we would need to change? We don't need to add any new properties; we can just pass different values via the existing properties.

With this in mind, think about how we might add new stories for not showing a label or disabling the component. How might we change the story values? To give you a head start, here are a couple of hints:

- We only need to add one new property; all others do not need to change.

- The documentation parameters don't need to be changed – they will still point to the same file, no matter which variant we use.

Check out the `Input.stories.mdx` file in the code download for the answers if you are stuck!

Okay – time to move on; let's turn our attention to creating our next component: the humble checkbox. It's a component that features everywhere, on millions of forms and pages all over the Internet; it's straightforward to construct something as a starting point for future development.

Constructing the Checkbox Component

We've made good progress so far – it might seem like we've covered a lot for a simple Input field component, but don't worry: things will get easier as we go through the next few components.

For this next tool in this chapter, we will use the same principles as before to help keep things simple and prepare the base for future development. First, let's start setting up the core component, ready for deployment into Storybook.

BUILDING THE BUTTON COMPONENT

Adding a checkbox component is easy to do – we can use similar techniques to the Input component we created earlier in this chapter. To do so, follow these steps:

1. First, create a folder called `Checkbox` under the `components` folder.

2. Next, crack open your text editor, and create a new file called `Checkbox.svelte`. Add the following code to this file, beginning with the `<script>` block, to import a stylesheet and define some exported variables:

```
<svelte:options tag="cobalt-checkbox" />

<script>
  export let checked = true;
  export let label = "This is a default checkbox";
  export let disabled = false;

  function onChange(event) {
    event.target.dispatchEvent(new
CustomEvent("onchange", { composed: true }));
  }

  $: checked = checked !== false;
</script>
```

3.   We can now add in the markup that will form the basis of our component – for this, add this code below the `<script>` block, missing a line first:

```
<div class="cobalt">
  <input
    type="checkbox"
    id="name"
    {checked}
    {disabled}
    on:change = {onChange}
    {...$$props}
  />
  <label for="name">
    {label}
  </label>
</div>
```

4. There is one last step for us to complete, which is to add some styling. Leave a line blank after the closing </label> tag, then add this block of code:

```
<style>
  .cobalt {
    display: flex;
    align-items: center;
    font-family: Arial, Helvetica, sans-serif;
  }

  input[type="checkbox"] {
    -webkit-appearance: none;
    appearance: none;
    margin: 0;
    font: inherit;
    color: currentColor;
    width: 18px;
    height: 18px;
    border: 2px solid currentColor;
    border-radius: 2px;
    transform: translateY(-1px);
    display: grid;
    place-content: center;
  }
  input[type="checkbox"]::before {
    content: "";
    width: 10px;
    height: 10px;
    clip-path: polygon(14% 44%, 0 65%, 50% 100%, 100%
    16%, 80% 0%, 43% 62%);
    transform: scale(0);
    transform-origin: bottom left;
    transition: 120ms transform ease-in-out;
```

```
      box-shadow: inset 16px 16px #6666ff;
    }

    input[type="checkbox"]:checked::before {
      transform: scale(1);
    }

    input[type="checkbox"]:disabled {
      color: #959495;
      cursor: not-allowed;
    }

    label {
      margin-left: 5px;
    }
  </style>
```

5. Save the file and close it – the component is now in place.

We now have a component in place, ready to test – granted, it's not a complex one, but the key here is to focus on creating the basis for something we can then develop over time. In the meantime, let's pause for a moment to review the code we added in the last demo – you will see some similarities to the previous component, but it's worth reiterating through them as practice!

Exploring the Code

The first task was to create a folder for our new component – inside this, we added Checkbox.svelte, which contains the code for our component. We added an import for the stylesheet, followed by exports for several variables, including checked and label, which we make available for consumption in code, such as in Storybook.

We then added the HTML markup for the component before switching to extracting a copy of the stylesheet from the code download and adding it to our component folder.

Although our code uses the same format as the previous component, there are three things I want to highlight: the order of properties, the use of on:change, and the use of the {...$$props} spread operator.

I'm a great believer in keeping consistency when it comes to coding – not only is using a proper naming convention worthwhile but keeping the same order of values is equally important. It keeps things tidier and makes it easier to trace issues if you have random values being passed between components! You will notice that I put the on:change event handler after the properties and then leave the $$props spread operator until last. It helps to ensure we collect all prop values in the right order.

Okay – let's move on: it's time to test our component using the Storybook instance we set up in the previous chapter. We'll use similar techniques as before, which helps make it quicker to add – let's dive in and explore the steps required in more detail.

Adding Variations in Storybook

From the first component, we've already seen that setting up an instance in Storybook is relatively straightforward. Once we get past choosing which formats to use when creating the first component, we can reuse most of its code for subsequent additions to the library. To see what I mean, check out the next exercise, where we add the newly created Checkbox component to Storybook.

ADDING VARIATIONS

To add in variations for our Checkbox component, follow these steps:

1. First, crack open a new file in your text editor, then add in this code – as before, we will go though it in blocks, starting with the declarations:

```
import Checkbox from "./Checkbox.svelte";
import CheckboxDocs from "./CheckboxDocs.mdx";
import {
    Meta,
    Story } from '@storybook/addon-docs';
```

2. Next, leave a line blank, then add the title for the page where we will render our component in Storybook:

```
<Meta
    title="Cobalt UI Library/Basic Components/Checkbox"
    component={Checkbox}
    parameters={{page: null}}
/>
```

3. To tender the component, we need to first define a template – that is taken care of with this markup:

```
export const Template = (args) => ({
    Component: Checkbox,
    props: args,
});
```

4. We can now render the Checkbox component – we will add it as a Default instance, with no additional parameters, save for a checked property, and an onChange event:

```
<Story
  name="Default"
  args={{
  checked: true,
    onClick: () => alert('this is a text field')
  }}
  parameters={{
    docs: {
      page: CheckboxDocs
    }
  }}>
  {Template.bind({})}
</Story>
```

Note here that the onChange reference is not the actual event handler but a reference to the one in our component – we use this parameter to pass the function through to the actual event handler in the component.

5. Save the file as `Checkbox.stories.mdx` in the Checkbox folder.

6. We have one further step to complete before we can preview the results – we need to add the `CheckboxDocs.mdx` file, referenced in step 4. Extract a copy of this file from the code download, then drop it in the `Checkbox` folder.

7. Next, switch to your Node.js terminal session, then make sure the working folder is set to our cobalt project area.

8.   At the prompt, enter `npm run storybook` and hit Enter – if all is well, we should see Storybook display in our browser at `http://localhost:6006/`. Click on the Checkbox link on the left to display the Default variant we just created, as shown in Figure 2-3.

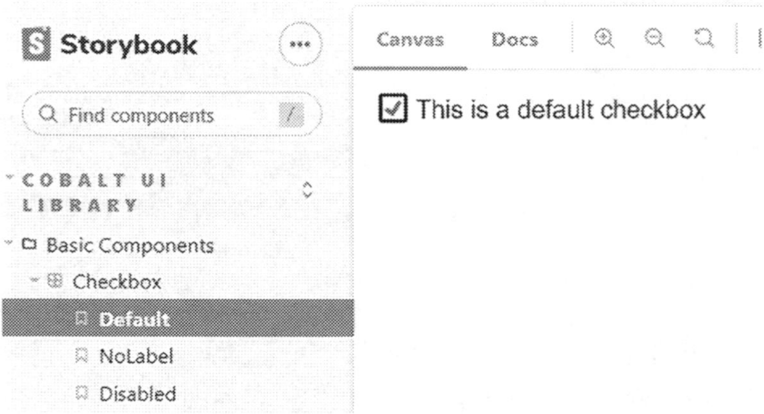

Figure 2-3. *Displaying the new Checkbox component in Storybook*

9.   We've added one variant into Storybook for this component, but what others could we add? I've given you a big clue in Figure 2-3. As another hint, we only need to switch around which properties we pass into the component from within each Story that we add to the Checkbox instance in Storybook.

The code download contains the expanded version if you need any inspiration!

We've now added our second component; we've almost finished the Basic Components section for our library! There is one more we will add shortly, but before doing so, let's first break for a moment to review the code we added in the last demo in more detail.

Breaking the Code Apart

So – what did we achieve in the last demo? We began by adding some imports to the Storybook file for the component itself, plus the `CheckboxDocs.mdx` documentation file and some tags required for displaying our component. Next up, we added a title for the Storybook page and a simple template; we need the latter to tell Svelte how to render our component.

With the template in place, we then added the Story. It uses `<Story>` tags from Storybook into which we pass an `args` object, with values for the `checked` and `onChange` properties. We also pass in a `parameters` option – we use this to tell Storybook to parse in the `CheckboxDocs.mdx` documentation file as a replacement for the one it creates by default for Svelte.

In the `<Meta...>` tag object, you will notice that we pass a similar parameters value, but this time set `docs: null`. It probably isn't necessary, but it is a useful belt-and-braces approach to ensuring we display the correct documentation in Storybook.

We then rounded out the demo by adding the `Checkbox.mdx` documentation file before executing the command to build and run Storybook with the latest updates for our components.

Okay – let's move on: we're done with Checkbox, so it's time to start on the next component: Slider. We could build one from the ground up, but that seems an overly complicated way to do it; why not use an alternative that is available natively in most modern browsers?

Adapting for Radio Buttons

Hold on a moment – before we do that, I want to try a little experiment.

As I'm sure you're aware, HTML markup for radio buttons is based on the ubiquitous <input...> tag, but instead, we pass in a type of radio. Logic says that based on our current code, we should therefore be able to create something similar, right?

Well, the answer is yes and no – the basic principle stays the same, but there are a few changes we need to make. Figure 2-4 shows how a radio component would appear if we added one to Storybook.

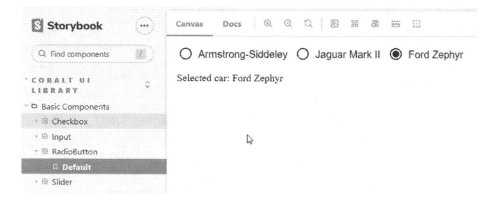

Figure 2-4. *Adding a RadioButton component*

If we had used the same process as the checkbox component, we would have ended up with just one radio button: not right! The changes we need to make will create a group of radio buttons instead, which will be more aligned with our needs. To understand these changes, let's walk through a version I've set up in more detail.

WALKTHROUGH: ADDING A RADIO COMPONENT

To set up our component, let's walk through the steps required:

1. First, go ahead and extract a copy of the `RadioButton` folder code from the code download – add the folder to the root of the components folder in our project folder.

2. Crack open the `RadioButton.svelte` file – inside, we can see an import for styles (similar to our previous components).

3. The first change is to specify (and export) options and `userSelected`. We use the former to iterate through the `options` object that contains the "data"; we use `userSelected` to grab the value of the selected option.

We also have the `slugify` constant, but this is just to help provide an ID for each radio button, should we need to test for the contents.

---

4. The real change comes, though, in the markup – inside the `cobalt` `<div>` element (which we use for each component), we first use a Svelte `#each` statement to iterate through each value in the options array and create `<input>` options for each returned value (in this case, 3). Note that we changed the type to `radio`, which we would expect to do anyway for radio buttons.

5. However, we do have the addition of `bind:group` – this is a Svelte directive that does pretty much what it says on the tin. It binds a reference to each value in the group and updates `userSelected` each time we change which option is selected.

The rest of the code is self-explanatory or similar to other components – this includes the use of the `...$props` spread operator that we've used elsewhere in this chapter. So – what does this mean for Storybook? Let's walk through how we would import our component into Storybook:

1. Crack open a copy of `Radiobutton.stories.mdx` from the code download that comes with this book.

2. We have similar imports – the first references functions required for Storybook to operate, and the second imports the component into our code.

3. We then specify two values – one to store the selected option in our radio button and an options array object to store the data required for our radio buttons.

4. A little further down, we use the same `<Meta...>` tag as before for the title.

5. The real change comes in the template – this time, we need to specify both the options array and add `bind:userSelected` to update `radioValue` each time we change it in the demo.

6. The `<Story...>` block also looks a little empty of code – we've not implemented any variants this time, nor need to pass in any extra parameters. However, we could add code to create a variant, such as disabling the radio buttons individually or as a group.

So – as you can see from the code, there are some subtle but important differences: it means that while it would be nice to use the same format as in previous components, it's not always possible!

Okay – let's crack on: for this chapter's third and final component, we will explore creating a Slider component. It's not one you're likely to see as often as the others, particularly on e-commerce sites, but it is still an equally important tool to have in the toolbox. Let's dive in and take a closer look at how we might set up such a component.

Constructing the Slider Component

If we're tasked with constructing a Slider component, it's easy to think we might have to build something from the ground up. It's a perfectly valid supposition; we can control what features to add and how we construct them. It will result in a lot more code, though, when most browsers already natively support the HTML range element – let's see what happens when we use it to create our next component.

BUILDING THE SLIDER COMPONENT

To build the final component for this chapter, follow these steps:

1. First, create a new folder called `Slider` under the `components` folder, at the same level as the previous two components.

2. Next, crack open your text editor, then add this code – we'll do this in blocks, starting with importing the stylesheet and setting some exported declarations:

```
<svelte:options tag="cobalt-slider" />

<script>
  export let id = undefined;
  export let min = 0;
  export let max = 100;
```

```
    export let step = 1;
    export let val = 50;
    export let disabled = false;
</script>
```

3. With the declarations in place, we can now add the markup used to render our component:

```
<div class="cobalt">
  <input
    type="range"
    id="{id}" {min} {max} {step}
    name="{id}"
    bind:value={val}
    disabled = {disabled}
  />
  <label for="{id}">{val}</label>
</div>
```

4. There is one last change to make, which is to add some styling. Leave a line blank after the closing </div> tag, then add this code:

```
<style>
  .cobalt {
    display: flex;
    flex-direction: row;
    font-family: Arial, Helvetica, sans-serif;
  }

  input[type="range"] {
    -webkit-appearance: none;
    width: 160px;
    height: 20px;
    margin: 10px 50px;
```

```css
  background: linear-gradient(to right, #19247c 0%,
  #19247c 100%);
  background-size: 150px 10px;
  background-position: center;
  background-repeat: no-repeat;
  overflow: hidden;
  outline: none;
}

input[type="range"]::-webkit-slider-thumb {
  -webkit-appearance: none;
  height: 20px;
  width: 20px;
  border-radius: 50%;
  cursor: ew-resize;
  box-shadow: 0 0 2px 0 #555;
  transition: background 0.3s ease-in-out;
  background: #6666ff;
  position: relative;
  z-index: 3;
  box-shadow: 0 0 5px 0 rgba(0, 0, 0, 0.3);
}

input[type="range"]::-moz-range-thumb {
  -webkit-appearance: none;
  height: 20px;
  width: 20px;
  border-radius: 50%;
  background: #6666ff;
  cursor: ew-resize;
  box-shadow: 0 0 2px 0 #555;
  transition: background 0.3s ease-in-out;
}
```

```css
input[type="range"]::-ms-thumb {
  -webkit-appearance: none;
  height: 20px;
  width: 20px;
  border-radius: 50%;
  background: #6666ff;
  cursor: ew-resize;
  box-shadow: 0 0 2px 0 #555;
  transition: background 0.3s ease-in-out;
}

input[type="range"]::-webkit-slider-thumb:hover,
input[type="range"]::-moz-range-thumb:hover,
input[type="range"]::-ms-thumb:hover {
  background: #9393ff;
}

/* Input Track */
input[type="range"]::-webkit-slider-runnable-track {
  -webkit-appearance: none;
  box-shadow: none;
  border: none;
  background: transparent;
}

input[type="range"]::-moz-range-track {
  -webkit-appearance: none;
  box-shadow: none;
  border: none;
  background: transparent;
}
```

```
input[type="range"]::-ms-track {
  -webkit-appearance: none;
  box-shadow: none;
  border: none;
  background: transparent;
}
</style>
```

5. Save the file as slider.svelte, then close all
    open files.

Cool – our slider component is now in place. We need to add it to our
Storybook instance to see it operate. Fortunately, this is easy to do – we can
use similar code to that used for the previous two components; let's look at
what's required for the next exercise.

Adding the Component to Storybook

Adding in the new Slider component is straightforward – thanks to careful
planning, we can reuse a copy of the previous code for Checkbox and Input
but change the references to Slider.

Taking this approach cuts down the development time – sure, we
will likely want to update content to make it a little more unique, but that
comes later. Let's focus on getting the basics in place as part of the next
exercise.

SETTING UP THE SLIDER IN STORYBOOK

With the component now in place, we can now add the component and
documentation to Storybook:

1. First, create a new file called Slider.stories.mdx at the
    root of the Slider folder.

2. Next, go ahead and add this code – we'll break it down section
    by section, beginning with the relevant imports:

```
import Slider from './Slider.svelte';
import SliderDocs from './SliderDocs.mdx';
import { Meta, Story, Template } from '@storybook/
addon-docs';
```

3. We now need to add a title for our Storybook page – add this
    Meta tag in, first leaving a blank line:

```
<Meta
  title="Cobalt UI Library/Basic Components/Slider"
  component={Slider}
  parameters={{page: null}}
/>
```

4. As before, we need to add a template to tell Svelte how to
    render the component:

```
export const Template = (args) => ({
  Component: Slider,
  props: args,
});
```

5. With the template in place, we can now add in the Story code to
    render our new Slider component:

```
<Story name="Default"
  args={{
    val: 1,
    min: 0,
    max: 100,
    step: 10
  }}
```

```
parameters={{
  docs: {
    page: SliderDocs
  },
}}>
{Template.bind({})}
</Story>
```

6. Let's add a variant – take a copy of the code from step 5, then miss a line and paste it into the file. Change the Story name to "Disabled," then add `disabled: true` below the line `step: 10` (and before the closing brackets).

7. Save the file. Next, we need to grab a copy of the documentation file for this component – it's in the code download as `SliderDocs.mdx`, so save a copy into the Slider folder.

8. Once done, switch to your Node.js terminal session, then make sure the working folder is set to our cobalt project area.

9. At the prompt, enter `npm run storybook` and hit Enter – if all is well, we should see Storybook fire up in our browser at `http://localhost:6006/`. Click on the Checkbox link on the left to display the Default variant we just created, as shown in Figure 2-5.

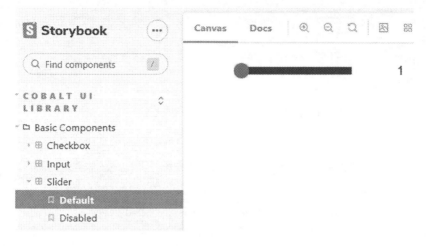

Figure 2-5. *Displaying the Slider component in Storybook*

Great – we've created the first set of components for our library! Things are shaping up well; we have a solid basis for developing the code at a later date. In the next chapter, we will focus on adding the next batch of components, but for now, let's round out this chapter with a final look at the changes made in the last exercise.

Exploring the Code

Adding components to our Storybook instance should be a little more familiar now – the key to it is preparing the code for the first, which we can reuse in subsequent components.

Keeping that thought in mind, we started by creating the Slider. stories.mdx file for Storybook, into which we first added some imports (component, documentation, and some features required from Storybook). We then added a title using the <Meta.../> tag, into which we told it how to set up the navigation in Storybook and that we would be using the Slider component. At the same time, we also set the page value to null to hide the default documentation page generated by Storybook.

Next up, we then created a template – something we built for the first component and which you will see added for all future components. We then set up our initial `<Story..>` block, which we labeled Default. Usually, we would use this to refer to a component out of the box, with no changes – this isn't possible here, though, as we need to provide some values: something to bear in mind!

We then switched to creating a variant – we talked about how this should be straightforward, given our desire to use consistent code, and that this should make adding variants easier. We then rounded out the demo by adding a prepared `SliderDocs.mdx` documentation file before firing up Storybook and previewing the results in a browser.

Summary

In Chapter 1, I mentioned that creating components and a library can be a rollercoaster. As we develop what will become our final library, there will be highs and lows, successes, and challenges to overcome. Over these last few pages, we've started that journey to add in our component – let's take a moment to review what we learned in this chapter.

The focus throughout this chapter was creating the code for each component – we started with constructing the code for a typical Input field before hooking it into our Storybook instance and adding in some variants to showcase how we can make our component more useful.

We then moved to create our second component, the Checkbox: this followed essentially the same format, but we also touched on how we might adapt the code to create a RadioButton component. As both share similar properties, one might forgive us for thinking it should be easy, but a closer inspection revealed this is not the case!

The third and final component we covered for this chapter was the Slider – we worked through creating the core component. Adding it to Storybook was more straightforward, though, as this is one of those components where we have to provide values for it to operate at all, not just because we want to change how it works; it's something to bear in mind when creating tools for our toolbox.

Okay – let's move on: it's time for a bit of action! You might have to pardon the pun there, as it wasn't the best lead-in to what we will cover in the next chapter. Suffice to say, we will focus on components that show a little action in some way (yes – there's the link). Intrigued? Stay with me, and I will reveal it all in the next chapter.

CHAPTER 3

Building
Action Components

Lights, camera, action…

Okay – we're not about to create the next movie blockbuster! Instead, it's the turn of the next batch of components we will be building, which all have some form of action (if you pardon the pun).

In the previous chapter, we started by creating some simple components based on standard HTML5 elements, but which we could refine into more complex versions as the library grows more mature over time. Our next batch of components are a little more involved and show a moving part in (most) respects – hence the reference to the title of this chapter!

Over the following few pages, we will, in turn, create SelectBox, Spinner, and Accordion components – let's begin with the SelectBox.

Creating the SelectBox Component

The typical select box type component is one you will find everywhere online. It, of course, is perfect for choosing options on e-commerce websites, such as the size of shoes, quantity of a particular item, or whether we want standard or expedited delivery. To construct this component, I've elected to use the standard HTML `<select>` element; let's make a start on building it as part of the next exercise.

© Alex Libby 2023
A. Libby, *Developing Web Components with Svelte*,
https://doi.org/10.1007/978-1-4842-9039-2_3

BUILDING THE SELECTBOX COMPONENT

To build our SelectBox component, follow these steps:

1. First, create a new folder called `SelectBox` at the root of the
   `lib` folder.

2. Next, crack open a new file and add this code – we'll start
   with adding a tag to turn our code into a web component and
   creating a few variables for export:

   ```
   <svelte:options tag="cobalt-selectbox" />

   <script>
     export let options = [];
     export let displayText = a => a.text;
     export let index = 0;
   ```

3. Miss a line, then add in this little function and the closing
   script tag:

   ```
   function onChange(event) {
       event.target.dispatchEvent(new
   CustomEvent("onchange", { composed: true }));
     }
   </script>
   ```

4. We can now add the markup for our component – much of this
   standard HTML markup, but it does include some Svelte tags:

   ```
   <div class="cobalt">
     <select bind:value={index} {disabled}
   on:change={onChange}>
       {#each options as option, i}
         <option value={i}>{displayText(option)}</option>
   ```

```
    {/each}
  </select>

</div>
```

5. Next, we need to add some styling. Leave a line blank, then add this code:

```
<style>
  .cobalt {
    display: flex;
  }

  select {
    padding: 5px 100px 5px 5px; /* 100px required to make
sure image displays */
    font-size: 16px;
    border: 1px solid #19247c;
    height: 34px;
    border-radius: 10px;
    -webkit-appearance: none;
    -moz-appearance: none;
    appearance: none;
    background: url("./icon.png") 96% / 15% no-repeat
#9393ff;
  }
</style>
```

6. Save the file as `SelectBox.svelte`, then close the file.

7. We also need one more file – in the code download, go ahead and extract a copy of `icon.png` from the SelectBox folder. You will have seen a reference to it in the styling from the previous step: all will become clear once we hook our component into Storybook.

We now have our component in place, although you will notice that we've not yet tested it – we will do that once we hook the component into our Storybook instance. For now, let's take some time out to review the code in more detail – there are some exciting features present, which are helpful to know!

Understanding What Happened

So far, we've added three components to our library – hopefully, by now, you will start to see some similarities in the steps we take, which will help speed up the process of getting out an initial version of a component!

The SelectBox component we created in the last exercise is no different – we first created a component folder before setting up the file for our component. We then exported several variables required for operating our SelectBox component in this file.

Next up, we added the markup for our component – most of this is standard HTML for select boxes, but there are a couple of points of note. We first `bind` the value of `value` to the `<select>` element; data flows typically from parent to child in Svelte, but this allows it to flow both ways (and update on any change). We then have a Svelte `#each.../each` block, which iterates through the `<option...>` tag to display the values from our options array that we will pass into the component. The `displayText` function extracts the relevant value from the options array. The SelectBox component knows which display value to show and what to set as the value property for that entry.

Last but by no means least, we also added a set of style rules for our component – these use our theme color plus set a few attributes so that our component at least renders correctly on the page.

Okay, let's crack on: we have our component in place and some rudimentary styling. It's time to test our code, so let's fire up Storybook and set up an entry for our component.

Adding the Component to Storybook

Right – where were we? Ah yes…adding our component to Storybook.

One of the benefits of careful planning is that we can reuse existing code – to date, we've created three components, which all use the same format when hooking them into Storybook. It might seem a little repetitious, but don't forget: reusability means we can be a lot more agile! I will come back to this when we review the changes made shortly, but for now, let's work through setting up our new component in Storybook as part of the next demo.

LINKING INTO STORYBOOK

Adding the component into Storybook is straightforward – we will reuse the existing code format from previous examples, with only minor changes needed. To see what I mean, let's set up the SelectBox component we created just now using these steps:

1. First, go ahead and create a new file, then add this code – as before, we have a reasonable chunk to add. Let's start with the initial `<script>` block to import the component and documentation, along with some functions from Storybook:

   ```
   import SelectBox from "./SelectBox.svelte";
   import SelectBoxDocs from "./SelectBoxDocs.mdx";
   import { Meta, Story } from '@storybook/addon-docs';
   ```

2. Next, leave a line blank, then add this `<Meta>` tag – it adds a title, sets the component we want to use, and blocks the default documentation page from being displayed:

   ```
   <Meta
     title = "Cobalt UI Library/Action Components/SelectBox"
     component={SelectBox}
     parameters={{ page: null }}
   />
   ```

3. With the initial configuration in place, we can now focus on our
    component – as before, we first need to add a template. Skip a
    line, then add this block in – it's similar to previous examples,
    with only a minor change of component:

```
export const Template = (args) => ({
  Component: SelectBox,
  props: args,
});
```

4. We can now render our component – for this, we will use the
    `<Story>` tag. Go ahead and add this block:

```
<Story name="Default"
  args={{
    options: [{"text":"aaa"},{"text":"bbb"},{"text":"
    ccc"}],
  }}
  parameters={{
    docs: {
      page: SelectBoxDocs
    },
  }}
/>
```

5. Let's also add a second story – this one will disable the
    component:

```
<Story name="Disabled"
  args={{
    options: [{"text":"aaa"},{"text":"bbb"},{"text":"
    ccc"}],
    disabled: true
  }}
```

```
parameters={{
  docs: {
    page: SelectBoxDocs
  },
}}
/>
```

6. Save the file as `SelectBox.stories.mdx`, then close the file.

7. You will see from the code that we've specified a file as our documentation but haven't yet added it. We need to extract a copy of `SelectBoxDocs.mdx` from the code download, then drop it into the SelectBox folder.

8. We have everything in place, so let's test it! Switch to a Node. js terminal session, then set the working folder to our `cobalt` project area.

9. At the prompt, enter `npm run storybook` and hit Enter – if all is well, we should see Storybook launch and display in our browser at `http://localhost:6006/`. Click on the Default link under SelectBox on the left to display the variant we just created, as shown in Figure 3-1.

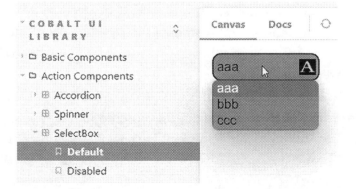

Figure 3-1. *The SelectBox component on display in Storybook*

And voila! Our new component is rendering in Storybook.... But hold on: I see some interesting effects there...an image and curved borders? Indeed – while researching for this book, I came across a nifty little trick to display an icon and restyle the drop-down box.

Granted, I've not added properties to the code to allow us to set these changes as part of initializing the component, but it shouldn't be too difficult to do so at a later date. In the meantime, let's dig into the code in more detail before we continue with creating the next component in this chapter.

Exploring the Code in Detail

To hook our SelectBox component, we began by creating our Storybook page – into this, we imported our component, along with the documentation (written in Markdown format) and some functions from Storybook to help support the documentation.

Next, we added a `<Meta>` tag, which contains the tags needed to display the component page in the correct order. The Cobalt UI Library is a reference to the top title, with Basic as the subtitle and, of course, SelectBox as the name for our component's page.

We then moved on to the critical part – our template. It's primarily the same as previous components; after all, there is no need (at this time) to make it any more complicated! We then added a Story block, into which we passed our `options` array as an `args`, along with setting the page value to `SelectBoxDocs` to display our custom documentation page. We repeated this step to add a second story – this time, we marked it as `Disabled` and added the `disabled` parameter to disable our component. This parameter we set as false by default, so we only need to specify it when we need to override the property.

As the final few steps, we saved and closed all files before extracting a copy of the `SelectBoxDocs.mdx` documentation file, before launching Storybook and previewing the results in our browser.

Before we change tack and explore our next component, I want to cover a few points of note:

- You will have noticed that we used the HTML5 native element as a basis for our component. It does present a question: Is this the best approach? I don't think there is a right or wrong answer: it will depend on the browsers you want (or have) to support. I hope that they will be recent (within the last two to three years), so the issue of supporting HTML5 should not even be an issue. The great thing about our MVP approach is that we could decide to convert to a custom, ground-up component; only time will tell!

- You will also notice that I've included vendor-prefixed versions of the appearance property within our CSS. In this case, they aren't strictly necessary; we could easily remove them, as long as we don't need to support older browsers. There is an icon displayed within our SelectBox component in our component – this was not part of the original plan but a bonus. It came from an article posted by someone on Stack Overflow as an example of how we might want to customize our SelectBox component – this all depends on how we want to develop the codebase in the future. In the same vein, we set the `padding-right` value (as part of `padding`) to `100px`. This change was only necessary to display the icon correctly – if we didn't want to include an icon, we could change it to something else later.

If, however, we should find ourselves supporting older ones, then a quick check at `https://caniuse.com/?search=appearance` will confirm if we need to make any changes!

Right, let's move on – we're making great progress, with our second component now in place and working. It's for us to look at the next one in this bunch. It's one where we could get into a spin if we're not careful (oops – sorry about the pun!). Yes, our next one is a spinner – essential if you need to render a lot of data on the page that might take a while to load.

Creating the Spinner Component

I'm sure you will have seen data returned on some websites that takes a while to display, right?

We could display that data, but a better UX experience is to render a loading element (or spinner) while we retrieve that data. Fortunately, it's easy enough to create the basis for something we can develop later – let's look at the code required to construct our component.

BUILDING THE SPINNER

To set up our spinner component, follow these steps:

1. First, create a new folder called `Spinner` inside the `\src\lib` folder of our project area – this is where we will store the code for our component.

2. Next, crack open a new file, and add this code – we'll go through it block by block, starting with some declarations we export for using within the component:

```
<svelte:options tag="cobalt-spinner" />
<script>
  export let color = "#19247c";
  export let duration = "0.75s";
  export let size = "60";
</script>
```

3. Next, we need to add the markup for our component, so leave a
    line blank and add this code:

```
<div class="cobalt">
  <div
    class="circle"
    style="--size: {size}px; --color: {color};
--duration: {duration}" />
</div>
```

4. To finish off the basic component, we need to add some
    styling – go ahead and leave a line blank, then add these rules:

```
<style>
  .circle {
    height: var(--size);
    width: var(--size);
    border-color: var(--color) transparent var(--color)
    var(--color);
    border-width: calc(var(--size) / 12);
    border-style: solid;
    border-radius: 50%;
    animation: var(--duration) linear 0s infinite normal
    none running rotateCircle;
  }

  @keyframes rotateCircle {
    0% {
      transform: rotate(0);
    }
```

```
    100% {
        transform: rotate(360deg);
    }
  }
</style>
```

5. Save the file as `Spinner.svelte` in the `Spinner` folder, then close it.

We now have our Spinner component in place – although a large part of it is standard HTML and CSS, it does include a few exciting techniques of note. Let's pause for a moment and review the code to understand how it all hangs together in more detail.

Understanding What Happened

We began by creating our Spinner component folder, into which we started to assemble the core component code – the first task was to add a bunch of exports for properties we will use later, such as `color`, `duration`, and `size`. These have default string values applied, but two of these will change; more on this in a moment.

Next, we then added the markup for our component – this uses the CSS variables function `var()` to turn what are string-formatted values (`size`, `color`, and `duration`) into variables in the format `var(--XX)`. The XX is the variable's name; in this case, we use all three exported variables to style our spinner – for example, `color` would appear in the markup as `var(--color)`.

The remaining CSS code is standard, so it should be reasonably self-explanatory – we use a custom `@keyframe` called `rotateCircle` to animate our spinner. The only property of interest, though, is `border`, where we specify three properties – we can effectively treat these as three parts of the circle. Change one, and we change a third of the wheel, which can lead to some interesting effects!

We then finished by adding the markup – spinners typically don't need anything more than an empty <div> element; as long as we style it correctly, it will show as our intended spinner in a browser.

Adding the Component to Storybook

We have the code in place for our component, so it's time to add it to our Storybook instance. The process for doing this is pretty much the same as the previous components, so the code will look a little more familiar by now – let's dive in and take a look in more detail.

```
HOOKING THE COMPONENT INTO STORYBOOK
```

Adding our Spinner into Storybook is straightforward as we're able to reuse much of the same code as before – to see what I mean, follow these steps:

1. First, go ahead and create a new file, then add this code – as before, we have a reasonable chunk to add. Let's start with the initial import block to import the component and documentation, along with some functions from Storybook:

    ```
    import Spinner from './Spinner.svelte';
    import SpinnerDocs from './SpinnerDocs.mdx';
    import { Meta, Story, Template } from
    '@storybook/addon-docs';
    ```

2. Next, we need to add our <Meta> tag – as before, it adds a title, sets the name of the component we want to use in the navigation, and blocks the default documentation page from being displayed:

    ```
    <Meta
        title="Cobalt UI Library/Action Components/Spinner"
    ```

```
    component={Spinner}
    parameters={{page: null}}
/>
```

3. With the initial configuration in place, we can set up our
    component – we first need to add our template, which only
    requires a minor change of component:

```
export const Template = (args) => ({
  Component: Spinner,
  props: args,
});
```

4. We can now render our component – for this, we will use
    the `<Story>` tag and pass into it the properties required to
    configure our spinner component. Go ahead and add this block:

```
<Story name="Default"
  args={{
    color: "#19247c",
    duration: "0.75s",
    size: "40"
  }}
  parameters={{
    docs: { page: SpinnerDocs },
  }}
/>
```

5. Save the file as `Spinner.stories.mdx` in the `\src\lib\`
    storybook `folder`, then close the file.

6. You will see from the code that we've specified a file as our
    documentation but haven't yet added it. We need to extract a
    copy of `SpinnerDocs.mdx` from the code download and then
    drop it into the `\src\lib\storybook` folder.

7. We have everything in place, so let's test it! Switch to a Node. js terminal session, then set the working folder to our cobalt project area.

8. At the prompt, enter npm run storybook and hit Enter – if all is well, we should see Storybook launch and display in our browser at http://localhost:6006/. Click on the Default link under Spinner on the left to display the variant we just created, as shown in the screenshot in Figure 3-2.

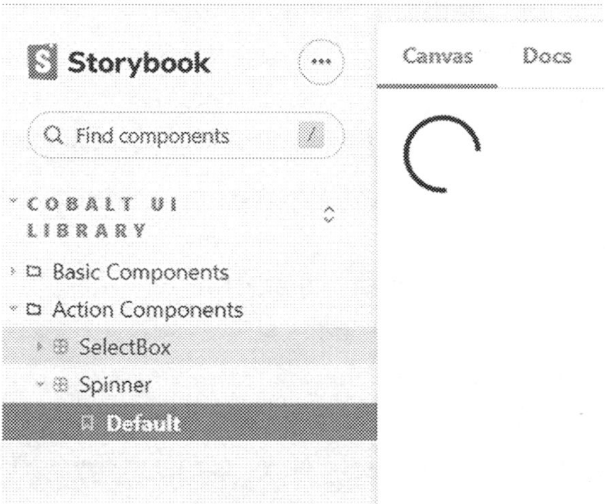

Figure 3-2. *Displaying the Spinner component in Storybook*

Excellent – the Spinner is now hopefully in and working: it's a shame that we can't see it spin in print, so hopefully, it works as expected for you on screen! One thing to note about this component is that we can add variants, but there is a twist.

Remember how with SelectBox, we added a disabled property as a variant? We disable the component, but it still looks like the same SelectBox. If we add a variant with Spinner, it will look different from our original spinner – to see what I mean, we will add a variant shortly. Before we do that, let's quickly review the code changes we made in the last demo in more detail. Much of what we added will start to look familiar (remember that point earlier about reusability!), but it's still worth looking to recap what we added in the demo.

Breaking Apart the Code

Adding our Spinner control to Storybook should now be a relatively familiar process – as before, we start by creating our Storybook page and importing the component, documentation, and some functions from Storybook to help support the documentation.

We then added a `<Meta>` tag with properties to display the component page in the proper order. In the same way, as we did for SelectBox, we set `Cobalt UI Library` for the top title, with `Action Components` as the subtitle for our group and, of course, `Spinner` as the name for our component's page.

We then moved on to the critical part – our template; here, we added a Story block, into which we passed the `color`, `size`, and `duration` properties. At the same time, we also set the `page` value to `SpinnerDocs` to display our custom documentation page. As the final few steps, we saved and closed all files before extracting a copy of the `SpinnerDocs.mdx` documentation file and launching Storybook to preview the results in our browser.

Creating Variants

We set up the Spinner component to operate in Storybook in that last demo. The process should be relatively familiar, as we've tried to keep it similar for all components. However, remember how I stated that if we added a variant for Spinner, it would likely be very different from something added for SelectBox?

Spinner is one of those components where we probably wouldn't enable or disable a component, such as for SelectBox. Instead, we focus on timing, color, size, and duration, resulting in a different look and feel! It might sound a little confusing, but trust me – the following exercise will make it much more apparent, so let's dive in and take a look.

"CHANGING THE LOOK"

I've titled this next exercise slightly differently than the others, but with good reason. Although we will be creating a variant, it looks so different from the original that it could equally be a separate component in its own right! That aside, here's what we need to do to add that new variant to our demo:

1. First, crack open `Spinner.svelte`, then locate the last export statement, and add this line before the closing `</script>` tag:

```
const range = (size, startAt = 0) =>
[...Array(size).keys()].map(i => i + startAt);
```

2. Scroll down to the line starting @keyframes `rotate`..., then change the word rotate for `rotateCircle`.

3. In the `.circle` declaration just above it, go to the end of the line, then change the word rotate to `rotateCircle`.

4. Next, we need to add the CSS for our variant – go ahead and add this below the `rotate` block:

```
.jumper {
  height: var(--size);
  width: var(--size);
  border-radius: 100%;
  animation-fill-mode: both;
  position: absolute;
```

```
      opacity: 0;
      background-color: var(--color);
      animation: bounce var(--duration) linear infinite;
    }

    @keyframes bounce {
      0% { opacity: 0; transform: scale(0); }
      5% { opacity: 1; }
      100% { opacity: 0; transform: scale(1); }
    }
```

5. Scroll down to pretty much the bottom – we need to add markup and tweak the existing code. First, find this line: `<div class="cobalt">`

6. Amend the original `<div class = "circle"…>` block to look like this – changes are marked in bold:

```
<!-- Circle spinner -->
{#if variant == "circle"}
  <div>
    <div
      class="circle"
      style="--size: {size}px; --color: {color};
--duration: {duration}"
    />
  </div>
{/if}
```

7. Leave a line blank after that closing `{/if}` tag, then add this code for our variant:

```
<!-- Jumper spinner -->
{#if variant =="jumper"}
    <div style="--size: {size}px; --color: {color};
--duration: {duration};">
```

```
{#each range(3, 1) as version}
  <div
    class="jumper"
    style="animation-delay: {(1 / 3) * (version -
1) + "px"};"
  />
  {/each}
</div>
{/if}
```

Note   This should be before the closing `</div>` tag at the end of the page!

8. Save and close the file. Fortunately, the changes required for Storybook are not so complex! For this, crack open `Spinner.stories.mdx`, then scroll to the bottom of the page and add this block:

```
<Story name = "Jumper"
  args={{
    color: "#19247c",
    duration: "1s",
    size: "60",
    variant: "jumper"
  }}
  parameters={{
    docs: { page: SpinnerDocs },
  }}
/>
```

9. We have everything in place, so let's test it! Switch to a Node. js terminal session, then set the working folder to our cobalt project area.

10. At the prompt, enter npm run storybook and hit Enter – if
     all is well, we should see Storybook launch and display in our
     browser at http://localhost:6006/.

11. Click on the Jumper link under Spinner on the left to display
     the variant we just created, as shown in the screenshot in
     Figure 3-3.

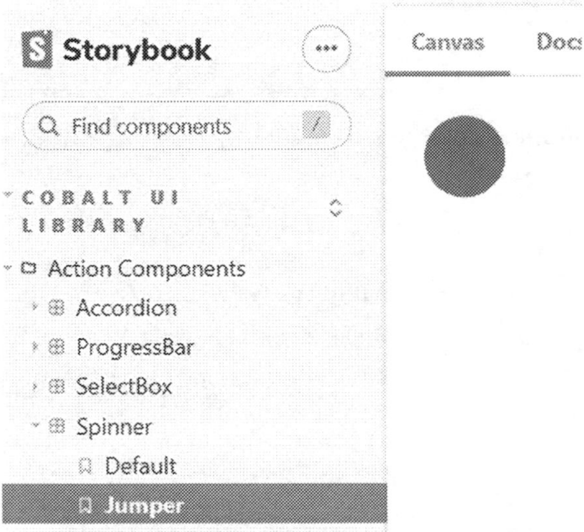

Figure 3-3. *Displaying the Spinner variant*

Wow – our Spinner looks different now! This is the beauty of this
component: even though the core markup is largely the same, varying the
properties we pass in can render something completely different.

Breaking Apart the Code

We began with adding an exported variable called variant, which we will
use to specify which variant to run when calling our component. We also
added a new const for range – this is used in the new effect to create a
splash effect as part of our animation. At the same time, we renamed the

original rotate @keyframes block to rotateCircle – this wasn't essential, but it helps provide a better separation of concerns once we add the @keyframes block for our new variant.

We then switched to adding the CSS styles required for the variant – this came in two parts, starting with creating the basis for the spinner, followed by that new @keyframes block to animate it.

We then modified the markup – first, we wrapped the original markup in a Svelte {#if}...{/else} block before adding the new markup for our variant.

Take a closer look at the markup for our variant: there are a couple of interesting points of note. We use CSS variables throughout, such as --size or --color. We also defined exported variables at the top of the file in the same name, so a statement such as --color: {color} becomes --color: #19247c in code. The feature of interest, though, is the #each block:

```
{#each range(3, 1) as version}
  <div
    class="jumper"
    style="animation-delay: {(1 / 3) * (version - 1)
    + "px"};"
  />
{/each}
```

Here, we use a standard Svelte {#each…as} block, similar to React but with slightly different syntax. But the real magic happens in the animation-delay style. Our block iterates through three instances of the div (range(3,1) equates to 3, 2, 1); the calculation provides a gradual step effect, similar to jumping into a puddle of water, hence the name of the animation!

Creating the Accordion Component

Let me ask you a question.

Hands up, how often have you been on a website where the author (or company) has added a ton of information but given no thought about its display? You take one look and think, "ugh – time to vote with my feet...," as they say!

That example might sound a little extreme, but I've been on thousands of sites over the years, where I still see designers display a lot of information with little regard to how they lay it out on the page. One way to fix that could be to use an instance of what we will be developing next: an Accordion.

These are great for storing a lot of information – such as product specs, reviews, and the like – in a compact manner, and we can select which tab to display for further details. Accordions are not challenging to create, although they require more code than we've done so far. To see what I mean, let's dive in and look at creating one as our next component.

BUILDING THE ACCORDION COMPONENT

To set up our Accordion component, follow these steps:

1. First, create a new folder called `Accordion` inside the `\src\lib\` folder within our project area – this is where we will store the code for our component.

2. At the same time, create a new folder called `AccordionItem` – this should be stored inside the `\src\lib` folder.

3. Next, crack open a new file and add this code – we'll go through it block by block, starting with some declarations we export for use within the component:

```
<svelte:options tag="cobalt-accordion" />
<script>
  import AccordionItem from './AccordionItem.svelte'
  export let data = [];
</script>

<div class="cobalt-accordion">
  {#each data as entry}
    <AccordionItem title={entry.title} entry={entry.
text} />
  {/each}
</div>
```

4. Next, miss a line, then add this block – it will provide some basic styling for our Accordion container:

```
<style>
  .cobalt-accordion {
    display: flex;
    flex-direction: column;
    width: 500px;
  }
</style>
```

5. Save the file as `Accordion.svelte`, then close the file.

6. You will notice from that code a reference to `AccordionItem` – we now need to create that component. For this, go ahead and crack open a new file, then add this code:

```
<svelte:options tag="cobalt-accordionitem" />
<script>
  import { slide } from "svelte/transition";
  import accordionData from "./accordiondata.json";
  export const data = accordionData;
```

```
export let entry = "";
export let title = "";
let isOpen = false
const toggle = () => isOpen = !isOpen
</script>
```

7. Last but by no means least, we need to add the markup for our component – this first block defines the button used to open and close each list item:

```
<button on:click={toggle} aria-expanded={isOpen}>
  <svg
    width="20"
    height="20"
    fill="none"
    stroke-linecap="round"
    stroke-linejoin="round"
    stroke-width="2"
    viewBox="0 0 24 24"
    stroke="currentColor">
      <path d="M9 5l7 7-7 7"></path>
  </svg>
  {entry[0]}
</button>
```

8. This second part triggers an animation if the button is opened by the user:

```
{#if isOpen}
  <ul transition:slide={{ duration: 300 }}>
      {#each entry[1] as item}
      <li>{item}</li>
      {/each}
  </ul>
{/if}
```

9. We need to add some styling – for this, miss a line after the closing {/if}, then add this code:

```
<style>
  svg { transition: transform 0.2s ease-in; }

  [aria-expanded="true"] svg {
    transform: rotate(0.25turn);
  }

  button.accordionItem { display: flex; align-items:
center; background-color: #6666ff; color: #ffffff;
border: none; }

  button[aria-expanded="false"].accordionItem
{ margin-bottom: 2px; }

  button.accordionItem:hover { background-color:
#19247c; }

  ul { border: 1px solid #6666ff; margin: 0; margin-
bottom: 2px; padding: 20px 20px 20px 40px; }
</style>
```

10. Save the file as `AccordionItem.svelte` in the `AccordionItem` folder, then close it.

Great – we can knock another component off the list of tasks to create our library! This one is a little special, though, as it is a composite component, or one made up of more than one subcomponent (all of the others are single component based).

This structure change does present one interesting point – how do we pass data down and make sure any that should stay local to their parent do stay local? Before we move on to the next and final component for this chapter, now's a perfect opportunity to review the code to see how our component hangs together in more detail.

Understanding What Happened

So far, all of the components we've added have had one thing in common. They are effectively unitary components, or, for those of you familiar with it, atomic components (if you follow the Atomic Design principles created by Brad Frost, which you can see at `https://bradfrost.com/blog/post/atomic-web-design/`). Our Accordion component is the odd one out, as this is a molecule – we combined several elements to form our component.

To understand the difference, let's break down the steps we took: we started with the requisite folder creation (as before) before creating `Accordion.svelte` – this contained an import to the `AccordionItem` atom (or subcomponent), along with some test data for the Accordion.

```
<script>
  import AccordionItem from './AccordionItem.svelte'
  export let data = []
</script>
```

It's worth noting that we could change the format of the data presented in our Accordion – for example, we could replace the data export shown previously with this:

```
import accordionData from "./accordiondata.json";
export let data = accordionData;
```

This would allow us to import data from an external JSON file – why is this significant? Well, the answer lies in how we can pass data to a Svelte web component – it can only be in string format, so passing boolean values, for example, isn't allowed!

Moving on, we then set up the markup for each item within the Accordion. We iterate through the `data` block using a Svelte `#each` function while at the same time destructuring each item as an instance of `entry`. This we pass into the AccordionItem component as a value for the `title` prop.

When we explore the AccordionItem component, things get more interesting – here, we have two imports: one for the slide transition effect and another for the stylesheet. We then export entry (which we use to pass down the values to each instance of AccordionItem) and title (the heading for each bar in the Accordion) before defining a scoped variable isOpen for use within the Accordion component.

Next up, we then moved on to creating the markup for the button that acts as the trigger for each Accordion item. It contains an SVG of the chevron icon wrapped inside a button, followed by a Svelte #if.../ if block to iterate through each entry and display it in the body of the Accordion item.

Adding the Component to Storybook

We have the code in place for our Accordion, so let's add it to our Storybook instance without further ado. The process for doing this is pretty much the same as the previous components, so hopefully, the code will start to look more familiar by now – let's jump in and explore what's required in more detail.

LINKING INTO STORYBOOK

Setting up the Accordion to work in Storybook should be straightforward as we're using the same code process as other components. We only need to make small changes to our code to reflect using a new component – to see what I mean, follow these steps:

1. First, go ahead and create a new file in the same way as we've done before, then add this code – we'll start with the initial `<script>` block to import the component and documentation, along with some functions from Storybook:

```
import AccordionDocs from "./AccordionDocs.mdx";
import Accordion from "./Accordion.svelte";
import AccordionItem from "./AccordionItem.svelte";
import { Meta, Story } from '@storybook/addon-docs';
```

2. Next, we need to add our <Meta> tag – as before, it adds
   a title, defines the navigation for our Storybook page, sets
   the name of the component, and prevents Storybook from
   displaying the default documentation page:

```
<Meta
  title="Cobalt UI Library/Action Components/Accordion"
  component={Accordion}
  parameters={{page: null}}
/>
```

3. With the initial configuration in place, we can set up the
   Accordion – we first need to insert the template, with only
   minor changes of component name required:

```
export const Template = (args) => ({
  Component: Accordion,
  props: args,
});
```

4. We can now render our component – for this, we will use the
   same <Story> tag as before and into it pass the properties
   required to configure our Accordion component. Go ahead and
   add this block:

```
<Story name="Default"
  args={{
    open: false,
    data: [
      {
        "title": "Heading 1",
```

```
        "text": "aorem ipsum dolor sit amet, consectetur
adipiscing elit. Sed malesuada, nulla sed lacinia
accumsan, ligula arcu interdum urna, eget rhoncus sapien
orci scelerisque metus."
      },
      {
        "title": "Heading 2",
        "text": "In bibendum commodo orci nec semper.
Nam magna mauris, ornare eu semper sit amet, vehicula
sed metus"
      },
      {
        "title": "Heading 3",
        "text": "Mauris tortor mi, scelerisque nec metus
nec, finibus euismod lacus. Maecenas non porttitor arcu"
      }
    ]

  }}
  parameters={{
    docs: { page: AccordionDocs },
  }}
/>
```

5. Save the file as `Accordion.stories.mdx` in the `\src\lib\storybook` folder, then close the file.

6. As with previous components, we need to extract a copy of `AccordionDocs.mdx` from the code download and then drop it into the Accordion folder. The markdown in this file will add a page ready for us to insert documentation for our component.

7. Switch to a Node.js terminal session, then set the working folder to our `cobalt` project area.

8. At the prompt, enter npm run storybook and hit Enter – if
    all is well, we should see Storybook launch and display in our
    browser at http://localhost:6006/. Click on the Default
    link under Spinner on the left to display the variant we just
    created, as shown in Figure 3-4.

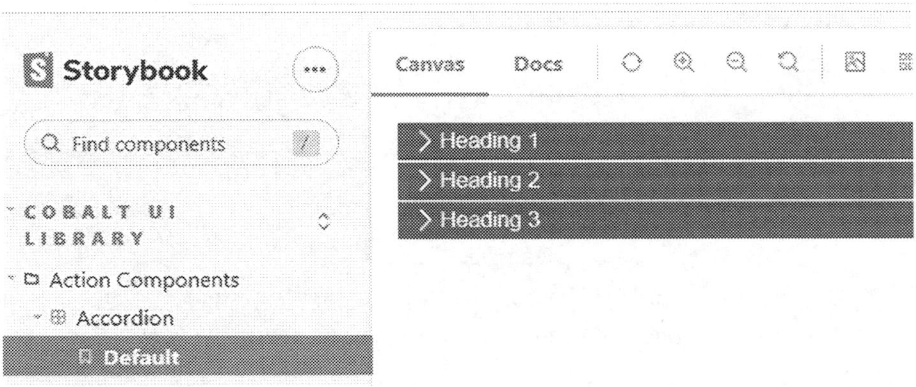

Figure 3-4. *The Accordion component on display in Storybook*

We're starting to cook now, to coin that phrase! We've created the code
for all three components for this chapter and added them to our Storybook
instance. Before moving on to the next chapter and exploring our next
batch of features, let's review the changes made in the last demo to see
how our Accordion component hooks into Storybook.

Reviewing the Code

Adding an Accordion component to Storybook should now be a relatively
familiar process – as before, we start by creating our Storybook page and
importing the feature, documentation, and some functions from Storybook
to help support the documentation.

We then added a <Meta> tag with properties to display the component
page in the correct order. In the same way, as we did for SelectBox,

we set `Cobalt UI Library` for the top title, with `Action Components` as the subtitle for our group and Accordion as the name for our group component's page.

We then moved on to the critical part – our template; here, we added a Story block, into which we passed the `open` and `data` properties to control when the Accordion is open and the data to display. At the same time, we also set the `page` value to `AccordionDocs` to display our custom documentation page. As the final few steps, we saved and closed all files before extracting a copy of the `AccordionDocs.mdx` documentation and launching Storybook to preview the results in our browser.

Summary

"And that's a wrap…!"

Yes, indeed – we've added all three Action components to our library; each has its respective page in our Storybook instance. It means we've reached the halfway point in constructing features for our library, with only two more categories to add later in the book. Before we get on building the next category of components, let's take a moment to review what we have learned in this chapter.

As we saw back in the previous chapter, the focus is on adding each component to our library and setting it up in Storybook. We started with the SelectBox component before swiftly moving on to creating the Spinner component. It was a little more involved as we explored adding a new variant – we learned that even though we use the same markup, changes in styling effectively meant we had the equivalent of a new component.

We explored setting up an Accordion component for the third and final component in this chapter. It was a little more complex, as we had to create two components: the main Accordion as the parent container and AccordionItem for displaying each item in the Accordion component.

Okay, let's crack with creating the next batch: next up is our navigation-based component group. We'll look at creating components such as a navigation bar and buttons, a menu and tabs, and more – intrigued? Stay with me, and I promise to navigate you through all in the next chapter if you pardon that terrible pun!

CHAPTER 4

Building the Navigation Components

"I may not have gone where I intended to go, but I think I have ended up where I needed to be."

That quote by the author Douglas Adams, from his 1988 detective novel, *The Long Dark Tea-Time of the Soul*, may have had a somewhat humorous edge, but I think it's an apt phrase to describe the theme for this chapter – they are all about navigation.

Good navigation is essential for any site – we can produce all manner of different components (such as the ones we've built so far) for different pages, but if we can't navigate to them, we might as well pack up and go home!

Over the following few pages, we will build three components – a set of Tabs, a Breadcrumb trail, and a SideBar menu. We will use similar methods throughout to help keep consistency and make it easier to develop; let's start with the Breadcrumb component.

© Alex Libby 2023
A. Libby, *Developing Web Components with Svelte*,
https://doi.org/10.1007/978-1-4842-9039-2_4

Creating the Breadcrumb Component

Hands up – how often have you had to navigate around a large website that has less than ideal navigation? I'm sure you will have done it at least once....

We would typically navigate using links or menu options, but we might also use breadcrumbs. This latter navigation scheme shows where we are on a site, making it easier to go back and forth without remembering which menu option to choose or which link to click. Breadcrumbs (or breadcrumb trails) have only been around for around 20 years, but the term comes from the Hansel and Gretel tale, where two children leave a breadcrumb trail to find their way home. It seems somewhat ironic that a feature synonymous with larger websites dates back from the early 19th century!

But I digress. We're going to create a simple Breadcrumb component for our first navigation component. We'll base it around a standard HTML unordered list, with a bit of styling and the option to use a custom image for the divider. Let's dive in and look at how to create it in more detail.

For the custom image, I've used two SVG icons from the Ionic library at `https://ionic.io/ionicons`; they are `arrow-forward-outline.svg` and `chevron-forward-outline.svg`. Both are in the code download; feel free to use alternatives if you prefer, but you will need to adjust the code to suit.

BUILDING THE BREADCRUMB TRAIL COMPONENT

To build our Breadcrumb component, follow these steps:

1. First, create a new folder called `Breadcrumbs` at the root of the `components` folder.

2. Next, crack open a new file and add this code – we'll start with importing the stylesheet, creating a few variables for export, and adding some default data from a JSON file:

```
<svelte:options tag="cobalt-breadcrumbs" />
<script>
  import arrow from './icons/arrow-forward-outline.svg';

  export let divider = "/";
  export let image = false;
  import breadcrumbItemsData from "./
breadcrumbsdata.json";

  export let breadcrumbItems = [];

  if (breadcrumbItems == []) {
    breadcrumbItems = breadcrumbItemsData;
  }
</script>
```

3. We can now add the markup for our component – much of this standard HTML markup, but it does include some Svelte tags. The first takes care of checking to see if we display a custom image or plain text as a divider:

```
<div class="cobalt">
  <ul class="breadcrumb">
    {#each breadcrumbItems as breadcrumbItem, i}
      <li>
        <!-- Breadcrumb divider -->
        {#if i !== 0}
          {#if !image}
            <span>{divider}</span>
          {/if}

          {#if image}
```

```
            <img src={arrow} alt='arrow' height=15
width=15 />
         {/if}
       {/if}
```

4. The second part of this block iterates through each item, to
    determine if it is the link or end tag:

    ```
            <!-- Render each breadcrumb -->
            {#if i === breadcrumbItems.length - 1}
                {breadcrumbItem.text}
            {:else}
                <a href={(breadcrumbItem.href)}>
                  { breadcrumbItem.text}
                </a>
            {/if}
          </li>
       {/each}
     </ul>
    </div>
    ```

5. Next, miss a line after the closing </div>, and add these
    style rules:

    ```
    <style>
      .cobalt { display: flex; font-family: Arial, Helvetica,
      sans-serif; }

      ul.breadcrumb { padding: 10px 16px; list-style: none;
      background-color: #eee; }

      ul.breadcrumb li { display: inline; font-size: 18px; }

      ul.breadcrumb li a { color: #19247c; text-
      decoration: none; }

      ul.breadcrumb li a:hover {
    ```

```
      color: #9393ff;
      text-decoration: underline;
    }

  ul.breadcrumb li span {
      display: inline;
      padding: 8px;
    }
  </style>
```

6. Save the file as `Breadcrumbs.svelte`, then close any open files. We need two more files – go ahead and extract copies of `arrow-forward-outline.svg` and `chevron-forward-outline.svg` from the code download, and put them into a new folder called icons, under the `Breadcrumbs` folder.

Excellent – we have our component in place, along with the two icons we need to test the custom image option of our component. The next task is to try it to make sure it works; as before, we'll work through adding it to our Storybook instance. Before we get to that, let's take a moment to review the code changes made – most of it should be self-explanatory, but some interesting Svelte techniques within the code are worth exploring in more detail.

Understanding What Happened

At first glance, you might feel a little confused with the number of conditional blocks in this component – it does feel like we've gone a little overboard in using them!

The reality is that we need to perform a lot of checks – the key to making this component work lies in the #each block we use inside the cobalt `<div>` element. We started by creating our component folder before adding the core component file, which contains an import for an image used in the component. We then created two exported variables (`image` and `divider`) to control if we display an image or text-based divider. At the same time, we also added an import for data from a JSON file and an export for breadcrumbItems.

What's going on with these data checks, I hear you ask? The answer lies in *how* we source our data – we would provide this when calling the component (in our case, from Storybook). If, however, we **don't** provide data (and which assumes therefore that the object `breadcrumbItems` will be empty), we then source default data from a JSON file. I could have provided this in the component, but sourcing it from a JSON file allows us to maintain separation of concerns.

The real magic then happens in the `#each` block that comes next – we iterate through the object, first checking to see if we need to display a divider. If the position of `i` (the index) is zero, we don't show one; otherwise, we display either a text or image-based divider, depending on what we set in the `image` or `divider` properties.

Once we've confirmed what to display, we then iterate through the object – we show a text label if the index matches the position of the last item or a link for all other entries. We end up with links for each entry in the chain, except for the last item, which indicates our chosen page.

To round off the task, we added some basic styling in an external stylesheet, along with two images, ready for us to test when adding the component to Storybook.

Adding the Component to Storybook

I know I've mentioned this before, but one of the benefits of careful planning is making code reusable; we've used the same format for all of the components created so far. Keeping this level of reusability is perfect for making development more rapid; after all, why reinvent the wheel unnecessarily? On that note, let's continue with our Breadcrumb component and set it up to work in our Storybook instance.

ADDING TO STORYBOOK

To get our Breadcrumb component working in Storybook, follow these steps:

1. First, go ahead and create a new file, then add this code – as before, we have a reasonable chunk to add. Let's start with the initial declaration block to import the component and documentation, along with some functions from Storybook:

```
import Breadcrumbs from "../Breadcrumbs/Breadcrumbs.
svelte";
import BreadcrumbsDocs from "./BreadcrumbsDocs.mdx";
import { Meta, Story } from '@storybook/addon-docs';

</script>
```

2. This next bit should be very familiar by now – leave a line blank, then add this `<Meta>` tag. As before, it adds a title, sets the component we want to use, and blocks the default documentation page from being displayed:

```
<Meta
  title="Cobalt UI Library/Navigation Components/
Breadcrumbs"
  component={Breadcrumbs}
  parameters={{page: null}}
/>
```

3. With the initial configuration in place, we can now focus on our component – as before, we first need to add a template. Skip a line, then add this block in – it's similar to previous examples, with only a minor change of component:

```
<Template let:args>
  <Breadcrumbs {...args} />
</Template>
```

4. We can now render our component – for this, we will use the
    `<Story>` tag. Go ahead and add this block:

```
<Story
  name="Default"
  args={{
    image: false,
    image: false,
    breadcrumbItems = [
      { href: "/", text: "Dashboard" },
      { href: "/reports", text: "Annual reports" },
      { href: "/reports/2019", text: "2019" },
    ];  }}
  parameters={{
    docs: {
      page: BreadcrumbsDocs
    },
  }}
/>
```

5. Let's also add a second story – this one will show a custom
    image instead of a text-based character as our divider:

```
<Story
  name="Custom image"
  args={{
    image: true,
    breadcrumbItems = [
      { href: "/", text: "Dashboard" },
      { href: "/reports", text: "Annual reports" },
      { href: "/reports/2019", text: "2019" },
    ];
  }}
  parameters={{
    docs: {
```

```
    page: BreadcrumbsDocs
  },
 }}
/>
```

6. Save the file as `Breadcrumbs.stories.svelte` in the `/src/lib/storybook` folder, then close the file.

7. You will see from the code that we've specified `BreadcrumbsDocs.mdx` as our documentation file but haven't yet added it. Go ahead and extract a copy of the file from the code download, then drop it into the Breadcrumbs folder.

8. We have everything in place, so let's test it! Switch to a Node.js terminal session, then set the working folder to our `cobalt` project area.

9. At the prompt, enter `npm run Storybook` and hit Enter – if all is well, we should see Storybook launch and display in our browser at `http://localhost:6006/`. Click on the Default link under SelectBox on the left to display the variant we just created, as shown in Figure 4-1.

Dashboard // Aerial photography // DJI

Figure 4-1. *Displaying the Breadcrumb component with a standard divider*

10.   Click on the Custom image link on the left – this variant swaps
      out the double slash and replaces it with a custom image, as
      shown in Figure 4-2.

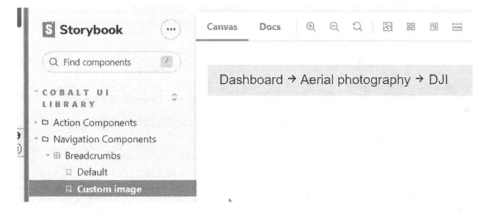

Figure 4-2. *The Breadcrumb variant displayed with a custom image*

You will note we added two images when creating the initial
component – try swapping the images over in the code. You may
need to adjust the styling a little, but the critical point here is that we
can use any SVG icon as our divider – we could even modify the code
to pass in an image name too!

It never ceases to amaze me how a standard element that has been
around for decades is something we can turn into a useful feature with
little more than a couple of functions and some styling!

List elements are incredibly versatile; Svelte's light touch means
that we can create all kinds of components with minimal extra code.
This concept was no different for the Breadcrumb component we've
just made – let's take a moment to review the code in more detail before
cracking on with our next navigation component.

Exploring the Code in Detail

Much of this component follows a similar pattern to the others that we've already created – we started with the now-familiar script block to import the placeholder documentation, an instance of the component, and some functions from the core Storybook framework. At the same time, we also added an `items` object with some sample data, which we use to display our Breadcrumb component.

Next up, we added the usual Meta tag, which contains the details needed for the navigation in Storybook, the name of the component we will use (`Breadcrumbs`), and an entry to block the default documentation page generated by Storybook. We also inserted our template – we changed the name of the component we use, but otherwise, it is identical to other components used in our library.

For the last part, we added two Story blocks to display instances of our Breadcrumb component – the first one, called `Default`, is set to render a double slash as our divider instead of an image. It is also the case in the second example (Custom image). However, as we also set the `image` property to `true`, this overrides the divider property to display an image when previewing the results in a browser.

Okay – let's move on: our next component is one you are likely to find more on a mobile device, but that doesn't matter. Sidebars still have a crucial role in helping us navigate a website, so they are a perfect tool to have in our library. They require more work to set up, but it's worth the effort: let's dive in and look at how we might create such a component for our library.

Building a SideBar Component

Cast your mind back quite a few years – remember the days when as developers, all we had to worry about navigation was to create something for desktops? With mobile usage exploding, it is ever more critical that we can create a usable navigation for this platform. There is no better way to do it than using a hamburger menu, such as our next component.

To create one, we will have to set up not one but two components: a hamburger icon and the sidebar itself. We'll do this over a two-part exercise, with breaks in between – let's crack on with part 1, which is to create the hamburger component.

BUILDING THE SIDEBAR MENU COMPONENT – PART 1: THE HAMBURGER

To construct the hamburger icon and menu button, follow these steps:

1. First, we need to create a SideBar folder for our component – go ahead and add one under /src/lib in our project area.

2. For this component, crack open a new file and add this code – we need to add two variables for export, along with the svelte:options directive and a check to determine if the sidebar is open or closed:

```
<svelte:options tag="cobalt-hamburger" />
<script>
    export let openSideBar = "false";
    export let open = false;

    openSideBar == "false" ? !open : open;
</script>
```

3. Next, miss a line, then add this markup for our button:

```
<button class:open on:click={() => open = !open}>
  <svg width=32 height=24>
    <line id="top" x1=0 y1=2  x2=32 y2=2/>
    <line id="middle" x1=0 y1=12 x2=24 y2=12/>
    <line id="bottom" x1=0 y1=22 x2=32 y2=22/>
```

```
    </svg>
</button>
```

4. With the button in place, all we need to add for this component is some styling – go ahead and drop these rules in the file, missing a line first:

```
<style>
    button { color: #a0aec0; margin-right: 16px; border-
    style: none; }

    button:hover { color: #4a5568; cursor:pointer;
    z-index: 20; }

    button:focus { outline: none }

    svg { min-height: 24px; transition: transform 0.3s
    ease-in-out; }

    svg line { stroke: currentColor; stroke-width: 3;
    transition: transform 0.3s ease-in-out }

    .open svg { transform: scale(0.7) }

    .open #top {
      transform: translate(6px, 0px) rotate(45deg)
    }

    .open #middle { opacity: 0; }

    .open #bottom { transform: translate(-12px, 9px)
    rotate(-45deg) }
</style>
```

5. Save the file as `Hamburger.svelte` in the same `SideBar` folder and close it.

That's component number one down, one left to go! We now have the hamburger button set up, so the only component left to create is our sidebar.

One of the great things about Svelte is that it doesn't try to overload HTML markup with a lot of extra cruft – this makes creating components such as our SideBar very clean! To see what I mean, let's look at what's involved in the next part of this exercise.

BUILDING THE SIDEBAR MENU COMPONENT – PART 2: THE SIDEBAR

To construct our final part of this component, the sidebar, follow these steps:

1. For this component, crack open a new file and add this code – unlike other components, we only need to add an open variable for export:

```
<svelte:options tag="cobalt-sidebar" />
<script>
  import { fly } from "svelte/transition";
  export let show = "true";
  let sidebar_show = show === "true";
</script>
```

2. Next up, miss a line, then add this markup for our component – this will render the menu in the sidebar, when opened, along with the contents of any HTML markup provided when calling the component:

```
<cobalt-hamburger on:click={() => (sidebar_show =
!sidebar_show)} />
```

```
{#if sidebar_show}
  <nav transition:fly={{ x: 250, opacity: 1 }}>
    <slot />
  </nav>
{/if}
```

3. To finish off the component, we need to add some basic
    styling – add these rules into the bottom of the file:

```
<style>
  nav {
    position: fixed;
    top: 0;
    right: 0;
    height: 100%;
    padding: 32px 16px 9.6px;
    border-left: 1px solid #aaa;
    background: #fff;
    overflow-y: auto;
    width: 160px;
    box-shadow: 2px 3px 3px 3px #000000;
  }
</style>
```

4. Save the file as SideBar.svelte in the same SideBar folder
    and close it.

That might have seemed like a lengthy exercise (even if it was over two
parts), but we now have our component in place! It looks like a lot of code,
and indeed, much of it is standard HTML markup and CSS styling. We do
use a few Svelte features within – let's take a closer look at the code we
used to understand how it all hangs together in our demo.

Breaking Apart the Code

Until now, most of the components we have created have been fairly simple affairs – the core functionality in a plug-in, styling in a supporting stylesheet, and documentation in a Markdown file. This last component turned things on its head, as we had to create two components, instead of just one – let's pause to review the code.

We began with creating our Hamburger icon component – inside this, we added a `svelte:options` directive to allow us to use it as a web component, before setting a variable `open` (which we default to false).

Next, we added a button with an `on:click` event handler – this we set to not only add or remove the `open` class (based on what the variable was set to) but also flip that `open` value to the opposite, each time we clicked the button. It means that we can set a class against the button to control how the sidebar is shown, as well as add some animation effects to the button. We then finish this part with adding the SVG for the hamburger lines and styling to control the animation.

In part 2, we focus on creating the star of the show (so to speak) – our sidebar. This contains some interesting Svelte code – we start with importing the `fly` animation from Svelte itself, along with exporting the `show` property, which we set to determine if the sidebar is hidden or visible when calling the component.

We then call the cobalt-hamburger component – note that we used the web component name here to ensure it works outside of a Svelte environment. At the same time, we added an event handler to trigger an `on:click` to flip the `sidebar_show` value to true or false. If it is the former, we fly in a `nav` element and display anything passed into the component, through the `<slot />` element – this is just a placeholder directive that displays anything, so we do need to be careful with what we tell the component to render! To finish off, we added some basic styling – this could be improved in time but will be sufficient to display our sidebar for the purposes of this book.

Using a Style Library – A Postscript

Before we move on to adding our new SideBar component, there is one more point I want to cover – our styling. You might be wondering where I'm heading with this, but there is a reason: Should we use a library? Let me explain what I mean.

While researching for this book, I played around with adding the ever-popular Tailwind CSS library, using this as a link:

```
<svelte:head>
  <link href="https://unpkg.com/tailwindcss@^1.0/dist/tailwind.
  min.css" rel="stylesheet"/>
</svelte:head>
```

Initially, this felt good – it's a well-known library used across thousands of sites. But something made me wonder if this was the route I wanted to take. Why? One key point: dependency. Sure, it's a sound library, but I'm old-fashioned when it comes to coding; I like to have more control over how my markup looks. Tailwind can add a lot of extra markup code and a dependency to my project, and I wanted to be in control of both, not the other way around!

Adding the Component to Storybook

By now, much of the code we need to use should be very familiar – it might seem like we're repeating ourselves, but this reusability makes it quicker to create our components. It's at this point that we would normally be adding our component to Storybook, in much the same way as we have done for previous examples. Only except this time, we're not going to do that.

Yes, you heard it correctly – we're going to break from the norm and run our demo outside of Storybook! This might sound a little weird, given the format we've used so far, but "there is method in the madness," as I'm sure someone once said. Building it this way does raise a few interesting questions, which we will explore later, but for now – let's crack on with setting up the demo for our SideBar component.

DEMOING THE SIDEBAR COMPONENT

We will construct this demo using the following files – these should be present already, but as a precaution, make sure you have these two files before continuing with this demo:

```
\index.html
\src\main.js
```

To get our Breadcrumb component working in a demo, follow these steps:

1. First, crack open `main.js` from within the `\src` folder – remove any code within, and replace it with this:

   ```
   export * from './lib/SideBar/SideBar.svelte'
   export * from './lib/SideBar/Hamburger.svelte'
   ```

2. Save the file and close it. Next, open the `index.html` file at the root of the project folder; we need to make a series of changes to this file. First, go ahead and change the content for the `<title>` tag:

   ```
   <title>Web Component Test Page</title>
   ```

3. Next, add this style block immediately below the `<title>` tags:

   ```
   <style>
     body { margin: 0; }

       main { font-family: sans-serif; margin: 0px 15px; }
   ```

```
#hamburger { background-color: #6666ff; display:
flex; padding: 5px; }
</style>
```

4. Scroll down to the opening <body> tag, then immediately below it, add this block:

```
<div id="hamburger">
  <cobalt-sidebar show="false">
    <p>About</p>
    <p>Work</p>
    <p>Blog</p>
    <p>Contact</p>
  </cobalt-sidebar>
</div>
```

5. For completeness, we should add some dummy text, so we can see what happens when we open the menu. Go ahead and add this block immediately below the code from the previous step:

```
<main>
  <h1>Testing Page:</h1>
  <p>This page is to test calling each web component
outside of a Svelte / Storybook environment</p>

  <p>Lorem ipsum dolor sit amet, consectetur
adipiscing elit. Ut vehicula nulla dolor, sed facilisis
nibh tincidunt vel. Maecenas vel ex nisi. Suspendisse
tincidunt gravida enim id viverra...<p>

  <p>Aenean vitae laoreet tellus. Aliquam et leo vel
justo lobortis feugiat eget ut purus. Curabitur molestie
tempus mauris sit amet viverra... </p>

  </main>
```

I've shortened the dummy text displayed here for brevity – the full version is available in the code download for this book.

6. Make sure you have this line present below the dummy text block – it should already be in the code:

```
<script type="module" src="/src/main.js"></script>
```

7. Save and close the file. We have everything in place, so let's test it! Switch to a Node.js terminal session, then set the working folder to our cobalt project area.

8. At the prompt, enter npm run dev and hit Enter – if all is well, we should see Storybook launch and display in our browser at http://localhost:5173/. Click on the button at the top left in the blue menu to open the menu (Figure 4-3) – the styling we've used is to provide a more authentic look and feel. I've added some Lorem Ipsum dummy text for a more authentic look and feel.

Testing Page:

This page is to test calling each web component outside of a Svelte / Storybook environment

Lorem ipsum dolor sit amet, consectetur adipiscing elit. Ut vehicula nulla dolor, sed facilisis nibh tincidunt vel. Maecenas vel ex nisi. Suspendisse tincidunt gravida enim id viverra. Donec non tortor iaculis, porttitor purus in, imperdiet tortor. Mauris vel accumsan urna. Sed eget tristique sem. Fusce sed interdum ligula, ac elementum enim. Morbi volutpat ligula orci, et vulputate justo rutrum id. Fusce porttitor leo at nisi elementum, eu facilisis ipsum iaculis. Praesent a purus sed leo rhoncus efficitur. Donec vulputate placerat blandit. Donec elementum diam tempor nisl malesuada maximus.

Aenean vitae laoreet tellus. Aliquam et leo vel justo lobortis feugiat eget ut purus. Curabitur molestie tempus mauris sit amet viverra. Duis sit amet libero tincidunt, fermentum dolor ut, eleifend neque. Praesent cursus massa ac laoreet scelerisque. In mauris nulla, convallis varius magna laoreet, accumsan iaculis sem. Morbi tempor pharetra leo, vel auctor quam.

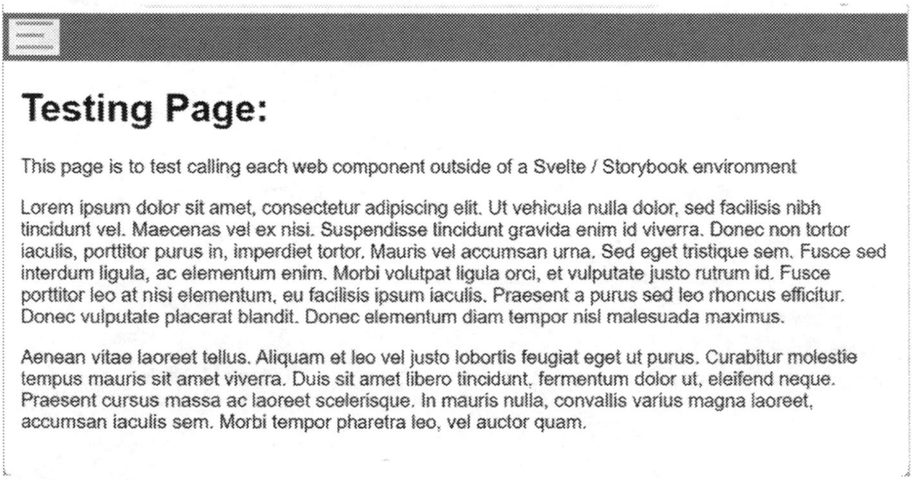

Figure 4-3. *Displaying the SideBar component with a standard divider*

9.   Click on the three-lined Hamburger icon on the left – our
     SideBar slides in to display four links (Figure 4-4).

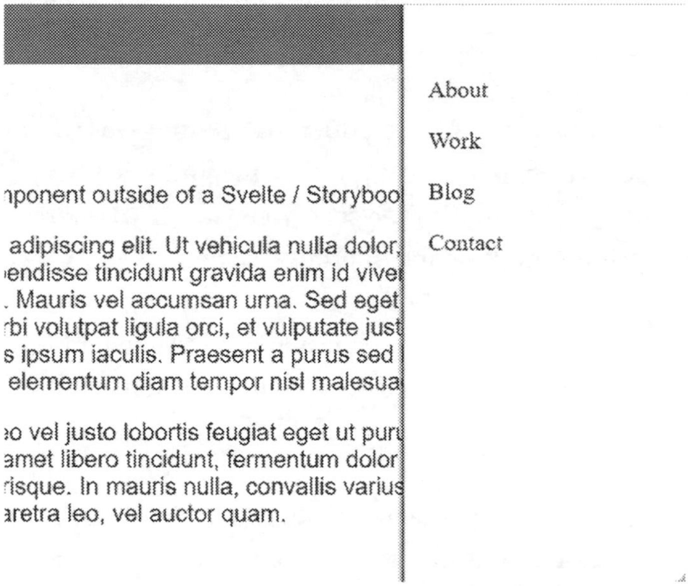

Figure 4-4. *The SideBar displayed, with four links present*

That might have seemed like a lot of work, but we now have a working
component on display. There is one thing, though – while the code
should be reasonably familiar by now, it does raise a couple of interesting
questions around how we implemented it, particularly with the call to the
second component in our template.

Before we crack on with the third and final component for this chapter,
let's take some time to review the code changes and understand how it all
works in more detail.

Understanding the Changes Made

This is one of those occasions where we break with habit and do something completely different – normally, we would have set up our component in Storybook, but adding it to a pure HTML demo makes for a nice change!

For this demo, we first had to set up `main.js` – this was to export all of the components from one central point, which makes it simpler to reference them in our calls. We then set up a basic HTML markup file with some simple styling – nothing too onerous, but enough to make the demo look somewhere near presentable!

Next up, we then added our sidebar markup – we first added a `<div>` with an `id` of hamburger, inside of which we then call the SideBar component using its web component name. The latter is important, as we're running the demo outside of Svelte, so the standard Svelte name won't work. It means though that we could call this component from inside any JavaScript framework, such as Vue, Angular, or React – I will come back to this later in the book.

To round off the demo, we then added some dummy markup inside a `<main>` block – this isn't essential, but it helps show off the effect of the sidebar better. We then checked to make sure we had a script reference to `main.js` – we noted this should already be present, but as it is a critical part of the demo, it was worth checking to make sure it was present. This completed the changes, so at this point, we fired up the development server to preview the results in our browser.

Okay – let's crack on: we have one more component to build in this chapter. This one should be no stranger, as it's used all over the web; it's time to take a look at how we might construct a Tabs component using Svelte, for our library.

Constructing the Tabs Component

If you buy anything online, such as books or products from the likes
of Amazon, then I can guarantee you will see instances of our next
component: Tabs. Tab components may only serve one purpose, but they
serve it well – they are a perfect way to display a lot of information in a
small area while allowing you to choose to view specific tabs as your needs
dictate.

For the last component in this chapter, we will build a simple Tabs
component. The basic structure is built around an unordered list and
<div> tags, but we need some Svelte magic to make it hang together – let's
look at how we create such a component in our next exercise.

BUILDING THE TABS COMPONENT

To construct our Tabs component, follow these steps:

1. To start, go ahead and create a new folder called Tabs, inside
   the \src\lib folder within our project area.

2. Next, crack open a new file and add this code – unlike other
   components, we need to add a little more code, plus a new
   function, onMount, and a click handler:

   ```
   <svelte:options tag="cobalt-tabs" />

   <script>
     import tabItems from "./tabsdata.json";
     export let activeTabValue = "0";
     export let items;
     export let vertical = false;

     if (items == null) {
       items = tabItems;
     }
   ```

```
    const handleClick = tabValue => () =>
(activeTabValue = tabValue);
</script>
```

3. Next up, miss a line, then add the markup to render our Tabs
    component:

```
<div class="cobalt" class:vertical>
  <ul>

      {#each Object.entries(items) as [id,item]}
        <li class={activeTabValue === id ?
        "active" : ""}>

          <span on:click={handleClick(id)}>
            {JSON.stringify(items[id].name).replace(/
            ['"]+/g, "")}
          </span>
        </li>
      {/each}
  </ul>

  <div class="content">
    {#each Object.entries(items) as [id, text]}
      {#if activeTabValue === id}
        {JSON.stringify(items[id].text).replace(/
        ['"]+/g, "")}
      {/if}
    {/each}  </div>
</div>
```

4. To finish off the component, we need to add some basic
    styling – we first add our library's theme colors, followed by
    some rudimentary styling:

```
.cobalt { display: block; }

ul {
```

```
  display: flex;
  flex-wrap: wrap;
  padding-left: 0;
  margin-bottom: 0;
  list-style: none;
  border-bottom: 1px solid #dee2e6;
}

.content {
  padding: 10px; }

span {
  border: 1px solid transparent;
  border-top-left-radius: 4px;
  border-top-right-radius: 4px;
  display: block;
  padding: 8px 16px;
  cursor: pointer;
}

span:hover {
  border-color: #e9ecef #e9ecef #dee2e6;
  background-color: #9393ff;
}

li.active > span { color: #ffffff; background-color:
#19247c;; border-color: #dee2e6 #dee2e6 #fff; }
```

5. Save the file as Tabs.svelte in the same Tabs folder and close it.

Great – that's the first part done! We now have a Tabs component ready to pull into Storybook and test that it works as expected. This next stage should be relatively familiar by now, so let's crack on with adding the new component to Storybook without further ado.

Exploring the Code Changes

In some ways, building a Tabs component is almost a game of two halves – although we are building one component, we have to construct code for two parts: the tab header (or tab itself) and the tab content area. Fortunately, Svelte makes this very easy, with not too much markup required!

We started by creating the requisite folder before starting to add code to what would become our core component. The first block took care of setting up two exported values – `items[]` and `activeTabValue` – as well as adding the `<svelte:options>` directive to tell Svelte we are creating a web component. At the same time, we also import an instance of our source data from a JSON file – this allows us to maintain separation of concerns. We then implement a check on `items` – if this happens to be null (as in we've not passed anything when calling the component), we set it to use the default data in the JSON file. We also add a `handleClick` event handler to switch between tabs, based on which `tabvalue` is set. Next up, we then added the markup for our component, which is based on an unordered list. We first iterate through each item and set an `active` class on the list item, depending on whether the tab has been clicked. At the same time, we display `item.value` as the header for each tab and then iterate through items and use `ActiveTabValue` to determine which content area to display as the tab in our browser.

You will notice the presence of `.replace(…)` when we display the text – this is purely to remove the quotes around each text entry from the JSON file. It's a little hacky and means we can't display quotes in the tab panel, but it works!

Accessibility – A Note

So far, we've developed a good set of components, but there is one thing we've not covered: accessibility.

Accessibility is of course an essential part of any component – with one in five people living with a disability, illness, or long-term impairment, we risk excluding up to 20% of the population if they can't use a site due to inaccessible components!

It does raise some important questions about how far we go – we can't cater for every impairment, so where do we draw the line? Making component accessible is a big task; not only do we need to add the right tags, but we also need to decide to what level we strive to attain.

It's part of the reason why I've not included accessibility for now; I felt it more important to get core functionality working and then add accessibility later. Some might argue that this isn't the right approach, but I think it's important to make sure any component you develop functions as expected, before fine-tuning it and making it more accessible.

Hooking the Component into Storybook

With the component now constructed, adding the Tabs component to our Storybook instance should be straightforward. We will use the same process as for previous components, which will help speed up the process. Let's look at the steps involved in more detail, so we can check to see if the Tabs component works as expected in Storybook.

HOOKING INTO STORYBOOK

To get our Tabs component working in Storybook, follow these steps:

1. First, go ahead and create a new file, then add this code – as before, we have a reasonable chunk to add. We'll start with adding the initial component imports, some functions from Storybook, and link in placeholder documentation:

    ```
    import Tabs from "../Tabs/Tabs.svelte";
    import TabsDocs from "./TabsDocs.mdx";
    import { Meta, Story } from '@storybook/addon-docs';''
    ```

2. This next bit should be very familiar by now – leave a line blank, then add this `<Meta>` tag. As before, it adds a title, sets the component we want to use, and blocks the default documentation page from being displayed:

    ```
    <Meta
      title = "Cobalt UI Library/Navigation Components/Tabs"
      component={Tabs}
      parameters={{ page: null }}
    />
    ```

3. With the initial configuration in place, we can now focus on our component – as before, we first need to add a template. Skip a line, then add this block in – it's similar to previous examples, but with a change of component and the passing of that example data into our component:

    ```
    export const Template = (args) => ({
      Component: Tabs,
      props: args,
    });
    ```

4. We can now render our component – for this, we will use the
    `<Story>` tag. Go ahead and add this block:

```
<Story
  name="Default"
  args={{
    vertical: false,
    items: [
      { "id": 1, "name": "Tab 1", "text": "This is
      a test"},
      { "id": 2, "name": "Tab 2", "text": "Here is
      tab 2"},
      { "id": 3, "name": "Tab 3", "text": "And this is
      tab 3"},
    ],
  }}

  parameters={{
    docs: {
      page: TabsDocs,
    },
  }}
/>
```

5. Save the file as `Tabs.stories.svelte`, then close the file.

6. You will see from the code that we've specified a file as our
    documentation but haven't yet added it. We need to extract a
    copy of `TabsDocs.mdx` from the code download and then drop
    it into the `Tabs` folder.

7. We have everything in place, so let's test it! Switch to a Node.
    js terminal session, then set the working folder to our cobalt
    project area.

8. At the prompt, enter npm run storybook and hit Enter – if all is well, we should see Storybook launch and display in our browser at http://localhost:6006/. Click on the Default link under the Tabs entry on the left to display the component we just created, as shown in Figure 4-5.

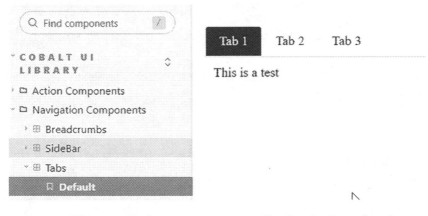

Figure 4-5. *The new Tab component on display in Storybook*

There – that doesn't look too shabby, does it? Granted, it doesn't have all of the features other Tabs components may have, but that will come in time; we've created a solid base for further development.

That isn't the end of it, though – there is scope to add a variation of our component, which we will do momentarily. Before we do so, let's pause for a moment to review the code changes we just made to see how the Tabs component renders in Storybook in more detail.

Understanding the Changes Made

By now, I'm sure you will be familiar with how we can add our component to Storybook – so much so that with a little trial and error, you could jump ahead and add it without too much help! Joking aside, it's good to review the changes we made, so let's dive in and check out the code in more detail.

We started by adding a call to the Tabs component, along with importing the placeholder Tabs documentation file and a few features from Storybook. So far, nothing particularly new; the only real change here is the `tabItems` data object we assign and will pass into the component.

The rest of the Storybook code is very similar to other components – we include the `<Meta>` tag as before (albeit referencing the Tab component this time) and a template for displaying the component on the page. We then add our Story block – for Tabs, it's a simple setup, with only the need to pass in the parameters to block the default documentation page produced by Storybook.

To round things off, we extracted a copy of the placeholder `TabsDocs.mdx` documentation file before running up the Storybook development server and previewing the results in our browser.

Creating a Variant

For the last demo in this chapter, we're going to modify how our Tabs component looks – in many cases, we would display the component horizontally, but there may be occasions where displaying the tab "heads" on the side would be a preferred option.

Fortunately, the changes needed to implement our new variant are pretty straightforward; let's crack on and implement them so we can see how our new variant appears in Storybook.

CREATING A VARIANT

To add our variant, follow these steps:

1. First, crack open the `Tabs.svelte` file, then add this line immediately below the last export:

    ```
    export let vertical = false;
    ```

2. Next, scroll down to the opening `<div>` tag for the markup;
    amend the code as highlighted:

    ```
    <div class="cobalt" class:vertical>
    ```

3. Save the file and close it. Switch to the `Tabs.stories.mdx`
    file, then scroll down to the end of the file.

4. In the Default story, add this immediately before the parameters
    call, like this:

    ```
    <Story name="Default"
      args={{
        vertical: false
        items: [
          { "id": 1, "name": "Tab 1", "text":
          "This is a test"},
          { "id": 2, "name": "Tab 2", "text":
          "Here is tab 2"},
          { "id": 3, "name": "Tab 3", "text":
          "And this is tab 3"},
        ],
      }}
    ```

5. Leave a line blank after that story, then add this new story code:

    ```
    <Story
      name="Vertical"
      args={{
        vertical: true,
        items: [
          { "id": 1, "name": "Tab 1", "text": "This is
          a test"},
          { "id": 2, "name": "Tab 2", "text": "Here is
          tab 2"},
    ```

```
    { "id": 3, "name": "Tab 3", "text": "And this
    is tab 3"},
  ],
}}
parameters={{
  docs: {
    page: TabsDocs,
  },
}}
/>
```

6. Save the file and close it. Crack open the `tabs.css` file, then
   scroll to the bottom – go ahead and add these style rules:

```css
/* variant */
div.cobalt.vertical { display: flex; }

div.cobalt.vertical ul {
  flex-direction: column;
  border-bottom: none;
  align-self: baseline;
  margin-top: 0;
}
div.cobalt.vertical div.content { width: 300px;
height: 200px; }

div.cobalt.vertical ul li span { border-top-left-radius:
0; border-top-right-radius: 0; }
```

7. We have everything in place, so let's test it! Save and close the
   file, then switch to a Node.js terminal session, and make sure
   the working folder points to our cobalt project area.

8. At the prompt, enter npm run storybook and hit Enter – if
    all is well, we should see Storybook launch and display in our
    browser at http://localhost:6006/. Click on the Vertical
    link under the Tabs entry on the left to display the component
    we just created, as shown in Figure 4-6.

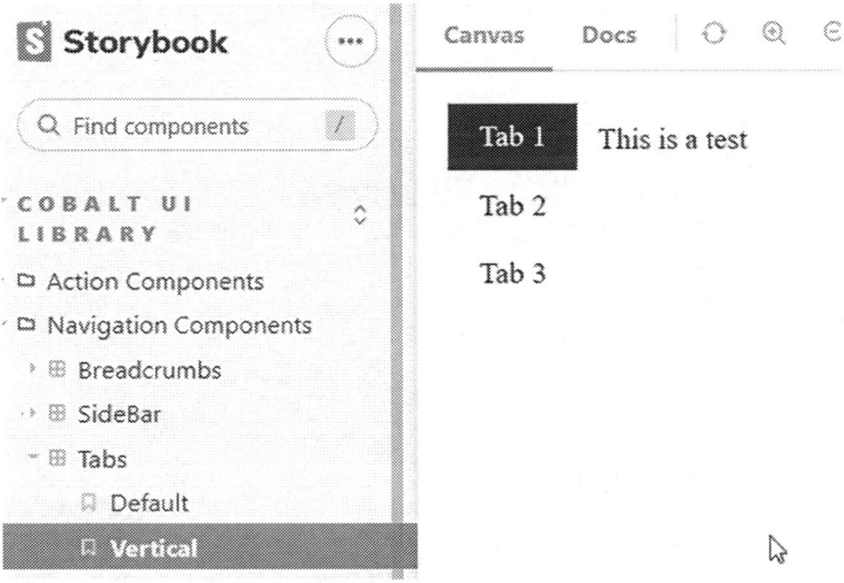

Figure 4-6. *The new variant for the Tabs component*

Perfect – with only a few minor changes (and of which most were CSS
based), we have a new variant for our Tabs component! Sure, this is only
one variant, and with a bit of work, we could add more variants (such
as different tabs, language support, and so on). It does show that with
minimal changes, we can turn an existing component into something
different and usable by developers consuming our library.

So – how did we get here? We started by adding an exported variable
vertical – this would be the trigger to tell the component to display our
tab set horizontally or vertically. We then updated the opening <div> tag

for our markup to use the class: directive; similar to before, this tells the component to include the `vertical` class if our variable `vertical` is true.

Next up, we then added a new markup block for our variant – into this, we pass the vertical variable, which is set to true. We then added a handful of styles to re-render the Tabs in a vertical format. That's one of the great things about Svelte – most of the work is done using CSS, with only minimal markup required to refactor our component!

Summary

"And that's the end of this journey, ladies and gentlemen. I hope you've enjoyed what you've seen…"

Creating excellent navigation for a site is essential – it's the bread and butter we need to help customers find what they want and keep them within the confines of our site. To help with that, we've created three Navigation components for our library; each has its respective page in our Storybook instance. We're now over halfway, with only one more component category to add to our library! Before we get on building the next category of components, let's take a moment to review what we have learned in this chapter.

As we saw back in the previous chapter, the focus is on adding each component to our library and setting it up in Storybook. We started with creating the Breadcrumbs trail component before swiftly moving on to building the more complex SideBar component.

We explored setting up a Tabs component for the third and final tool in our toolbox. It was a little more involved as we examined adding a new variant – we learned that even though we use the same markup, changes in styling effectively meant we had the equivalent of a new component.

Okay, let's crack with creating the penultimate batch of components: the notification group. We'll look at creating components such as an overlay, modal dialog boxes, and more – intrigued? Stay with me, and I'll reveal it all in the next chapter.

## CHAPTER 5

Creating Notification Components

I spend many an hour reading and researching for the books I've written – I've come across all manner of different articles, views, and ideas; too many to count! There was, however, one thing that I found that I think is very apt for this chapter:

"You can be happy with less and miserable with more."

This little gem, from the author and entrepreneur Robert Gill, is perfect for the following few pages – particularly when I say we're going to look at creating notification components! One hopes that we never get any indicating an error of some kind; indeed, the less we get, the more we're happy!

Keeping that thought, for now, we're going to work our way through creating three more components – an Alert, Dialog, and Tooltip. Much of what you are about to see will reuse many of the principles we've already covered, so without further ado, let's crack on with creating the first, which is the Alert component.

© Alex Libby 2023
A. Libby, *Developing Web Components with Svelte*,
https://doi.org/10.1007/978-1-4842-9039-2_5

Creating the Alert Component

An essential part of the user experience for anyone browsing a website is making sure we keep them informed. While we expect things to run smoothly, there will be occasions where we have to notify our customers if there is a problem! We need an Alert component – we're going to develop a suitable tool for our component toolbox using the standard HTML5 dialog element.

We could build something from the ground up, but there's no need to do so when most recent browsers natively support the dialog element. In our next exercise, we can use that to construct our Alert component. Before we assemble the code, there is one small point we should cover first, relating to the icons we use in the exercise.

Sourcing the Icons

Our Alert component will use a couple of SVG icons from the Ionicons library at `https://ionic.io/ionicons`, which we used back in Chapter 4. I've picked two, and edited versions of them for the exercise; these will be available in the code download, along with the (renamed) originals.

If you want to use different ones, browse to the link and enter "alert" or "warn" in the search box. It will come back with at least two options – to download the SVGs, click on one of the icons, then hit the SVG icon to the right of the brown box that appears at the foot of the screen in Figure 5-1.

Figure 5-1. *The download icon on the Ionic website*

122

You will need to update the SVG markup used in one of the files in the next exercise – I will point out which one, at the appropriate point. Okay – with that in mind, let's begin with the next exercise to construct our Alert component.

Building the Component

Although we're building what should be a simple Alert component, the code we need to use is a little more complex than some of our other components! We will have to create a few files and add the SVGs we talked about just now – we'll start with creating the core component first.

BUILDING THE ALERT COMPONENT

To construct our Alert component, follow these steps:

1. First, create a new folder called `Alert` at the root of the components folder.

2. Next, crack open a new file and add this code – we'll start with importing an Icon component and setting a few variables for export:

```
<svelte:options tag="cobalt-alert" />

<script>

  import Icon from "./Icon.svelte";

  export let show;
  export let icon;
  export let close;
  export let type = "";
  export let title = "";
```

```
export let description = "";
let showAnimation = true;
let typeClass;
```

3. Next, leave a line blank, then add the second part of our
    script block:

```
// Convert string value to boolean where appropriate
let showIcon = JSON.parse(icon);

switch (type) {
  case "warn":
    typeClass = "alert-warn";
    break;
  case "dark":
    typeClass = "alert-dark";
    break;
  case "error":
    typeClass = "alert-error";
    break;
  case "info":
    typeClass = "alert-info";
    break;
  case "success":
    typeClass = "alert-success";
    break;
  default:
    typeClass = "";
  }
  const classes = ["alert", typeClass, showAnimation ?
"fade-in" : ""]
    .filter((klass) => klass.length)
    .join(" ");

  const closeAlert = () => {
```

```
      show = false;
    };
</script>
```

4. We can now add the markup for our component – much of this
    standard HTML markup, but with a few Svelte tags in the mix.
    Miss a line, then add this block:

```
{#if show}
  <dialog open on:click={close} class={classes}
  role="alert">
    <div class="icon">
      {#if showIcon}<Icon iconType={type} />{/if}
    </div>
    <div class="message">
      <strong>
        {title}
      </strong>
      {description}
    </div>
    <div>
      <button on:click={closeAlert}>&#x2716;</button>
    </div>
  </dialog>
{/if}
```

5. We have one more section to add, which is the styling. For
    this, leave a blank line after the code from step 4, then add
    this block:

```
<style>
  dialog { min-width: 300px; display: flex;    justify-
  content: space-between; font-family: Arial, Helvetica,
  sans-serif; border: none; }
```

```
button { background: none; border: none; font-
size: 21px; }

.icon { margin-right: 10px; }

.message { display: flex; flex-direction:
column;    line-height: 24px; min-width: 300px; }

.fade-in { animation: fade-in 2000ms both; }

@keyframes fade-in {
  from {
    opacity: 0%;
  }
}

.alert-warn { background: #ffeb3b; color: #000000; }

.alert-info { background: #2196f3; color: #ffffff; }
</style>
```

6. Save the file as `Alert.svelte`, then close it. Next, crack open a new file and add this code – this time we first need to set three exported variables before adding what will be the markup for the first of two icons we add to our component:

```
<svelte:options tag="cobalt-icon" />

<script>
  export let width = "24px";
  export let height = "24px";
  export let iconType = "";

  let icons = [
    {
      box: 512,
      name: "info",
```

```
svg: `<path d="M248 64C146.39 64 64 146.39 64
248s82.39 184 184 184 184-82.39 184-184S349.61 64
248 64z" fill="none" stroke="currentColor" stroke-
miterlimit="10" stroke-width="32"/><path fill="none"
stroke="#ffffff" stroke-linecap="round" stroke-
linejoin="round" stroke-width="32" d="M220 220h32v116"/>
        <path fill="none" stroke="currentColor" stroke-
linecap="round" stroke-miterlimit="10" stroke-width="32"
d="M208 340h88" /><path d="M248 130a26 26 0 1026 26 26 26
0 00-26-26z" fill="#ffffff" />`,
    },
```

7. Next up, add these lines – this will form the second icon for
    our demo:

```
    {
      box: 512,
      name: "warn",
      svg: `<path d="M448 256c0-106-86-192-192-192S64
150 64 256s86 192 192 192 192-86 192-192z"
stroke="#000000" fill="none" stroke-miterlimit="10"
stroke-width="32"/><path d="M250.26 166.05L256
288l5.73-121.95a5.74 5.74 0 00-5.79-6h0a5.74 5.74 0
00-5.68 6z" fill="none" stroke="currentColor" stroke-
linecap="round" stroke-linejoin="round" stroke-
width="32"/><path d="M256 367.91a20 20 0 1120-20 20 20 0
01-20 20z" fill="#000000" />`,
    },
  ];

  let displayIcon = icons.find((e) => e.name ===
  iconType);
</script>
```

The markup is available in the code download, so you don't have to edit manually! If you were feeling brave enough and decided to use a different SVG, it's in this file you will need to update the markup. The values shown against the two `svg:` properties in this code block are the ones you will need to update.

8. With the SVG markup in place, we now need to call it – for this, miss a line, then add this markup:

```
<svg
  class={$$props.class}
  {width}
  {height}
  viewBox="0 0 {displayIcon.box} {displayIcon.box}">
    {@html displayIcon.svg}
</svg>
```

9. Save the file as `Icon.svelte` in the Alert folder, and close it.

10. Close any open files.

Great – we have our component in place, ready to test! Although much of the code consists of standard HTML markup and CSS styling, there are a few interesting points where we use Svelte syntax. Before we add our component to Storybook, let's take some time to review the code and understand how it all works – I know the SVG part will appear a little confusing at first!

Understanding What Happened

In an ideal world, we would never need to display alerts to people using a site or online application – everything would run smoothly, customers get what they want and where they need to be and leave happy and content....

However, the reality is that it is all a pipe dream and that we still need to display the occasional alert! With that in mind, and to construct our component, we started by creating the usual component folder before setting some variables for export. At the same time, we imported an `Icon` component and set two variables for use internally.

Next up, we set up a somewhat lengthy `switch` statement for type – this works out what class to set based on the value assigned to type. For example, if we had passed in `warn`, then the class applied to the component would be `alert-warn` and so on. We then concatenate all of the classes together, ready for use in our component.

We then moved on to adding the markup for our component – this is where things get a little more complex. We wrap everything in a Svelte `if` block; if `show` is set to `true`, we render the component; otherwise, we hide it. The core part of the component is built around an HTML5 dialog element, into which we pass the classes we set earlier, along with setting an `on:click` event handler to close the alert. The rest of the markup is standard HTML, with the exception of the second Svelte `if` block and the event handler assigned to the close button. To round off that part, we then add some basic styling, which includes a simple animation to render the alert.

Next up, we created `Icon.svelte` – this contained the markup for two SVGs, with three exported properties so we can control the `width`, `height`, and `iconType` from outside the component file. The magic happens in the `displayIcons` function, where we filter icons based on the `iconType` name passed into the component.

Once filtered, we render an SVG icon using the prop values and content from the `icons` object. We then rounded out the demo by adding a copy of the stylesheet alert.css from the code download – this contained the styles for the main Alert component and some additional styles we will use later in this chapter.

129

Right – let's crack on: we still have plenty to do! It's time we tested our component to ensure it works, so as with others, let's dive in and hook our component into Storybook.

Adding the Component to Storybook

So far, we've created the core Alert component, added some styling, and sourced three SVGs to act as icons when displaying the Alert. We're now at a stage where we can test the component, so as before, let's crack on with adding an instance to Storybook so we can prove it works as we expect.

ADDING TO STORYBOOK

To get our Alert component working in Storybook, follow these steps:

1. First, go ahead and create a new file, then add this code – as before, we have a reasonable chunk to add. Let's start with the initial block to import the component and documentation, along with some functions from Storybook:

```
import Alert from '../Alert/Alert.svelte';
import AlertDocs from "./AlertDocs.mdx";
import { Meta, Story } from '@storybook/addon-docs';
```

2. This next bit should be very familiar by now – leave a line blank, then add this <Meta> tag. As before, it adds a title, sets the component we want to use, and blocks the default documentation page from being displayed:

```
<Meta
   title = "Cobalt UI Library/Notification
Components/Alert"
   component={Alert}
   parameters={{page: null}}
/>
```

3. With the initial configuration in place, we can now focus on our component – as before, we first need to add a template. Skip a line, then add this block:

```
export const Template = (args) => ({
  Component: Alert,
  props: args,
});
```

4. We can now render our component – for this, we will use the now-familiar `<Story>` tag. Miss a line, then add this code:

```
<Story
      name="Info"
      args={{
            show: true,
            description: "An info description",
            title: "Simple Info",
            icon: "true",
            type: "info",
      }}
      parameters={{
            docs: {
                    page: AlertDocs
            }
      }}>
      {Template.bind({})}
</Story>
```

5. Save the file as `Alert.stories.mdx`, then close the file.

6. You will see from the code that we've specified a file as our documentation but haven't yet added it. We need to extract a copy of `AlertDocs.mdx` from the code download and then drop it into the Alert folder.

7. We have everything in place, so let's test it! Switch to a Node.
    js terminal session, then set the working folder to our `cobalt`
    project area.

8. At the prompt, enter `npm run storybook` and hit Enter – if
    all is well, we should see Storybook launch and display in our
    browser at `http://localhost:6006/`. Click on the Default
    link under Alert on the left to display the variant we just created,
    as shown in Figure 5-2.

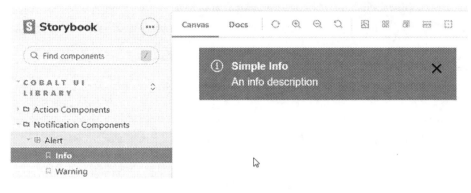

Figure 5-2. *Displaying the new Alert warning in Storybook*

Excellent – we now have a working component ready for others to
use. It's a simple affair (even if the code might say otherwise) but essential
addition to our library!

However, if we had to display any alerts, then it wouldn't just be
information ones – what about warnings, or success messages, for
example? Fortunately, these are easy to add as variants – we will add one
shortly. Let's first examine the code we created to get the component
working in Storybook in more detail.

Exploring the Code Changes

Much of this component follows a similar pattern to the others we've already created – we started with the now-familiar script block to import the placeholder documentation, an instance of the component, and some functions from the core Storybook framework. At the same time, we added an item object with some sample data, which we use to display our Breadcrumb component.

Next up, we added the usual Meta tag, which contains the details needed for the navigation in Storybook, the name of the component we will use (`Alert`), and an entry to block the default documentation page generated by Storybook. We also inserted our template – we changed the name of the component we use, but otherwise, it is identical to other components used in our library.

For the last part, we added a Story block to display an instance of our Alert component. This one, called `Info`, is set to render a simple informational alert against a predefined blue background (defined within the component itself). We pass into this component several values, such as title, description, and type, to define what the alert should display.

Okay – let's move on: our next component is one you are likely to find more on a mobile device, but that doesn't matter. Sidebars still have a crucial role in helping us navigate a website, so they are a perfect tool to have in our library. They require more work to set up, but it's worth the effort: let's dive in and look at how we might create such a component for our library.

Creating a Variant

Cast your mind back to the end of the last section but one – remember how I said it's easy to add different variants for the Alert component, such as displaying a warning message instead?

Well – we won't need to change the structure as such but tell the Alert component to use different values to display the desired message. It's easy enough to effect the changes, so let's dive in and add a variant to display a warning message in our component.

CONSTRUCTING THE VARIANT

To add our variant, follow these steps:

1. First, crack open `Alerts.svelte`, then scroll to the bottom of the page.

2. Add a blank line, then this code – this will display a warning style message in our component:

```
<Story
  name="Warning"
  args={{
    show: true,
    description: "An warning message",
    title: "Simple warning",
    icon: "true",
    type: "warn",
  }}
  parameters={{
    docs: {
      page: AlertDocs
    }
  }}>
  {Template.bind({})}
</Story>
```

3. We have everything in place, so let's test it! Save and close the file, then switch to a Node.js terminal session, and make sure the working folder points to our cobalt project area.

4. At the prompt, enter `npm run storybook` and hit Enter – if all is well, we should see Storybook launch and display in our browser at `http://localhost:6006/`. Click on the Warning link under the Alert entry on the left to display the component we just created, as shown in Figure 5-3.

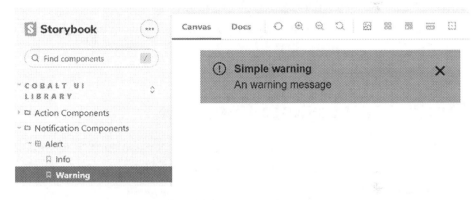

Figure 5-3. *Displaying the Warning variant of our Alert component*

Perfect – it shows that with only a few styling changes (and, of course, the message we display), we can express something that looks a little different and customize it to our needs.

A question, though: notice anything about the styling, say…how we achieved it? Some of you will undoubtedly see that we didn't add any styling for the variants, yet each appeared in its own colors. How *did* we manage to apply styling? That is indeed a good question and one that uses a clever feature in Svelte – let's take a moment to explore that and the rest of the variant code in more detail.

Breaking Apart the Code

As demos go, this is probably one of the simplest we've created so far – we've not even had to add any styles, as we made these available when we created the original component!

Most of the work hangs off step 2, where we added a new Story block to display a `warn` variant. In both cases, we changed only the `icon` and `type` parameters; the rest stayed the same as the original default Alert.

Let's move on: we still have two more components to add to our library. The next one we'll look at could still be classed as an Alert component but really suited for more complex occasions when you really need to present more dialog to your user.

Creating the Dialog Component

Okay, the lead-in to this chapter was a little corny, but on a more serious note, the name of our next component is a Dialog component! (It's good to talk, but I digress.)

Leaving aside any references to talking for the moment, the Dialog component is perfect for displaying more complex messages, although these will be disruptive. Dialogs are usually designed to be modal and must be cleared before a user can continue with their task. While they do provide feedback, it's also worth noting that we should not use dialogs to excess; they must be used when necessary, so we don't irritate our users!

The Dialog component is straightforward to create but needs a good chunk of code – let's dive in and take a look.

BUILDING THE TOAST COMPONENT

To build our Toast component, follow these steps:

1. First, create a new folder under `components`, called `Dialog`.

2. Extract a copy of the CloseIcon.svelte file from the code
    download that accompanies this book. Save it in the root of the
    Dialog folder.

3. Next, crack open a new file and add this code – we have a good
    chunk to cover, so we will add it in sections, starting with an
    export, one import, and setting a local variable:

```
<svelte:options tag="cobalt-dialog" />

<script>
  import CloseIcon from "./Close.svelte";
  export let show = "true";
  let showDialog = show == "true";
</script>
```

4. Next, leave a line blank, then add this markup:

```
<button on:click={() => (showDialog = !showDialog)}>Show
dialog</button>

{#if showDialog}
  <div class="cobalt">
    <div id="background" />
    <div id="modal">
      <div class="header">
        <h3>Modal title</h3>
        <button
          type="button"
          class="close"
          on:click={() => (showDialog = false)}
        >
          <CloseIcon />
        </button>
      </div>
      <p>Click on the X to close me</p>
```

```
    </div>
  </div>
{/if}
```

5. Finally (for this file), skip a line, then add this block of styles:

```
<style>
  .cobalt { font-family: Arial, Helvetica, sans-serif; }

  @keyframes fadein {
    from { opacity: 0; }
    to { opacity: 1; }
  }

  #background { position: fixed; z-index: 1; top:
0;    left: 0; width: 100vw; height: 100vh; background-
color: rgba(0, 0, 0, 0.7); animation: fadein 0.5s; }

  #modal { position: fixed; z-index: 2; top:
50%;    left: 50%; transform: translate(-50%,
-50%);  background: #fff; padding: 10px; width:
400px;    height: 250px; }

  .header { display: flex; justify-content: space-
between; border-bottom: 1px solid #c4c4c4; }

  #modal div button { display: contents; color:
#19247c; }

  #modal div button:hover { color: #9393ff; }
</style>
```

6. Save the file as Dialog.svelte, then close it.

Great – we have a component in place, but I can imagine what your first question will be: What does it all do? We've covered quite a bit of code over the last few pages, so let's kick back for a moment and take a closer look at the changes we made to understand how it all hangs together.

Understanding What Happened

So – what did we achieve in that last demo? We kicked off by first creating the now-familiar component folder and file before extracting a copy of the CloseIcon file from the code download – this we will use in our component. We then set up a script block in the component file, to import CloseIcon, and set an exported variable show and an internal showDialog variable.

Next up, we then set our markup – we started by defining a button element, which has an event handler to show or hide the Dialog component, each time we click the button. In the main markup, we wrap our code in a Svelte `if` block – this controls when the code is rendered based on the value of `showDialog`.

Inside the dialog markup, we set a title along with a button which we use to close the dialog and some content within. It's worth noting that (for now) the content has been hard-coded; in a future iteration, we should make these values more dynamic! We then round out the demo with some basic styling to set elements such as animation and the background for the modal dialog.

At this point, we now have a working component – the next step is to test it. As before, let's crack on and hook it into our Storybook instance.

Adding to Storybook

So now that we've created our Dialog component, how do we get it into Storybook? We'll use the same process as we've done before, but this time, we won't be adding any variants. Dialogs are more for displaying content, rather than producing different designs that are not consistent, which could confuse our users! With that in mind, let's jump in and take a look at the steps to set up our component in more detail.

ADDING TO STORYBOOK

To get our Dialog component working in Storybook, follow these steps:

1. First, go ahead and create a new file, then add this code – as before, we have a reasonable chunk to add. Let's start with the initial block to import the component and documentation, along with some functions from Storybook:

```
import Dialog from "../Dialog/Dialog.svelte";
import DialogDocs from "./DialogDocs.mdx";
import { Meta, Story } from '@storybook/addon-docs';
```

2. This next bit should be very familiar by now – leave a line blank, then add this <Meta> tag. As before, it adds a title, sets the component we want to use, and blocks the default documentation page from being displayed:

```
<Meta
  title="Cobalt UI Library/Notification Components/Dialog"
  component={Dialog}
  parameters={{ page: null }}
/>
```

3. With the initial configuration in place, we can now focus on our component – as before, we first need to add a template. Skip a line, then add this block in – it's similar to previous examples, with only a minor change of component and the addition of a button to trigger our alerts:

```
export const Template = (args) => ({
  Component: Dialog,
  props: args,
});
```

4. We can now render our component – for this, we will use the `<Story>` tag. Go ahead and add this block:

```
<Story name="Default"
  args={{
    showDialog: "false",
  }}
  parameters={{
    docs: {
      page: DialogDocs
    },
  }}
/>
```

5. Save the file as `Dialog.stories.svelte`, then close the file.

6. You will see from the code that we've specified a file as our documentation but haven't yet added it. We need to extract a copy of `DialogDocs.mdx` from the code download, then drop it into the Toast folder.

7. We have everything in place, so let's test it! Switch to a Node.js terminal session, then set the working folder to our `cobalt` project area.

8. At the prompt, enter `npm run Storybook` and hit Enter – if all is well, we should see Storybook launch and display in our browser at `http://localhost:6006/`. Click on the Success link under Toast on the left to display the variant we just created, as shown in Figure 5-4.

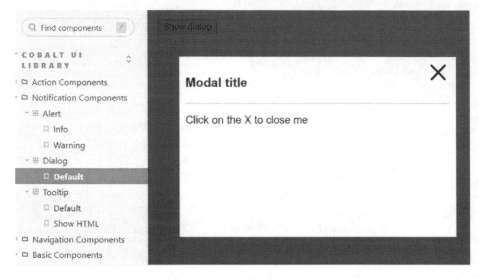

Figure 5-4. *Displaying our Dialog Alert component*

Perfect – that's the first iteration of our Dialog component done, ready for use! For now, we've not added any variants, although with a little care, we could perhaps change the formatting, or even add another button (such as an OK or Cancel), perhaps?

That thought aside, we're almost done with creating components for the Notifications part of our library; before we move on to the next category, there is one more we'll develop. This next component might seem an intriguing choice for some, but it does notify people – and you have to have one in your toolkit at some point! I'm talking about the Tooltip component – over the following few pages, we will develop our own version for the library.

Creating the Tooltip Component

The ubiquitous tooltip has been around for years – it's one of those components that just works! It's not meant to offer anything outrageously different or complex, but it is still valuable as a tool for our toolbox.

This time though, we're not going to use a standard HTML5 element like <dialog> (primarily as one doesn't exist for tooltip) but instead build our component from scratch. We're also not going to create a standard Tooltip component, but one we might use to help guide visitors through our site. For example, if we had to ask age (for age-restricted sites, such as breweries), we could explain why we need the information. Setting up the component is a little more complex, but most of the code required is standard HTML – let's dive in and take a look.

BUILDING THE TOOLTIP COMPONENT

To set up our Tooltip component, follow these steps:

1. First, create a new folder called `Tooltip` at the root of the `src/lib` folder.

2. Next, crack open a new file and add this code – we'll start with importing the fade function from Svelte, creating a few variables for export, and setting some placeholder variables for use within the component:

```
<svelte:options tag="cobalt-tooltip" />

<script>
  import { fade } from "svelte/transition";
  export let id = "tooltip";
  export let label;
  export let tip;
  export let timeout = "400";
```

```
export let showHTML = "false";

let displayHTML = JSON.parse(showHTML);

let active = false;
let enterTrigger;
let leaveTrigger;
```

3. We still need to add the second half of our script – for
    this, leave a line blank, then add this code. We have four
    functions, which take care of when the mouse or keyboard is
    used – the first two are the equivalent of onMouseEnter and
    onKeyboardDown:

```
function handleKeydown(e) {
  if (e.key === "Escape") {
    active = false;
    e.target.blur();
  }
}

function handleMouseEnter() {
  enterTrigger = setTimeout(() => {
    active = true;
  }, parseInt(timeout, 0));
}
```

4. Leave a line blank, then add the remaining two functions – they
    deal with onMouseLeave and handling interaction:

```
function handleMouseLeave() {
  if (enterTrigger) {
    clearTimeout(enterTrigger);
    enterTrigger = null;
  }
  leaveTrigger = setTimeout(() => {
```

```
    active = false;
  }, parseInt(timeout, 0));
}

function handleInteraction() {
  if (leaveTrigger) {
    clearTimeout(leaveTrigger);
    leaveTrigger = null;
  }
}
</script>
```

5. We can now add the markup for our component – much of this standard HTML markup, but it does include some Svelte tags. We'll do it in two sections – first, leave a new line blank, then add this code:

```
<div class="tooltip">
  <button
    aria-describedby={id}
    type="button"
    class="trigger"
    on:click={() => (active = true)}
    on:keydown={handleKeydown}
    on:mouseenter={handleMouseEnter}
    on:mouseleave={handleMouseLeave}
  >
    ?
  </button>
```

6. Immediately after the previous block, add the remaining code for our markup:

```
<div aria-hidden={!active} {id} role="tooltip" aria-label={label}>
  {#if active}
```

```
        <div
          transition:fade
          class="content"
          on:mouseenter={handleInteraction}
          on:mouseleave={handleMouseLeave}
        >
          {#if displayHTML}
            {@html tip}
          {:else}
            {tip}
          {/if}
        </div>
      {/if}
    </div>
</div>""""""""""""
```

7. For the last part of this component, we need to style it – we
   only need a handful of styles, so leave a line blank and add
   these rules:

```
<style>
  .tooltip { position: relative; z-index: 2; }

  .trigger { padding: 0; margin: 0; width: 19px; height:
19px; line-height: 15px; font-size: 17px; text-align:
center; background-color: transparent; border-radius:
50%; border: 3px solid #666666; color: #999999; cursor:
pointer; font-weight: bold; }

  .content { all: initial; position: absolute;    left: 0;
top: 100%; width: 300px; margin-top: 10px;
padding: 10px; border-radius: 8px; box-shadow: rgba(0, 0,
0, 0.24) 0px 3px 8px; font-size: 14px;    font-family:
Arial, Helvetica, sans-serif; }

  .trigger:focus { outline: 2px solid #000; }
```

```
[role="tooltip"]:empty { display: none; }
</style>
```

8.   Save the file as `Tooltip.svelte`, then close the file.

9.   Close any files you have open.

Excellent – we have our component in place. The next task is to try it to make sure it works; as before, we'll work through adding it to our Storybook instance.

Before we get to that, let's take a moment to review the code changes made – most of it should be self-explanatory, but some interesting Svelte techniques within the code are worth exploring in more detail.

Understanding What Happened

As components go, this is probably one of the more complex components to put together for our library – it's a real mix of HTML markup and Svelte script!

To get there, we created our file before adding a host of exported variables, to set values such as the tooltip message, `timeout`, and whether we want to show HTML or plain text in the tooltip. At the same time, we also set some internal variables to help manage the Tooltip component. We also created a set of functions – these are primarily to handle mouse or keyboard interaction when using the component.

Next up came the markup – as mentioned in the introduction, this is custom but made up of some key elements – we have a `button` element for the question mark. We pass various properties into this element, such as `type`, `class`, and `aria-describedby`. We also set several event handlers to manage keyboard and mouse interaction.

In the main block of markup, we set our container `div`, inside of which we have our tooltip – this is set to fade in or out depending on what value we set for `active`. This also contains an `if` block, to determine if we can show HTML code, or should show plain text; this is controlled by the `displayHTML` value. To finish, we then added a set of CSS style rules to make our tooltip look at least presentable when displayed in the browser.

Adding the Component to Storybook

You should hopefully know the drill by now – it's time to test our component!

We can do this in several ways; for our next exercise, we will use the default placement value at the bottom left of our example button. For the variant (which will come shortly), we will add a story to Storybook that allows the display of custom HTML in the tooltip. Let's start with setting up a default instance of our Tooltip component in Storybook.

ADDING TO STORYBOOK

To get our Tooltip component working in Storybook, follow these steps:

1. First, go ahead and create a new file, then add this code – as before, we have a reasonable chunk to add. Let's start with the initial block to import the component and documentation, along with some functions from Storybook:

```
import Tooltip from "../Tooltip/Tooltip.svelte";
import TooltipDocs from "./TooltipDocs.mdx";
import { Meta, Story } from '@storybook/addon-docs';
```

2. This next bit should be very familiar by now – leave a line blank, then add this `<Meta>` tag. As before, it adds a title, sets the component we want to use, and blocks the default documentation page from being displayed:

```
<Meta
  title="Cobalt UI Library/Notification Components/
  Tooltip"
  component={Tooltip}
  parameters={{ page: null }}
/>
```

3. With the initial configuration in place, we can now focus on our component – as before, we first need to add a template. Skip a line, then add this block in – it's similar to previous examples, but with a few changes:

```
export const Template = (args) => ({
  Component: Tooltip,
  props: args,
});
```

4. We can now render our component – for this, we will use the `<Story>` tag. Go ahead and add this block:

```
<Story
    name="Default"
    args={{
        tip: '<p>This is an informational tooltip - to
        learn more <a href="/tutorial">click here</a><p>',
        showHTML: "false",
        timeout": "400",
        label": "more info",
    }}
    parameters={{
        docs: {
            page: TooltipDocs,
        },
    }}
/>
```

5. Save the file as `Tooltip.stories.svelte`, then close the file.

6. You will see from the code that we've specified a file as our documentation but haven't yet added it. We need to extract a copy of `TooltipDocs.mdx` from the code download and then drop it into the `Tooltip` folder.

7. We have everything in place, so let's test it! Switch to a Node.js terminal session, then set the working folder to our `cobalt` project area.

8. At the prompt, enter `npm run Storybook` and hit Enter – if all is well, we should see Storybook launch and display in our browser at `http://localhost:6006/`. Click on the Default link under SelectBox on the left to display the variant we just created, as shown in Figure 5-5.

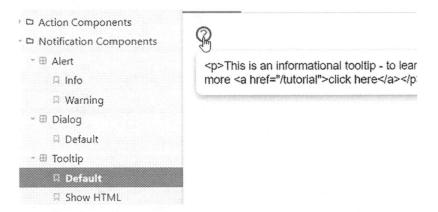

Figure 5-5. *Displaying the Tooltip component in Storybook*

9. When you run the demo for the first time, you may notice that the tooltip is not 100% visible; this is easy to fix. Crack open the `preview-head.html` file in the `./storybook` folder, and add this code at the bottom:

```
<style>
  .innerZoomElementWrapper {
    height: 200px;
  }
</style>
```

10. Save the file and refresh your browser – you will find that each Story preview window will now be larger, to better fit the demo.

As it so happens, this fix will also resolve the same issue with the Spinner component, which you may have seen earlier in the book!

Great – we should now have our Tooltip component displayed in Storybook! This is a useful addition to our library and one we should be able to expand in the future; we might want to control where the tip displays, for example. However, that's for another time – for now, let's take a moment to review the code changes before cracking on with the next component.

Exploring the Code Changes

At first glance, adding our Tooltip component should be easy. Indeed, we've added a few components already, so as we're using the same process, we should be able to add it and variants without too much difficulty.

To get us started, we first created our story file before adding the imports for the component, our placeholder documentation file, and some functions from Storybook.

This next part should be very familiar by now – we add the usual <Meta> tag, which sets the component we want to use and blocks Storybook from creating the default documentation page. We then added a template – it's very similar to previous ones, to tell it which component to use and to pass in any prop values set as arguments. We then finish the demo by adding a Story block for the default instance of our Tooltip component, along with our documentation file, before previewing the results in a browser.

Creating a Variant

Throughout this book, we've added a few variants to components along the way. In many cases, these have been as additional entries in Storybook.

Our Tooltip component is no different – although we will create a second "story" for it, we are in reality copying most of the code from the original story and changing a single value! To see what I mean, let's dive in and take a look.

CONSTRUCTING THE VARIANT

To add a variant for the Tooltip component, follow these steps:

1. First, go ahead and crack open `Tooltip.stories.svelte` – scroll down to the bottom of the file.

2. Leave a line blank, then add in this block of code:

```
<Story
  name="Show HTML"
  args={{
    tip: '<p>This is an informational tooltip - <a
    href="/tutorial">learn more</a></p>',
    showHTML: "true",
    timeout: "400",
    label: "more info",
}}
```

```
parameters={{
  docs: {
    page: TooltipDocs,
  },
}}
/>
```

3. Save and close any files open.

4. We have everything in place, so let's test it! Switch to a Node.
   js terminal session, then set the working folder to our `cobalt`
   project area.

5. At the prompt, enter `npm run storybook` and hit Enter – if
   all is well, we should see Storybook launch and display in our
   browser at `http://localhost:6006/`. Click on the Default
   link under SelectBox on the left to display the variant we just
   created, as shown in Figure 5-6.

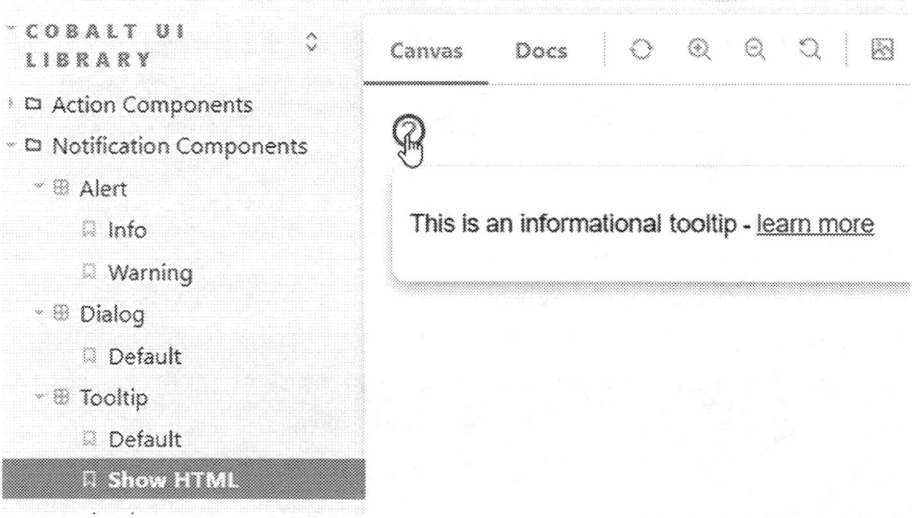

Figure 5-6. *Displaying the custom version of our Tooltip component*

Excellent – we've completed our Tooltip component and tested it: it's now ready for use. That brings us to the close of this chapter and where we move on to what will be the next batch of components to add, but before we do so, let's quickly cover off the changes made in this last demo. The only change we had to effect was to change `showHTML` from `"false"` to `"true"`; this triggers the `displayHTML` check in our code, so allowing us to use HTML. The rest of the code is the same, albeit with slightly different markup; you will notice though that the markup is rendered properly this time, not as plain text in our demo.

Summary

No one likes getting more notifications than is necessary – it's essential to get the balance right. Otherwise, we are likely to end up irritating our customers! We still need to have something available, and while getting the balance right is something that only comes with testing, we can at least ensure we have suitable components available for use.

To help with that, we've created three components for our library; each has its respective page in our Storybook instance. It brings us up to the penultimate component group in our library, with only one more component category to add to our library! Before we build the final category of components, let's take a moment to review what we have learned in this chapter.

As we saw in the previous chapter, the focus is on adding each component to our library and setting it up in Storybook. We started with creating the Alert trail component before swiftly moving on to building the more complex Notification component. Both follow the same principle of displaying a notification, but they each do it differently, and choosing the best one to use will depend on where we need to use it.

We explored setting up a Tooltip component as this category's third and final tool. This one ended up being a little more limiting, as we couldn't set up a separate variant in Storybook; this is something we should consider prioritizing in future development. Despite this, we found that we can still create a suitable variant with only minimal changes, even if we can't display it in Storybook at the same time as the default version.

Okay, let's crack with creating the final batch of components: the Grids group. It will depart a little from the usual practice as we're only going to make a single component this time! But – this is one component that will be flexible and allow us to create different layouts. Intrigued? Stay with me, and I will explain all in the next chapter.

CHAPTER 6

Creating Grid Components

So far, we've created a reasonably sized collection of components, most of which we've added to Storybook and checked that they run as expected in a browser. We have one more set of components to create before we update the documentation in the next chapter – the last batch of components is an ImageGrid.

Hold on a moment. That's just one component, right? Well, yes – and no: it is one component, but due to how Web Components work in Svelte, we need to make it from no less than three components!

I'm sure you're probably a little confused by now – don't worry: we will still use the same approach as before, but this time, I'll show you how with a bit of planning, we can bring all three components together to create a starting point for our ImageGrid component. Let's begin with setting the scene for the construction of this component.

Determining the Approach

When I started researching for this chapter, I had initially planned to create a layout grid component (or set of components). However, this soon proved too large for this book's scope – it would have meant subsuming

© Alex Libby 2023
A. Libby, *Developing Web Components with Svelte*,
https://doi.org/10.1007/978-1-4842-9039-2_6

a large part of the CSS Grid or CSS Flexbox layout concepts, which could almost form a book itself! So – how can I scale this back to something more manageable?

I was still keen to use native CSS standards where possible and not use third-party libraries to help keep the component light and dependency-free (so to speak). One component came to mind that fitted the bill – what about an ImageGrid? We can use these in e-commerce sites to display products; this is a perfect fit for using CSS Grid to build a working component. Sure, we could do this from scratch, but why reinvent the wheel when someone has something you can use?

So – how to make this a set of components? Well, two quirks helped in this respect:

- Svelte web components can only accept string-based prop values. You will undoubtedly see from each component we've created that we only pass string values; this is why!

- Storybook doesn't make it easy to showcase multiple components in a single story – there are cases for React, but support for Svelte doesn't seem to be at the same level (at least at the time of writing). To work around this, we can create a container component; into this, we can call the child components we need for creating our ImageGrid.

With this in mind, let's begin with building the first of our three components – the Table component, which will act as our container for the ImageGrid.

Building the Table Component

As always, we must start somewhere – we know Storybook doesn't make it easy to display composite components in the same format as individual ones, so it makes sense to create our container component for the ImageGrid.

This first component will be a relatively lightweight one, to begin with, but one I am sure we can develop in the future – along with the two child components we will create later in this chapter. Let's dive in and look at what is involved in more detail.

BUILDING THE TABLE COMPONENT

To construct our Table component, follow these steps:

1. First, create a new folder called Table at the root of the components folder.

2. Next, open a new file and add this code – save it as Table. svelte. We'll start with setting the svelte:options tag, followed by importing two components and setting four variables for export:

```
<svelte:options tag="cobalt-table" />

<script>
  import Grid from "./Grid.svelte";
  import Cell from "./Cell.svelte";

  export let columnCount = "4";
  export let rowCount = "4";
  export let itemCount = "";
  export let border = "";
  export let placeholderImages = "false";
</script>
```

3. Next, we have the markup – first, miss a line, then add this
    block of code:

```
<Grid columns={columnCount} rows={rowCount} {border}>
  {#each { length: parseInt(itemCount, 0) } as _, i}
    <Cell {placeholderImages} />
  {/each}
</Grid>
```

4. Please save the file and close it.

That was a short exercise – it doesn't look like it does much at face
value! It still performs an important role, though – to understand how it fits
into the larger picture, let's take a moment to review the code changes in
more detail.

Understanding What Happened

Although this last exercise was brief, it serves an important role – you may
remember earlier my comments about Storybook not making it easy to
host a component made up of subcomponents, such as ours. In this case,
we managed to get around it by using the Table component as a container
for everything else. We may use the Cell and Grid components too, but as
far as Storybook is concerned, we host everything inside Table.

In terms of code, there is very little going on in this component – we set
the now-familiar `svelte:options` tag before importing both the Grid and
Cell components into our component. We then set five variables for export,
including `columnCount`, `rowCount`, and `border`.

The (other) important part of this component, though, is in the call
to `<Grid...>` – here, we pass into it values for `columnCount` (number of
columns), `rowCount` (number of rows), and border (dictates if one should
be displayed). We then iterate through `itemCount`, having converted it

from a string to an integer; for each instance of `itemCount`, we call the Cell component and tell it whether it should display placeholder images when viewing the component in our browser.

Okay – let's move on: we've referenced the Grid and Cell components in our last demo, but the Table component won't work yet, as neither Cell nor Grid exists yet! That's easy to fix: let's dive in and look at setting up both; we'll start with Grid as the next component.

Creating the Grid Component

With the container component now complete, we can focus on the second component for this chapter – the Grid component. It will act as a container too, but this one reformats each cell into the correct order based on what we set using Flexbox. Setting up this component is a little more complex than the previous one, so let's dive in and take a look.

CONSTRUCTING THE GRID COMPONENT

We have the initial Table component in place – the next one to develop is the Grid component. To set this component up, work through these steps:

1. First, create a new file called `Grid.svelte` inside the `\src\ components\Table` folder.

2. Next, crack open a new file and add this code – we'll start with setting the `svelte:options` tag, followed by setting four variables for export and two for internal use in the component:

```
<svelte:options tag="cobalt-grid" />

<script>
  export let columns = "2";
  export let rows = "4";
  export let border = "1px solid #000000";
```

161

```
    let colInt = parseInt(columns, 0);
    let rowInt = parseInt(rows, 0);
</script>
```

3. Next, we need to add the markup for our component – skip a line, then add this code:

```
<div
  style="
    grid-template-rows: repeat({rowInt}, 1fr);
    grid-template-columns: repeat({colInt}, auto);
    border: {border};
  "
>
  <slot />
</div>
```

4. To finish off the component, let's add some styling – we're hard-coding most of the properties for now, but with the intention that if we develop the component further, we can make them dynamic:

```
<style>
  div {
    font-family: Arial, Helvetica, sans-serif;
    display: grid;
    grid-column-gap: 10px;
    grid-row-gap: 5px;
    grid-auto-flow: column;
    border: 1px solid black;
  }
</style>
```

5. Go ahead and save and close the file – the changes for this component are complete.

Excellent – that's two components down, one left to complete for our ImageGrid! We base most of this component around standard HTML markup and CSS styling, but there are a couple of exciting code features we've used – let's review the code changes we made to understand how they work in more detail.

Breaking Apart the Code

There is one thing I love about Svelte – we could have spent time creating an elaborate Grid component, but instead, Svelte allows us to use existing techniques such as CSS Grid, with very little need for extra coding to make it all work!

To build our Grid component, we began first by adding the now-familiar `svelte:options` tag before creating three variables for export: `columns`, `rows`, and `border`. These will take care of the number of `columns` we should display, the number of `rows` that should be present, and whether our table should have a `border`.

We then converted the column and row values from strings to integers – this is necessary, as we can only pass strings between Svelte web components. We get around it by converting these strings into the respective types within each component.

The key part of this component comes next – most of the hard work is done using CSS styling, which makes it super-efficient. We set a `<div>` element, to which we apply the CSS Grid `grid-template-rows` and `grid-template-columns` attributes. We use these to define the number of rows and columns to display on the page, using `1fr` to set cells of equal spacing in each case. At the same time, we also set some typical CSS styling that you might see when using CSS Grid elements – such as `display: grid` or `grid-row-gap`. These are hard-coded for now, but there is no reason why we might not want to make them more dynamic sometime in the future.

You will also notice the presence of `<slot />` – this we use to display whatever HTML or text is rendered inside the call to Grid when using the component.

Right, let's crack on – we have one more component to create, which is Cell.

Creating the Cell Component

At this stage, we now have two of the three components in place – there is one more component left to add: the Cell component.

This one isn't as complex as Grid – here, we need to create a container representing the cell of our grid and determine if we want to show a placeholder image or leave it blank.

Admittedly, the former is something we might want more control over, but that's the beauty of creating a component – it's something we can develop further at a later date. For now, though, let's focus on building the base cell component, which we will do as part of the next exercise.

CONSTRUCTING THE CELL COMPONENT

We've reached the third and final component for this chapter – to set it up, follow these steps:

1. First, crack open a new file, saving it as `Cell.svelte` in the `\src\components\Table` folder.

2. Next, go ahead and add this code to the top of that file:

```
<svelte:options tag="cobalt-cell" />

<script>
  export let placeholder = "false";
  let imgHolder = JSON.parse(placeholder);
</script>
```

3. We need to add markup for our component – miss a line after the code from step 2, then add this:

```
<div class="cell">
  {#if imgHolder}
    <div>
      <img src="https://loremflickr.com/150/160/camera"
      alt="placeholder" />
      <div class="description">This is a test image</div>
    </div>
  {:else}
    <slot />
  {/if}
</div>
```

4. As the last part, let's finish our component off with some styling:

```
<style>
  .cell { border: 1px solid black; text-align: center; }

  .description { color: #ffffff; background-color:
  #6666ff; padding: 2px 0; }

  img { padding: 5px; }
</style>
```

5. Save the file and close it – we have completed all of the necessary changes for now.

Perfect – we have everything in place, ready to link into Storybook! Although this last component wasn't substantial, we can still gain some valuable tips from this code, so let's review it in more detail before moving on to the next stage.

Understanding What Happened

In that last demo, we created the Cell component, which means we now have all the constituent elements we need for our ImageGrid component. This final component was a little more involved than the others – to construct it, we first added the usual `svelte:options` tag before setting two variables (including one for export, `placeholder`).

You may notice the somewhat interesting use of `JSON.parse`, mainly as we're not using any JSON content in our component! There is a reason for this – it's a little hack to convert the original string value for `placeholderImages` into a number value (and store it in `imgHolder`).

We then set a `div` element as a container before using `imgHolder` to determine if the component should display markup for a placeholder image. If so, we include an image that uses the LoremFlickr website to pick a random image as our placeholder; I've set it to use the `camera` as a search term, but we could change it to something else if required. The critical thing to note is that if a placeholder image is not needed, we use `<slot />` to render whatever markup is between the component tags.

Our next task is to add our new ImageGrid component to Storybook, so we can see how it looks in practice – before we do that, there is one small point I want to cover: `placeholderImages`.

You will see from the cell component markup that we've added an option to display placeholder images or our own but have not yet used it. The reason for this is that we will make use of it in Storybook when we come to add a variant later in this chapter. It's all about preparation and thinking ahead – as you will see, it makes adding our `placeholderImages` variant much easier!

Adding to Storybook

By now, I suspect this next part should be somewhat familiar to you –
we've added all of our components (except one) to Storybook, so there
isn't likely to be anything too new for our next task. We're now at a stage
where we can test the ImageGrid component, so as before, let's crack
on with adding an instance to Storybook so we can prove it works as
we expect.

HOOKING INTO STORYBOOK

Although we've created a component, we won't see how it works until we get
it into our demo. To do so, follow these steps:

1. First, create a new file, then add this code – as before, we have
   a reasonable chunk to add. Let's start with the initial block to
   import the component and documentation, along with some
   functions from Storybook:

```
import Table from "../ImageGrid/Table.svelte";
import TableDocs from "./TableDocs.mdx";
import { Meta, Story } from '@storybook/addon-docs';
```

2. Next, leave a line blank, then add the now-familiar Meta tag,
   as shown:

```
<Meta
  title="Cobalt UI Library/Grid Components/ImageGrid"
  component={Table}
  parameters={{page: null}}
/>
```

3. As in previous demos, we also need to add a template – go
    ahead and miss a line, then add this constant declaration:

```
export const Template = (args) => ({
  Component: Table,
  props: args,
});
```

4. We can now add the Story to our file, which will render the
    component on the page:

```
<Story name="Default"
  args={{
    columnCount: "1",
    rowCount: "4",
    border: "none",
    placeholderImages: "false",
    itemCount: "12",
  }}
  parameters={{
    docs: {
      page: TableDocs
    },
  }}
/>
```

5. Save the file as `Table.stories.mdx` in the \src\lib\storybook
    folder, then close the file.

6. You will see from the code that we've specified a file as our
    documentation but haven't yet added it. We need to extract a
    copy of `TableDocs.mdx` from the code download and then
    drop it into the Alert folder.

7. We have everything in place, so let's test it! Switch to a Node.
    js terminal session, then set the working folder to our `cobalt`
    project area.

8. At the prompt, enter `npm run storybook` and hit Enter – if
    all is well, we should see Storybook launch and display in our
    browser at `http://localhost:6006/`. Click on the Default
    link under Alert on the left to display the variant we just created,
    as shown in Figure 6-1.

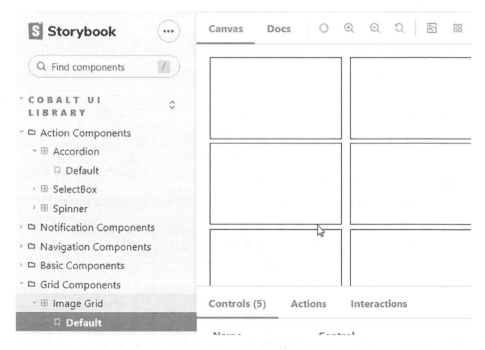

Figure 6-1. *Our newly created ImageGrid component in Storybook*

Great – we now have a working ImageGrid component available in our
component library! We've covered a good chunk of code in this last demo,
so while most of it will be similar to what we've already used earlier in the
book, let's take a quick look through it as a bit of a refresher for us.

Exploring in Detail

By now, you will hopefully be familiar with most of the steps we've used to add our component to Storybook – using the same format may seem a little repetitive, but the flip side is that it does make it quicker to replicate for other components.

In our case, we set up an instance of the Storybook page for the ImageGrid component, even though we're using Table as the main container for our component. We added three imports, namely, the Table component, documentation, and two functions from the Addon-Docs component for Storybook.

Next came the usual `<Meta>` tag – we used this to create a section called `ImageGrid` in Storybook and point it to the `Table` component as the entry point. We also disabled Storybook from automatically generating its documentation, as we will replace it shortly.

The most important part came next – we added a template for our component to render it on-screen; here, we set it to use the Table component and pass in `args` as a props call.

To combine it and complete the component, we added an instance of `<Story>` to tell Storybook how to render the component and which props values to use. We told it to use the `TableDocs.mdx` file as our documentation; this comes from the code download accompanying this book.

Adding a Variant

We now have our ImageGrid displayed in Storybook – it looks good and resizes well (or at least within the confines of Storybook). The trouble is it seems a little...well, plain. Can we do anything about this?

As it happens, yes, we can – you've probably guessed it: we could add a variant at this point! There is a variant I think would work well here – what about adding a placeholder image and maybe a label too?

ADDING A VARIANT

To add in both an image and label will require some changes to the story we set up in Storybook – to see what needs changing, follow these steps:

1. First, crack open `Table.stories.mdx` from within the `\src\lib\storybook` folder – take a copy of the **entire** "Default" Story block, and paste it below, leaving a line blank between stories.

2. Next, change the Story name property from "Default" to "Placeholder Images."

3. The value we need to change is `placeholderImages` – set this to `true`.

4. Save the file, then close it.

5. We need to test the change – to do so, revert to a Node.js command prompt, then make sure the working folder is set to our project area if it is not already there.

6. At the prompt, type `npm run storybook`, then press Enter.

7. Storybook's development server should fire up – if all is well, we can preview the results of our change at `http://localhost:6006/`. Find the Grid entry on the left, then click on ImageGrid ➤ Placeholder Images to view the new variant (Figure 6-2).

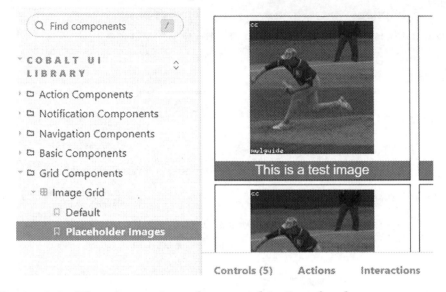

Figure 6-2. *The new variant showcased in Storybook*

This change looks a little more enticing, wouldn't you agree? There will be cases where we aren't ready to display our images, so having something in place gives a little more visual interest.

As you will have seen, we've used an image placeholder service, so images are not instant – this would be a perfect candidate for updating to a fetch feature (more on this later). For now, though, let's concentrate on the code changes we made – most of it should be self-explanatory by now, but it's still worth reviewing the code in more detail.

Understanding How It Works

This last demo has to be one of the simplest we've done – it might seem a little long at seven steps, but in reality, we only need to do one thing: copy and rename the story! A lot of this comes from a little careful preplanning; it shows that thinking ahead makes a repetitive task easier to complete.

Even though we only made one change, it's still an important one – we added a new instance of a Story block, but this time changed the `placeholderImages` property to `true`. It tells the component to render placeholder images from the LoremFlickr service we added earlier, along with the labels below each picture. This was the only change we needed to make – we finished by running the usual steps to preview the results in our browser.

Summary

Adding the ImageGrid/Table components marks a significant milestone – we now have all of the components set up in our library and available in Storybook. It might have taken a while to get there, but we are indeed there. Or are we? I'll come back to that question in a moment, but we've covered some important material in this chapter, so let's pause to review what we have learned.

We briefly looked at how we would approach this particular group. We noted a couple of limitations around only accepting string values and Storybook not making things easy for us, so we decided to create an ImageGrid component as a basis for the subcomponents in this chapter.

In total, we created three components based on the CSS Grid framework supported natively in most browsers, which makes them more lightweight and easier to develop. We started first with Table, which acts as our entry point for Storybook, and followed this with Grid, then Cell – all three used minimal markup with styling that you might typically use when styling with CSS Grid.

We then rounded off the chapter with a look at how to hook the components into Storybook as the ImageGrid, before adding a simple variant to display placeholder images in our component.

Phew – all the components are now up and running; what's next? We are there in terms of development, but it's time for one of those tasks that I know people don't always enjoy...documentation. Yes, it's time to do some writing; stay with me as I show you how we use Markdown to create our documentation within Storybook in the next chapter.

CHAPTER 7

Writing Documentation

Throughout this book, we've created a host of new components to form our component library – they may only be simple ones, but as they say: we must start somewhere!

There is one important task we need to perform, and that is to document how these components work. Given we're using Storybook (at least for most of them), then we can add some documentation files to each component, which are accessible from the Docs tab at the top of Storybook, as shown in Figure 7-1.

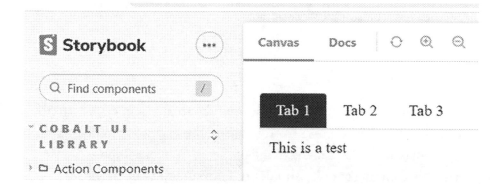

Figure 7-1. *An example of the Docs tab in Storybook*

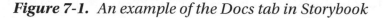

© Alex Libby 2023
A. Libby, *Developing Web Components with Svelte*,
https://doi.org/10.1007/978-1-4842-9039-2_7

You will no doubt notice that we've already done this for most (if not all) components – the trouble is they are placeholder pages and in dire need of updating! This updating is easy enough to do – the placeholder pages we've added so far use Markdown, similar to what you might use if you're creating pages in GitHub, for example.

Don't worry if you're not familiar with Markdown – most of it is text based, with a relatively simple syntax for creating items such as titles. I'll take you through everything step by step as we go through this chapter. Rather than being too prescriptive about the final article, we'll keep each relatively fluid, so you can use them as a basis for expanding and developing your versions in the future.

Okay – we have plenty to cover: rather than go through each category of components (which will get a little tedious, I'm sure), we're going to take a different approach. In this chapter, we'll work through two categories step by step. In Chapter 8, though, the focus will be on you! I'll provide the necessary labels and values, but it will be up to you to work through each of the remaining categories. Don't worry, though – if you get stuck, all the answers will be available in the accompanying code download. With all of that in mind, let's explore the process we will use for performing the update for each documentation page.

Setting the Scene

Cast your mind back to the last component we created – in each instance, we added a file called XXXXX.stories.mdx to the storybook folder for each component (where XXXXX is the name of the component, such as Slider).

This file contains our placeholder documentation – each will, of course, vary depending on the components and variants we create, but all will have some key elements for consistency:

- Title and introduction (we must start somewhere!)

- Jump links to each variant

- An example of the code for each component or variant

- Add-on badges to confirm status, for example, Stable, Experimental, etc.

- A list of argument types where appropriate

In addition, do you remember adding a `page:null` change into each Storybook file, such as this example?

```
<Meta
  title="Cobalt UI Library/Basic Components/Checkbox"
  component={Checkbox}
  parameters={{ page: null }}
/>
```

It allows us to create a custom documentation page for each component – if we don't, Storybook will produce most pages automatically. The autogeneration may not be too much of an issue, but I'm not sure how much control we will have over the results!

Okay – let's crack on: now that we know what we need to cover, we'll make a start by updating each documentation page. We'll begin with the easy Basic group first; before we do so, we need to perform a little housekeeping.

Copies of all the source files will be in the code download if you get stuck – but I recommend working through the changes bit by bit to learn how it hangs together! Documentation should evolve; we'll begin with something simple for now, but we can expand and develop in the future.

Adding Status Badges

Our first task is to set up badges – this is one of the features we listed back in the previous section as something we want to have on all component pages. The process comes in two parts – in the next exercise, we'll set up the feature for use in Storybook; we will add labels later as we go through the documentation for each component.

ADDING STATUS BADGES

To add status badges, follow these steps — we'll use the Checkbox component as our example:

1. First, we need to install the storybook-addon-badges package. To do this, crack open a Node.js terminal session, then change the working folder to our project area.

2. At the prompt, run this command:

   ```
   npm install @geometricpanda/storybook-addon-badges
   ```

3. Node will go away and install it — minimize the session, as we will need it later in this exercise.

4. Once we've installed the package, switch to your editor, and open the `main.js` file in the `\.storybook` folder.

5. We need to tell Storybook about our new package, so add the highlighted line as indicated:

   ```
   "addons": [
     "@storybook/addon-links",
     "@storybook/addon-essentials",
     "@storybook/addon-interactions",
       "@geometricpanda/storybook-addon-badges",
   ],
   ```

6.   We have one more configuration change to make – this one is
     in \.storybook\preview.js. Crack this file open in your
     editor, then add this block immediately before the last closing },
     like so:

```
matchers: {
  color: /(background|color)$/i,
  date: /Date$/,
},
badgesConfig: {
  beta: {
    styles: {
      backgroundColor: '#FFF',
      borderColor: '#018786',
      color: '#018786',
    },
    title: 'Beta',
  },
  deprecated: {
    styles: {
      backgroundColor: '#FFF',
      borderColor: '#6200EE',
      color: '#6200EE',
    },
    title: 'Deprecated',
  },
},
}
```

7.   Next, open Checkbox.stories.mdx from the \src\lib\
     storybook folder in your editor, then add this line immediately
     after the last import statement at the top of the file:

```
import { BADGE } from '@geometricpanda/storybook-
addon-badges';
```

8. Scroll down to the parameters section in the Default story – go ahead and add the badges: line, as shown:

```
parameters={{
  docs: {
    page: CheckboxDocs
  },
  badges: [BADGE.EXPERIMENTAL]
}}>
{Template.bind({})}
```

9. Save and close all open files. Revert to the Node.js terminal session from earlier; then at the prompt, enter npm run storybook and browse to http://localhost:6006/. If all is well, we should see the Experimental badge shown in Figure 7-2.

Figure 7-2. *An example of a Storybook add-on badge*

Great – we can now add badges to our site! At first glance, one marked EXPERIMENTAL might scare a few people – don't worry: it's not intended! What's more important here – for now – is the *principle* of adding badges; we can easily add new custom badges or override the styles of existing ones at a later date.

As it happens, we've already added two examples (see step 6), so if you change BADGE.EXPERIMENTAL to BADGE.BETA (from step 8), you will hopefully see something a little less scary! That aside, this is a valuable feature in Storybook, so let's spend a few moments reviewing the changes in more detail.

Understanding What Happened

Since I started working with Storybook several years ago, adding badges has always been one of my top tasks for customizing Storybook. It gives a clear, unambiguous way to show what state a plug-in is in, such as Stable, Experimental, or even (dare I say it) Deprecated.

It is an easy plug-in to install – we first ran a typical `npm install` command to download and set up the plug-in. The install is only part of the story, though, as next, we had to tell Storybook about the plug-in; we added it to the list of add-ons in the `.\storybook\preview.js` configuration file. We then added an interesting block – it's not something we will use immediately, but I will return to this in a moment.

To finish the demo, we added an import statement to `Checkbox.stories.mdx` (our demo file for this exercise). We followed this by inserting a `badges:` property into the `<Story>` object before saving the file and restarting Storybook to view the results in our browser.

Customizing the Badges Plug-in Configuration

Now – cast your mind back a few lines from that explanation: remember I said we added a block but didn't use it just yet?

This block was a good example of customizing the configuration for the Storybook Addon Badges plug-in; here is a reminder of the code:

```
badgesConfig: {
  beta: {
    styles: {
      backgroundColor: '#FFF',
      borderColor: '#018786',
      color: '#018786',
    },
    title: 'Beta',
    },
```

```
deprecated: {
  styles: {
    backgroundColor: '#FFF',
    borderColor: '#6200EE',
    color: '#6200EE',
  },
  title: 'Deprecated',
},
...
```

At first glance, it might take a moment to work out how it all hangs together, but it's simpler than it might appear. We have the `badgesConfig` object, inside which we can add as many badge types as we require.

Our example has two at present: beta and deprecated – we might want to add labels such as Alpha, Windows Only, Mac Only, and so on. Whatever labels we add will entirely be based on our requirements, although I would recommend not adding more labels than is necessary!

The key to making it all work is two properties: `styles` and `title`. Both should be self-explanatory, but to confirm, they contain the CSS styles and title name for each label.

Try changing the `BADGE.EXPERIMENTAL` to `BADGE.BETA`, which we set up in the last exercise – it should look something like this:

```
parameters={{
  docs: {
    page: CheckboxDocs
  },
  badges: [BADGE.BETA]
}}>
{Template.bind({})}
```

If all is well, we should see the EXPERIMENTAL label replaced with a BETA one, as shown in Figure 7-3.

Canvas   Docs   ○ ⊕ ⊖ ⊘ | ▨ ░ ▨ ░ ⊡ | [BETA]

☑ This is a default checkbox

Figure 7-3. *The new BETA label on the Checkbox docs page in StoryBook*

The remaining styles for each label are just standard CSS color properties – this will vary according to the color palette you're using for your site.

I would recommend using HEX values, though – a scan through the DOM of an example suggests that most values for this plug-in surface as HEX values anyway, plus the documentation isn't clear as to whether the plug-in supports RGBA or other color values.

Okay – let's crack on with updating the documentation! There is plenty to do, but as a fair bit is very similar, we're not going to work through all the steps for adding documentation. Instead, I will take a different approach involving some audience participation. Yes, we're already doing that, but bear with me, and I will explain.

Updating Our Documentation – Our Approach

While researching for this book, it struck me that although we're adding relatively simple pages, we still have to work through many steps – many of which are repetitive, so it will get a little tedious after a while!

That's not something I want, so we're going to take a different approach. We'll work through two examples together step by step; for the remaining three, I'll only provide specific details required, such as links or variant names. There is a good reason for doing it this way: not only can you create copies very easily using search and replace, but also it gives you a chance to practice creating the pages so that you can be more self-sufficient.

I know this might sound scary, but trust me – it won't be! We can easily create most of the pages using search and replace; the trick is to keep a consistent layout throughout. Let's keep that thought in mind while we make a start on the first group – you will soon see that we use the same layout for each component, which makes updating very easy.

Don't worry if you get stuck — I will provide copies of all documentation in the code download accompanying this book.

Writing Documentation for Basic Components

For the first set of documentation pages, we will focus on the components from the Basic group, namely, Checkbox, Input, and Slider.

Most of what we add should be self-explanatory, although I recommend keeping the spacing as laid out in the examples in the code download. Markdown text is space specific – not including the correct spaces can frequently lead to Markdown formatting errors.

For logistical purposes, we'll work through the process of updating the documentation as a three-part exercise; each part will focus on a specific component. With that thought in mind, let's start working through the steps required in more detail.

To help with Markdown syntax, I recommend installing a plug-in for your editor: if you use Visual Studio Code (like I do), then the official plug-in is called MDX and is free to download and install.

DOCUMENTING BASIC COMPONENTS – PART 1: CHECKBOX

To update the documentation for the Checkbox component, follow these steps:

1. First, go ahead and open the `CheckBoxDocs.mdx` file from within the `\src\lib\storybook` folder. You can delete the contents within the file – we will replace them with more up-to-date content. There is a good chunk of code to add, so we'll begin with an import for Storybook and the `CheckBox.svelte` component itself:

    ```
    import { ArgsTable, Canvas, Meta, Story } from '@
    storybook/addon-docs';
    import CheckBox from '../CheckBox/CheckBox.svelte';
    ```

2. Next up, miss a line, then add this title – this will ensure we set up the correct navigation for our plug-in, as well as tell Storybook which component we're using:

    ```
    <Meta title="Basic Components/CheckBox"
    component={CheckBox} />
    ```

3. Once you've added that line, miss another line, then add this block – it contains some introductory text and some jump links to the relevant section for each variant (in this case, three):

    ```
    # CheckBox

    Checkbox is the primary component. It has three
    possible states.
    ```

- [Default](#default)
- [No Label](#no-label)
- [Disabled](#disabled)

4. Next, skip a line, then add this block – this takes care of the Default variant for our component:

```
<a id="default" />

## Default

This is the default version of the checkbox component.

<Canvas>
  <Story id="cobalt-ui-library-basic-components-checkbox-
  -default-story" />
</Canvas>
```

5. Repeat the same action as before, but this time, add this block – this one covers the No Label variant of our Checkbox component:

```
<a id="nolabel" />

## No Label

This variant hides the label normally seen with the
CheckBox component.

<Canvas>
  <Story id="cobalt-ui-library-basic-components-checkbox-
  -no-label" />
</Canvas>
```

6. Last but by no means least – here's the code for the Disabled variant:

```
<a id="disabled" />

## Disabled Input

This variant disables the CheckBox.

<Canvas>
  <Story id="cobalt-ui-library-basic-components-checkbox-
  -disabled" />
</Canvas>
```

7. To finish it all off, we need to add one more section – this lists the various arguments and properties available for this component:

```
## Properties of component

Below is a list of arguments available for this
component:

<ArgsTable of={CheckBox} />
```

8. Save the file and close it – fire up a Node.js command prompt; then at the prompt, switch the working folder to the project area and run this command: `npm run storybook`.

9. If all is well, we should see the documentation appear if we browse to `http://localhost:6006/` and click on the Default entry for Checkbox on the left, then the Docs tab at the top (as shown in the extract in Figure 7-4).

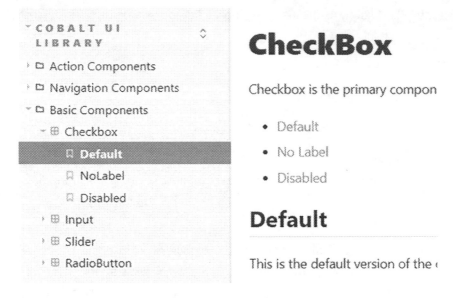

Figure 7-4. *An extract of the Checkbox documentation in Storybook*

Excellent – we've completed the documentation for the first of our components! Granted, it's not the complete works of War and Peace, but it's a starting point: it also looks a little more presentable. Take a few moments to catch your breath, grab a drink, and we'll continue with the next part of this exercise.

DOCUMENTING BASIC COMPONENTS – PART 2: INPUT

To add the documentation for the Input component, follow these steps:

1. First, go ahead and open the `InputDocs.mdx` file from within the `\src\lib\storybook` folder. You can delete the contents within the file – we will replace them with more up-to-date content. There is a good chunk of code to add, so we'll begin with an import for Storybook and the `Input.svelte` component itself:

```
import { ArgsTable, Canvas, Meta, Story } from '@
storybook/addon-docs';
import Input from '../Input/Input.svelte';
```

2. Next up, miss a line, then add this title – this will ensure we set up the correct navigation for our plug-in, as well as tell Storybook which component we're using:

```
<Meta title="Basic Components/Input" component={Input} />
```

3. Once you've added that line, miss another line, then add this block – it contains some introductory text and some jump links to the relevant section for each variant (in this case, four):

```
# Input

Input is the primary component. It has four
possible states.

- [Default](#default)
- [Email](#email)
- [No Label](#no-label)
- [Disabled](#disabled)
```

4. Next, skip a line, then add this block – this takes care of the Default variant for our component:

```
<a id="default" />

## Default

This is the default version of the Input component.

<Canvas>
  <Story id="cobalt-ui-library-basic-components-input--
  default-story" />
</Canvas>
```

5. Next, skip a line, then add this block – this deals with the Email
    variant for our component:

```
<a id="email" />
```

```
## Email
```

```
This variant formats the Input as an email-driven field.
```

```
<Canvas>
  <Story id="cobalt-ui-library-basic-components-input--
  email" />
</Canvas>
```

6. Next, skip a line, then add this block – this section covers the
    No Label variant for our component:

```
<a id="no-label" />
```

```
## No Label
```

```
This variant hides the label normally seen with the Input
component.
```

```
<Canvas>
  <Story id="cobalt-ui-library-basic-components-input--
  no-label" />
</Canvas>
```

```
<a id="disabled" />
```

7. Last but by no means least, skip a line, then add this block –
   this takes care of the Disabled variant for our component:

```
## Disabled Input
```

```
This variant disables the Input component.
```

```
<Canvas>
  <Story id="cobalt-ui-library-basic-components-input--
  disabled" />
</Canvas>
```

8. To finish it all off, we need to add one more section – this
   lists the various arguments and properties available for this
   component:

```
## Properties of component
```

```
Below is a list of arguments available for this
component:
```

```
<ArgsTable of={Input} />
```

9. Save the file and close it – fire up a Node.js command prompt;
   then at the prompt, switch the working folder to the project
   area and run this command: `npm run storybook`.

10. If all is well, we should see the documentation appear if we
    browse to `http://localhost:6006/` and click on the
    Default entry for Checkbox on the left, then the Docs tab at the
    top (as shown in the extract in Figure 7-5).

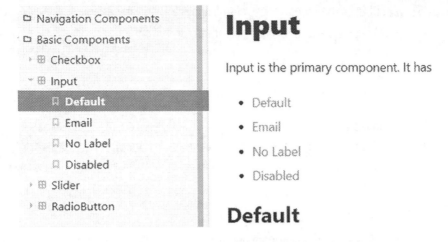

Figure 7-5. Extract of the documentation for Input

Great – two down, one more to go...at least for this group! As before, take a moment to catch your breath, then let's continue creating documentation for this group's third and final component.

DOCUMENTING BASIC COMPONENTS – PART 3: SLIDER

To add the documentation for the Slider component, follow these steps:

1. First, go ahead and open the `SliderDocs.mdx` file from within the `\src\lib\storybook` folder. You can delete the contents within the file – we will replace them with more up-to-date content. There is a good chunk of code to add, so we'll begin with an import for Storybook and the `Slider.svelte` component itself:

    ```
    import { ArgsTable, Canvas, Meta, Story } from '@
    storybook/addon-docs';
    import Slider from '../Slider/Slider.svelte';
    ```

2. Next up, miss a line, then add this title – this will ensure we
    set up the correct navigation for our plug-in, as well as tell
    Storybook which component we're using:

```
<Meta title="Basic Components/Slider"
component={Slider} />
```

3. Once you've added that line, miss another line, then add this
    block – it contains some introductory text and some jump links
    to the relevant section for each variant (in this case, two):

```
# Slider

Slider is the primary component. It has two
possible states.

- [Default](#default)
- [Disabled](#disabled)
```

4. Next, skip a line, then add this block – this block deals with the
    Default variant for our component:

```
<a id="default" />

## Default

This is the default version of the Slider component.

<Canvas>
  <Story id="cobalt-ui-library-basic-components-slider--
  default-story" />
</Canvas>
```

5. Next, skip a line, then add this block – this takes care of the
    Email variant for our component:

    ```
    <a id="disabled" />
    ```

    ```
    ## Disabled
    ```

    ```
    This variant disables the Slider component.
    ```

    ```
    <Canvas>
      <Story id="cobalt-ui-library-basic-components-slider--
      disabled" />
    </Canvas>
    ```

6. As before, to finish it all off, we need to add one more section –
    this lists the various arguments and properties available for this
    component:

    ```
    ## Properties of component
    ```

    ```
    Below is a list of arguments available for this
    component:
    ```

    ```
    <ArgsTable of={Slider} />
    ```

7. Save the file and close it – fire up a Node.js command prompt;
    then at the prompt, switch the working folder to the project
    area and run this command: `npm run storybook`.

8. If all is well, we should see the documentation appear if we
    browse to `http://localhost:6006/` and click on the
    Default entry for Checkbox on the left, then the Docs tab at the
    top (as shown in the extract in Figure 7-6).

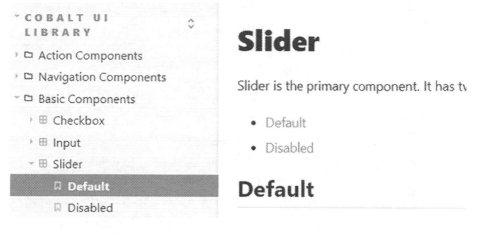

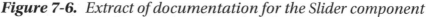

Figure 7-6. *Extract of documentation for the Slider component*

Perfect – that completes the documentation for our first group! Although we've covered a lot of steps in this lengthy exercise, many of them are very similar.

It might have felt a little repetitive, but that's no bad thing – after all, practice makes perfect, right? That aside, we've covered some essential steps in each part of this exercise, so let's take a moment to review the changes we made in more detail.

Breaking Apart the Changes

Adding documentation is an essential task for any component library – I've seen dozens of repositories in GitHub, for example, where documentation varies from detailed to practically nonexistent! It's something that often doesn't get the love and attention it needs – after all, who likes writing documentation?

That aside, over the last exercise, we spent time updating the help content for each of the Basic group of components. The process was the same for each, so to avoid repetition, we'll cover the method used for all three as a collective, not individually.

We first started with deleting the contents of the original Markdown file we created earlier in the book – this we replaced with an import from Storybook's addon-docs plug-in and the relevant import for the affected component (such as Input). We then added the `Meta` tag entry, which we use to give the page a title, define the navigation in Storybook, and tell the story file which component we're using. At the same time, we also added an introduction and jump links to each variant for the component.

We then worked through adding the variants – in each example, we started with the Default (i.e., out-of-the-box) instance before adding anywhere between one and three different variants. Each variant consisted of a named anchor, title, introductory sentence, and a `Canvas` example of the variant. In the Canvas example, we specified the story's ID (taken from the URL) – Storybook then inserts an instance of that story into our documentation page. To finish the page, we added an `ArgsTable` entry for the component before previewing the results in a browser.

The story ID links are case sensitive – they must match what is in the address bar, including the case. Otherwise, they will not operate correctly.

Okay – let's crack on with the next set of components: it's the turn of the Action group. The process will be very similar to the one we've just used, if not near identical – let's dive in and take a look.

Updating Documentation for Action Components

So far, we've completed the documentation for the first group of components – this is an excellent step in the right direction. We still have more to do, so let's focus on the second set of documentation pages, which cover the Accordion, SelectBox, and Spinner components.

As before, most of what we add should be self-explanatory; keep in mind my earlier comment about keeping the spacing as laid out in the examples in the code download. Markdown text is space specific – not including the right spaces can frequently lead to Markdown formatting errors!

In the same way we did for the previous exercise, we'll work through the process of updating the documentation in three parts. Each part will focus on a specific component. With that thought in mind, let's start working through the steps required in more detail.

DOCUMENTING ACTION COMPONENTS – PART 1: ACCORDION

To add the documentation for the Accordion component, follow these steps:

1. First, go ahead and open the `AccordionDocs.mdx` file from within the `\src\lib\storybook` folder. You can delete the contents within the file – we will replace them with more up-to-date content. There is a good chunk of code to add, so we'll begin with an import for Storybook and the `Input.svelte` component itself:

   ```
   import { ArgsTable, Canvas, Meta, Story } from '@storybook/addon-docs';
   import Accordion from '../Accordion/Accordion.svelte';
   ```

2. Next up, miss a line, then add this title – this will ensure we set up the correct navigation for our plug-in, as well as tell Storybook which component we're using:

   ```
   <Meta title="Basic Components/Accordion"
   component={Accordion} />
   ```

3. Once you've added that line, miss another line, then add this
   block – it contains some introductory text and some jump links
   to the relevant section for each variant (in this case, just one):

```
# Accordion

Accordion is the primary component. It does not yet have
any variants.

- [Default](#default)
```

4. Next, skip a line, then add this block – this takes care of the
   Default variant for our component:

```
<a id="default" />

## Default

This is the default version of the Accordion component.

<Canvas>
  <Story id="cobalt-ui-library-action-components-
  accordion--default-story" />
</Canvas>
```

5. As before, to finish it all off, we need to add one more section –
   this lists the various arguments and properties available for this
   component:

```
## Properties of component

Below is a list of arguments available for this
component:

<ArgsTable of={Accordion} />
```

6. Save the file and close it – fire up a Node.js command prompt;
   then at the prompt, switch the working folder to the project
   area and run this command: npm run storybook.

7. If all is well, we should see the documentation appear if we browse to `http://localhost:6006/` and click on the Default entry for Accordion on the left, then the Docs tab at the top (as shown in the extract in Figure 7-7).

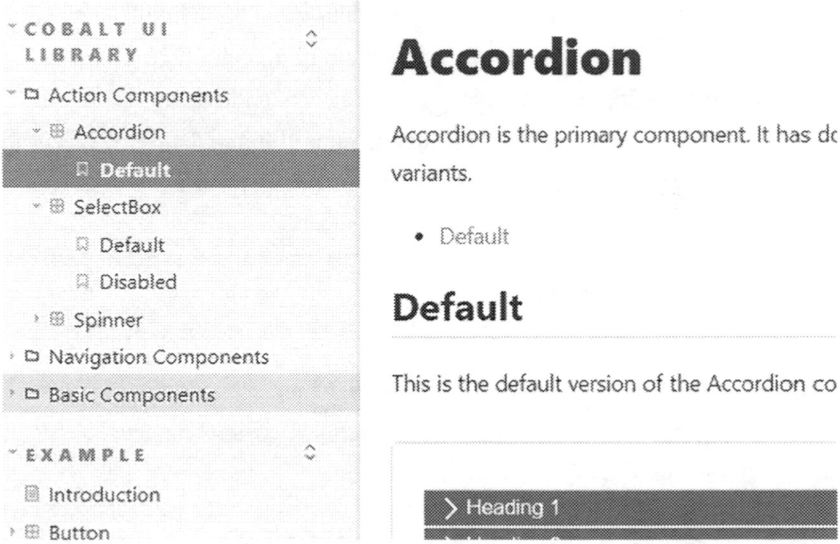

Figure 7-7. *An extract of documentation for the Accordion component*

Perfect – that's component number four done, but still plenty more to do! Take a breather for a moment, or grab a drink – when you're ready, we'll continue with the next component.

DOCUMENTING ACTION COMPONENTS – PART 2: SELECTBOX

To add the documentation for the SelectBox component, follow these steps:

1. First, go ahead and open the `SelectBoxDocs.mdx` file from within the `\src\lib\storybook` folder. You can delete the contents within the file – we will replace them with more up-to-date content. There is a good chunk of code to add, so we'll begin with an import for Storybook and the `SelectBox.svelte` component itself:

    ```
    import { ArgsTable, Canvas, Meta, Story } from
    '@storybook/addon-docs';
    import SelectBox from '../SelectBox/SelectBox.svelte';
    ```

2. Next up, miss a line, then add this title – this will ensure we set up the correct navigation for our plug-in, as well as tell Storybook which component we're using:

    ```
    <Meta title="Basic Components/SelectBox"
    component={SelectBox} />
    ```

3. Once you've added that line, miss another line, then add this block – it contains some introductory text and some jump links to the relevant section for each variant (in this case, two):

    ```
    # SelectBox

    SelectBox is the primary component. It has two
    possible states.

    - [Default](#default)
    - [Disabled](#disabled)
    ```

4. Next, skip a line, then add this block – this takes care of the
    Default variant for our component:

```
<a id="default" />
```

```
## Default
```

```
This is the default version of the SelectBox component.
```

```
<Canvas>
  <Story id="cobalt-ui-library-action-components-
  selectbox--default-story" />
</Canvas>
```

5. Next, skip a line, then add this block – this takes care of the
    Disabled variant for our component:

```
<a id="disabled" />
```

```
## Disabled
```

```
This variant disables the SelectBox component.
```

```
<Canvas>
  <Story id="cobalt-ui-library-action-components-
  selectbox--disabled" />
</Canvas>
```

6. As before, to finish it all off, we need to add one more section –
    this lists the various arguments and properties available for this
    component:

```
## Properties of component
```

```
Below is a list of arguments available for this
component:
```

```
<ArgsTable of={SelectBox} />
```

7. Save the file and close it – fire up a Node.js command prompt; then at the prompt, switch the working folder to the project area and run this command: `npm run storybook`.

8. If all is well, we should see the documentation appear if we browse to `http://localhost:6006/` and click on the Default entry for SelectBox on the left, then the Docs tab at the top (as shown in the extract in Figure 7-8).

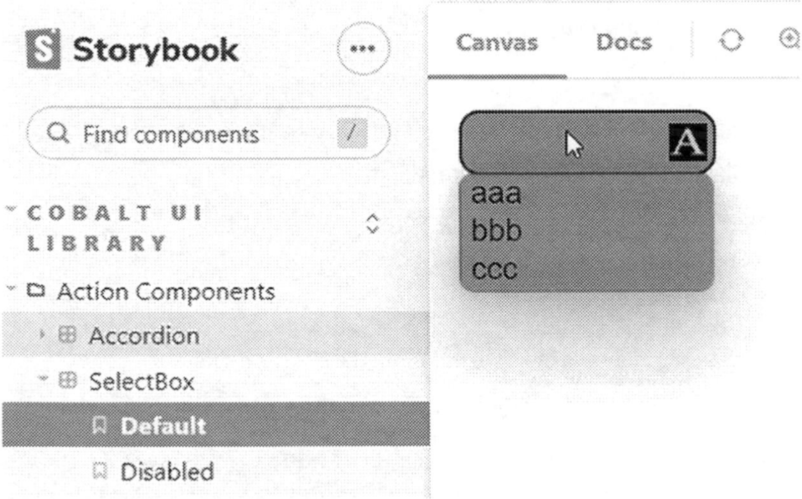

Figure 7-8. *An extract of the documentation for SelectBox*

Great – that's another one done: five so far! We still have plenty more to do, so take a breather for a moment or grab a drink – when you're ready, we'll continue with component number six.

DOCUMENTING ACTION COMPONENTS – PART 3: SPINNER

To add the documentation for the Spinner component, follow these steps:

1. First, go ahead and open the `SpinnerDocs.mdx` file from within the `\src\lib\storybook` folder. You can delete the contents within the file – we will replace them with more up-to-date content. There is a good chunk of code to add, so we'll begin with an import for Storybook and the `Spinner.svelte` component itself:

    ```
    import { ArgsTable, Canvas, Meta, Story } from '@
    storybook/addon-docs';
    import Spinner from '../Spinner/Spinner.svelte';
    ```

2. Next up, miss a line, then add this title – this will ensure we set up the correct navigation for our plug-in, as well as tell Storybook which component we're using:

    ```
    <Meta title="Basic Components/Spinner"
    component={Spinner} />
    ```

3. Once you've added that line, miss another line, then add this block – it contains some introductory text and some jump links to the relevant section for each variant (in this case, just two):

    ```
    # Spinner
    ```

    ```
    Spinner is the primary component. It has two
    possible states.
    ```

    ```
    - [Default](#default)
    - [Jumper](#jumper)
    ```

4. Next, skip a line, then add this block – this takes care of the
    Default variant for our component:

```
<a id="default" />
```

```
## Default
```

```
This is the default version of the Spinner component.
```

```
<Canvas>
  <Story id="cobalt-ui-library-action-components-spinner-
  -default-story" />
</Canvas>
```

5. Next, skip a line, then add this block – this takes care of the
    Jumper variant for our component:

```
<a id="Jumper" />
```

```
## Jumper
```

```
This variant disables the Spinner component.
```

```
<Canvas>
  <Story id="cobalt-ui-library-action-components-spinner-
  -jumper" />
</Canvas>
```

6. As before, to finish it all off, we need to add one more section –
    this lists the various arguments and properties available for this
    component:

```
## Properties of component
```

```
Below is a list of arguments available for this
component:
```

```
<ArgsTable of={Spinner} />
```

7. Save the file and close it – fire up a Node.js command prompt; then at the prompt, switch the working folder to the project area and run this command: `npm run storybook`.

8. If all is well, we should see the documentation appear if we browse to `http://localhost:6006/` and click on the Default entry for SelectBox on the left, then the Docs tab at the top (as shown in the extract in Figure 7-9).

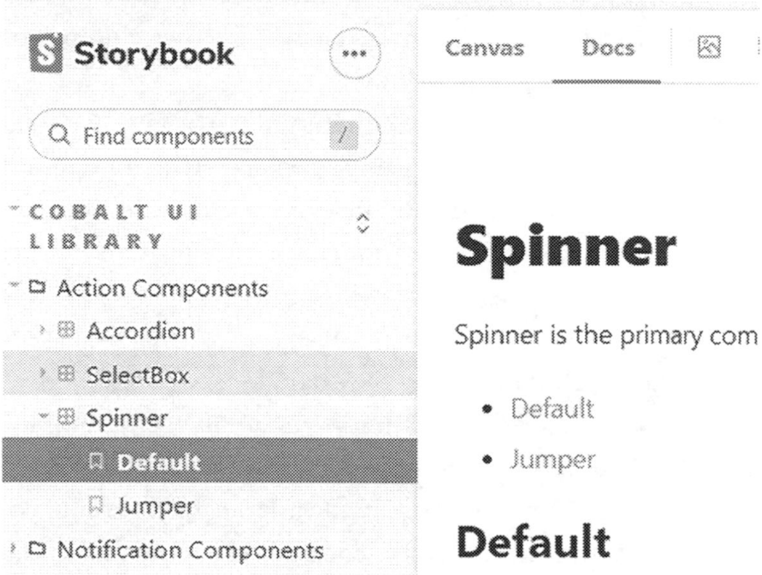

Figure 7-9. *An extract of the documentation for the Spinner component*

And we can breathe easy now! That's the end of the Action components group – we now have six components in our library. We still have more to do, but before we do so, let's quickly review the changes made in the last demo in more detail.

Exploring the Changes Made

Adding documentation is an essential task for any component library – I've seen dozens of repositories in GitHub, for example, where documentation varies from detailed to practically nonexistent! It's something that often doesn't get the love and attention it needs – after all, who likes writing documentation?

That aside, over the last exercise, we spent time updating the help content for each of the Basic group of components. The process was the same for each, so to avoid repetition, we'll cover the methodology used for all three as a collective, not individually.

We first started with deleting the contents of the original Markdown file we created earlier in the book – this we replaced with an import from Storybook's addon-docs plug-in and the relevant import for the affected component (such as Input). We then added the `Meta` tag entry, which we use to give the page a title, define the navigation in Storybook, and tell the story file which component we're using. At the same time, we also added an introduction and jump links to each variant for the component.

We then worked through adding the variants – in each example, we started with the Default (i.e., out-of-the-box) instance before adding anywhere between one and three different variants. Each variant consisted of a named anchor, title, introductory sentence, and a `Canvas` example of the variant. In the Canvas example, we specified the story's ID (taken from the URL) – Storybook then inserts an instance of that story into our documentation page. To finish the page, we added an `ArgsTable` entry for the component before previewing the results in a browser.

The story ID links are case sensitive – they must match what is in the address bar, including the case. Otherwise, they will not operate correctly.

Summary

Documentation of how a component works is an oft-neglected but essential part of any component library; I've lost count of the number of libraries I've seen where the developer provides the bare minimum, making things awkward for working out how to achieve a task.

Gaps may exist in the documentation from the get-go, but it should at least be accurate. We covered a lot of material in this chapter, so review what we have learned.

We started by exploring how to add Storybook badges – we saw how this is a helpful tool to help identify the state of any component, such as Experimental, Stable, or (heaven forbid), Deprecated. Adding this feature was a simple change to make; at the same time, we learned about how to customize the labels so that we could display our text.

Next up, we began the lengthy process of updating the documentation files for each component. Given the number involved and the high level of duplication, we focused on the Basic and Action groups. This was all in preparation for working through the remaining pages as practice in the next chapter – I'll list the details needed, ready for you to work them into your own version. We'll then finish with a quick note about tidying up some loose ends before we begin testing in Chapter 9.

Don't worry – it might seem complex, but if you remember that I've designed the pages to use the same format, it will be easier than you might expect! With that thought in mind, stay with me, and let's move on to starting those changes in the next chapter.

## CHAPTER 8

Documenting More Components

Throughout this book, we've created a host of new components to form our component library – they may only be simple ones, but as they say: we must start somewhere!

With all the components in place, we had one important task to document how each works. We began this in Chapter 7, but we still have a few groups to complete. It's at this stage where I turn things over to you! This chapter will focus on making the remaining changes as practice.

Adding the Remaining Documentation

Right – it's at this point where it really is over to you!

So far, we've worked through almost half our components – we have pages in place in Storybook, which we can develop and refine over time. We still have three categories left to do, which are Notification, Navigation, and Grid. We will come to the details for each shortly, but first, we must deal with a minor issue.

Remember how we deliberately didn't add SideBar as a component to Storybook? It was primarily because the latter got in the way; we had to build a demo outside Storybook to show off this component. While we can create some documentation for this component, it's unlikely to be effective without a fully working demo inside Storybook! It is why the documentation is minimal for this component – once we get it into Storybook, we can begin to develop the documentation for it properly.

Keeping that thought in mind, you will hopefully have seen that for the first two categories, we used the same format throughout. With a bit of care, we can create copies for the remaining components using search and replace; now is an excellent time to put that theory to the test.

Adding Documentation for Notification Components

For the first of the remaining three groups, we'll focus on the Notification components: Dialog, Alert, and Tooltip. We can use a similar process for all three, as we have already done so far; let's begin with the Dialog component.

DOCUMENTING NOTIFICATION COMPONENTS – PART 1: DIALOG

To get the documentation for our Dialog component up to scratch, follow these steps:

1. First, crack open the `DialogDocs.mdx` file from within the `\src\lib\storybook` folder – go ahead and replace the existing `@import` and `<Meta>` tags lines with this:

```
import { ArgsTable, Canvas, Meta, Story } from '@
storybook/addon-docs';
import Dialog from "../Dialog/Dialog.svelte";

<Meta title="Cobalt UI Library/Notification Components/
Dialog" component={Dialog} />
```

2. Next, leave a line blank, then add this code – there is a good chunk to add, so we'll go through it block by block, beginning with the shortcut links for each variant:

```
# Dialog

Dialog is the primary component. It has one
possible state.

- [Default](#default)
```

3. Next is the text for the Default variant:

```
<a id="default" />

## Default

This is the default version of the Dialog component.

<Canvas>
  <Story id="cobalt-ui-library-notification-components-
  dialog--default-story" />
</Canvas>
```

4. Miss a line, then add this block – it takes care of displaying the properties of our component:

```
## Properties of component

Below is a list of arguments available for this
component:

<ArgsTable of={Dialog} />
```

A tip – although we've worked through code, you may notice that you can create a lot of these files using copies of the Spinner.mdx file and search/replace with the appropriate component name. Take care though if you do – some properties are case sensitive! All of the completed files are in the code download that accompanies this book.

5.   Save the file, then close it.

6.   Once you run the demo in Storybook, we should see something akin to the screenshot shown in Figure 8-1.

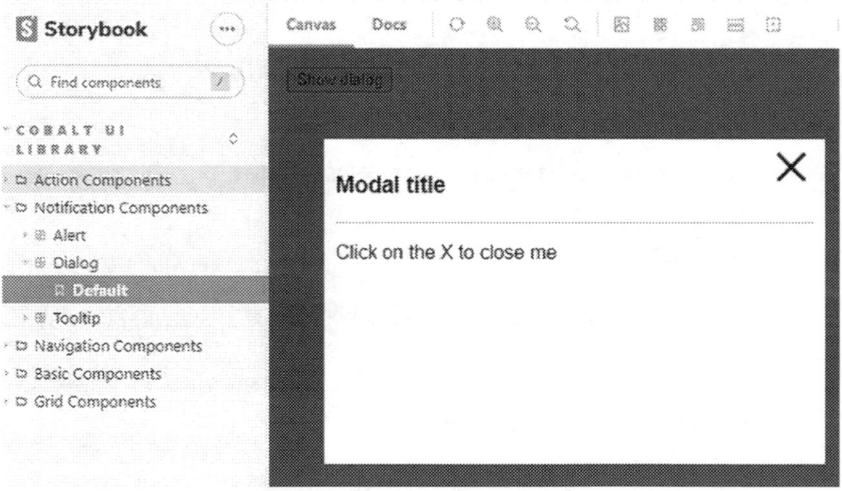

Figure 8-1. *The Dialog component on display in Storybook*

Perfect – if all went well, we should have the documentation file in place for our Dialog component. Take a breather for a moment, and then when you are ready, let's continue with Part 2.

DOCUMENTING NOTIFICATION COMPONENTS – PART 2: ALERT

To get the documentation for our Alert component up to scratch, follow these steps:

1. First, crack open the `AlertDocs.mdx` file from within the `\src\lib\storybook` folder – go ahead and replace the existing `@import` and `<Meta>` tags lines with this:

```
import { ArgsTable, Canvas, Meta, Story } from
'@storybook/addon-docs';
import Alert from "../Alert/Alert.svelte";

<Meta title="Cobalt UI Library/Notification Components/
Alert" component={Alert} />
```

2. Next, leave a line blank, then add this code – there is a good chunk to add, so we'll go through it block by block, beginning with the shortcut links for each variant:

```
# Alert

Alert is the primary component. It has two
possible states.

- [Info](#info)
- [Warning](#warning)
```

3. Next is the text for the Info variant:

```
<a id="info" />

## Info

This is the default version of the Alert component.

<Canvas>
```

```
<Story id="cobalt-ui-library-notification-components-
alert--info" />
</Canvas>
```

4. This next block is the text for the Warning variant of our component:

```
<a id="warning" />
```

```
## Warning
```

```
This variant displays the Alert component styled as a
warning.
```

```
<Canvas>
  <Story id="cobalt-ui-library-notification-components-
  alert--warning" />
</Canvas>
```

5. Miss a line, then add this block – it takes care of displaying the properties of our component:

```
## Properties of component
Below is a list of arguments available for this
component:
```

```
<ArgsTable of={Alert} />
```

6. Save and close the file.

7. Once you run the demo in Storybook, if all is well, we should see something akin to the screenshot shown in Figure 8-2, where we see the blue Info alert.

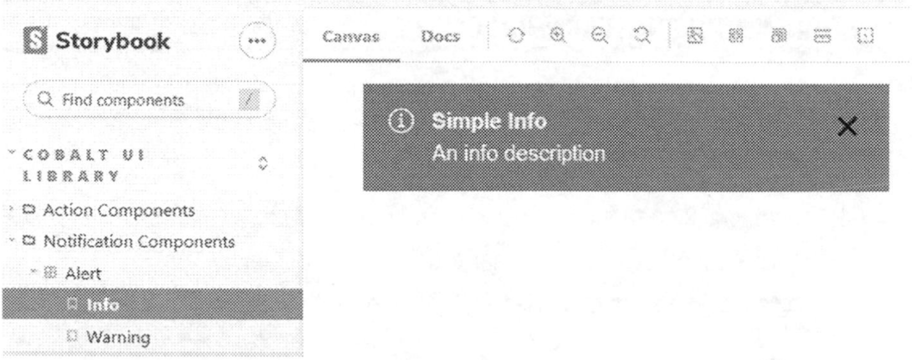

Figure 8-2. *Storybook displaying the Alert component*

8.   Clicking on Warning should show the yellow Warning variant
(Figure 8-3).

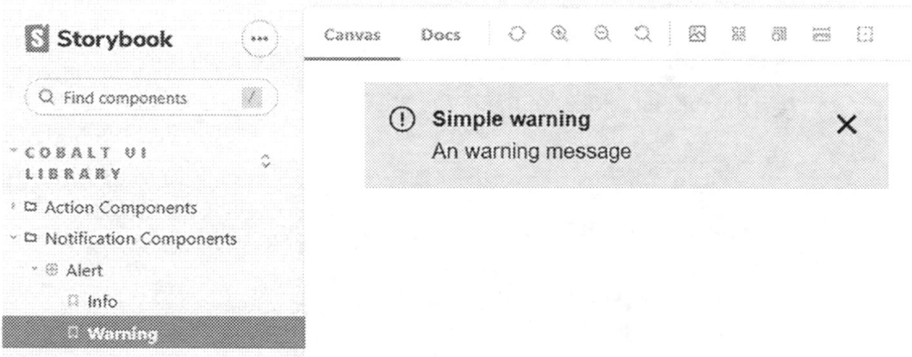

Figure 8-3. *Storybook displaying the yellow Warning alert variant*

Perfect – if all went well, we should have the documentation file in
place for our Alert component. Take a breather for a moment, and then
when you are ready, let's continue with the final part of this group: Part 3.

DOCUMENTING NOTIFICATION COMPONENTS – PART 3: TOOLTIP

To get the documentation for our Tooltip component up to scratch, follow these steps:

1. First, crack open the `TooltipDocs.mdx` file from within the `\src\lib\storybook` folder – go ahead and replace the existing @import and <Meta> tags lines with this:

```
import { ArgsTable, Canvas, Meta, Story } from
'@storybook/addon-docs';
import Alert from "../Tooltip/Tooltip.svelte";

<Meta title="Cobalt UI Library/Notification Components/
Tooltip" component={Tooltip} />
```

2. Next, leave a line blank, then add this code – there is a good chunk to add, so we'll go through it block by block, beginning with the shortcut links for each variant:

```
# Tooltip

Tooltip is the primary component. It has two
possible states.

- [Default](#default)
- [Custom HTML](#customhtml)
```

3. Next is the text for the Default variant:

```
<a id="default" />

## Default

This is the default version of the Tooltip component.

<Canvas>
```

```
<Story id="cobalt-ui-library-notification-components-
tooltip--default-story" />
</Canvas>
```

4. We need to add the code for our variant – miss a line, then add this block:

```
<a id="customhtml" />
```

```
## Custom HTML
```

```
This variant allows us to display HTML in the Tooltip
component.
```

```
<Canvas>
  <Story id="cobalt-ui-library-notification-components-
  tooltip--show-html" />
</Canvas>
```

5. Last but by no means least, we need to add the block to take care of listing the properties for our component:

```
## Properties of component
```

```
Below is a list of arguments available for this
component:
```

```
<ArgsTable of={Tooltip} />
```

6. Save and close the file. Once you run the demo in Storybook, if all is well, we should see something akin to the screenshot shown in Figure 8-4, where we see the tooltip display our content (and what will happen if we use HTML in the default mode).

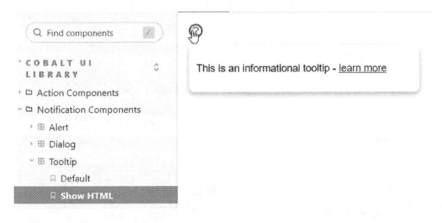

Figure 8-4. *The Tooltip component on display in Storybook*

7. If all is well, we should have a variant on show, too, in
    Storybook – this is what it should look like when running
    (Figure 8-5).

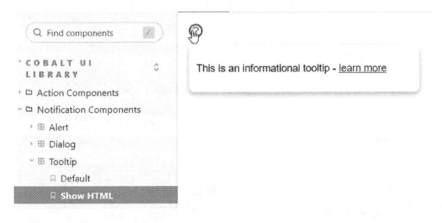

Figure 8-5. *The Tooltip variant on display in Storybook*

Perfect – if all went well, we should have the documentation file in place for our Tooltip component. We've covered a lot of code; while much of it is similar for each component, it's still important to understand what we've done. With that in mind, let's review the code changes I hope you will now have in your documentation files in more detail.

Exploring the Code Changes in Detail

Documentation, documentation – it's a thankless task, but someone has to do it! We shouldn't gloss over the importance of producing it, though, as this is what helps others to use it and not waste time trying to find the answer to a fundamental issue.

Leaving that aside, over the last exercise, we spent time updating the help content for each of the Notification group of components. The process was the same for each, so to avoid repetition, we'll cover the methodology used for all three as a collective, not individually.

As in the last demo, we started first with deleting the contents of the original Markdown file we created earlier in the book – this we replaced with an import from Storybook's addon-docs plug-in and the relevant import for the affected component (such as Input). We then added the Meta tag entry, which we use to give the page a title, define the navigation in Storybook, and tell the story file which component we're using. At the same time, we also added an introduction and jump links to each variant for the component.

In the same way, as we did previously, we then worked through adding the variants – in each example, we started with the Default (i.e., out-of-the-box) instance before adding anywhere between one and three different variants. Each variant consisted of a named anchor, title, introductory sentence, and a Canvas example of the variant. In the Canvas example, we specified the story's ID (taken from the URL) – Storybook then inserts an instance of that story into our documentation page. To finish off the page, we added an ArgsTable entry for the component before previewing the results in a browser.

The story ID links are case sensitive – they must match what is in the address bar, including the case. Otherwise, they will not operate correctly.

Okay – let's crack on with the next set of components: it's the turn of the Action group. The process will be very similar to the one we've just used, if not near identical – let's dive in and take a look.

Updating Documentation for Navigation Components

We've done one of the groups as an interactive exercise – hopefully, it wasn't too scary! We still have two groups to cover, which will be an excellent way to practice what we learned earlier in this chapter. Let's begin with the first of these two groups: the Navigation Components.

DOCUMENTING NAVIGATION COMPONENTS – PART 1: BREADCRUMBS

To update the documentation for our Breadcrumb component, follow these steps:

1. First, crack open the `BreadcrumbsDocs.mdx` file from within the `\src\lib\storybook` folder – go ahead and replace the existing @import and <Meta> tags lines with this:

```
import { ArgsTable, Canvas, Meta, Story } from
'@storybook/addon-docs';
import Breadcrumbs from "../Breadcrumbs/Breadcrumbs.
svelte";

<Meta title="Cobalt UI Library/Navigation Components/
Breadcrumbs" component={Breadcrumbs} />
```

2. Next, leave a line blank, then add this code – there is a good chunk to add, so we'll go through it block by block, beginning with the shortcut links for each variant:

```
# Breadcrumbs

Breadcrumbs is the primary component. It has two
possible states.

- [Default](#default)
- [Custom Image](#customimage)
```

3. We have the documentation for two variants to add to our file – let's miss a line and then add the first, for the default:

```
## Default

This is the default version of the Breadcrumbs component.

<Canvas>
  <Story id="cobalt-ui-library-navigation-components-
  breadcrumbs--default-story" />
</Canvas>
```

4. Here's the code for the variant – Custom Image:

```
<a id="customimage" />

## Custom Image

This variant displays the Breadcrumbs component with a
custom image.

<Canvas>
  <Story id="cobalt-ui-library-navigation-components-
  breadcrumbs--custom-image" />
</Canvas>
```

5. To finish off this documentation file, we need to add the
    code that will take care of listing all of the properties for the
    component:

```
## Properties of component
```

```
Below is a list of arguments available for this
component:
```

```
<ArgsTable of={Breadcrumbs} />
```

6. Save and close the file. Once you run the demo in Storybook,
    if all is well, we should see something akin to the screenshot
    shown in Figure 8-6, where we see the breadcrumbs on
    display.

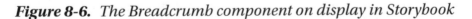

Figure 8-6. *The Breadcrumb component on display in Storybook*

7. We should not forget the variant for this component – if all is
    well, that will appear in Storybook as the screenshot shown in
    Figure 8-7.

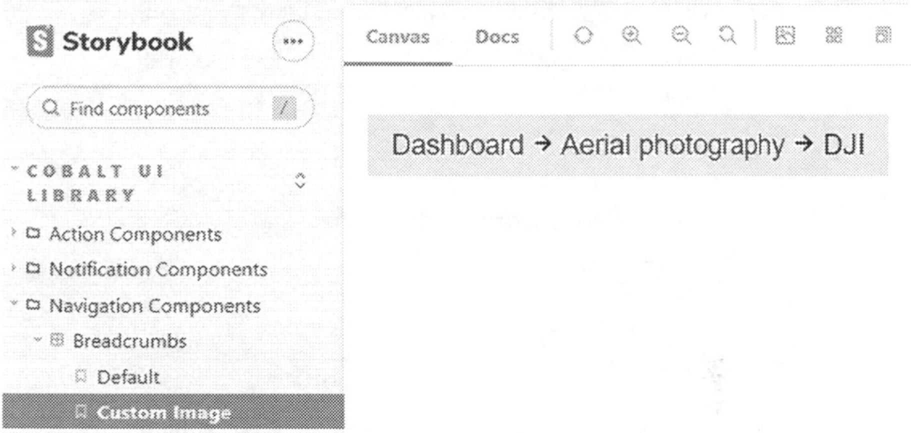

Figure 8-7. *The Breadcrumb variant on display in Storybook*

If all went well, we should have the documentation file in place for our Breadcrumb component. Take a breather for a moment, and then when you are ready, let's continue with the second part of this group: Tabs.

DOCUMENTING NAVIGATION COMPONENTS – PART 2: TABS

To update the documentation for our Tabs component, follow these steps:

1. First, crack open the `TabsDocs.mdx` file from within the `\src\lib\storybook` folder – go ahead and replace the existing `@import` and `<Meta>` tags lines with this:

```
import { ArgsTable, Canvas, Meta, Story } from
'@storybook/addon-docs';
import Tabs from "../Tabs/Tabs.svelte";

<Meta title="Cobalt UI Library/Navigation Components/
Tabs" component={Tabs} />
```

2.   Next, leave a line blank, then add this code – there is a good
     chunk to add, so we'll go through it block by block, beginning
     with the shortcut links for each variant:

```
# Tabs

Tabs is the primary component. It has two
possible states.

- [Default](#default)
- [Vertical](#vertical)
```

3.   We need to add the documentation for the first of two variants –
     let's begin with the Default:

```
<a id="default" />

## Default

This is the default version of the Tabs component.

<Canvas>
  <Story id="cobalt-ui-library-navigation-components-
  tabs--default-story" />
</Canvas>
```

4.   Next, let's add the code for the second – this will display the
     tabs in a vertical format:

```
<a id="vertical" />

## Vertical

This variant displays the Tabs component in a
vertical format.

<Canvas>
  <Story id="cobalt-ui-library-navigation-components-
  tabs--vertical" />
</Canvas>
```

5. For the last step, we need to add a section to take care of displaying the properties of the component:

```
## Properties of component
```

```
Below is a list of arguments available for this
component:
```

```
<ArgsTable of={Tabs} />
```

6. Save the file, then close it.

7. Once you run the demo in Storybook, if all is well, we should see the Tabs appear, as shown in Figure 8-8.

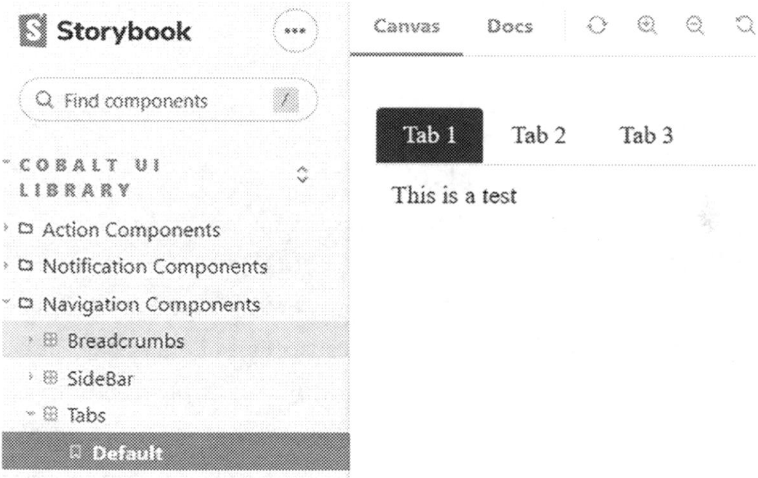

Figure 8-8. *The Tabs component on display in Storybook*

8. The Tabs component comes with a variant – this is what it will look like in Storybook (Figure 8-9).

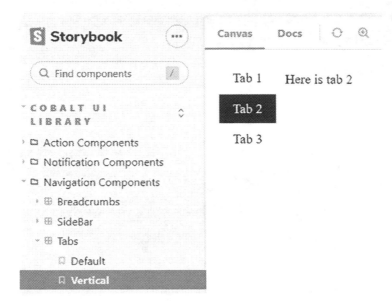

Figure 8-9. *The Tabs variant in Storybook*

Hopefully, all went well, and you now have the documentation file in place for the Tabs component! Take a breather for a moment, and then when you are ready, let's continue with the final part of this group: Part 3.

So far, we've created documentation for each component that follows a consistent format – the last one for this group will be a little different. Remember how we built and tested our SideBar component outside Storybook, owing to issues with rendering it inside the application?

Well, that change also has a knock-on effect here – as we're not able to run the component in Storybook correctly (at least not yet), we won't be able to include some of the properties we need so that the documentation will be shorter.

It's not ideal, but something we need to look at – for now, let's create something that we can refine over time as we develop the component.

DOCUMENTING NAVIGATION COMPONENTS – PART 3: SIDEBAR

To update the documentation for our SideBar component, follow these steps:

1. First, crack open the `SideBarDocs.mdx` file from within the `\src\lib\storybook` folder – go ahead and replace the existing `@import` and `<Meta>` tags lines with this:

    ```
    import { ArgsTable, Canvas, Meta, Story } from '@
    storybook/addon-docs';
    import Tabs from "../SideBar/SideBar.svelte";

    <Meta title="Cobalt UI Library/Navigation Components/
    SideBar" component={SideBar} />
    ```

2. Next, leave a line blank, then add this code – there is a good chunk to add, so we'll go through it block by block, beginning with the shortcut links for each variant:

    ```
    # SideBar

    SideBar is the primary component. It only has one
    possible state.

    - [Default](#default)
    ```

3. Next, miss a line, then add this code in for the variant:

    ```
    <a id="default" />

    ## Default

    This is the default version of the SideBar component.
    ```

4. For the last step, we need to add a section to take care of displaying the properties of the component:

    ```
    ## Properties of component
    ```

Below is a list of arguments available for this component:

```
<ArgsTable of={SideBar} />
```

5. Save the file, then close it.

Some may ask why we went to the lengths of adding documentation – it's a good question! My answer would be that we're thinking ahead; the documentation may not be good now, but we need to work on the basis that we will get SideBar into Storybook. If we can do this, we will have something we can develop in the future.

Perfect – if all went well, we should have the documentation file in place for our Breadcrumb component. We've added a fair chunk of code; while much of it is similar for each component, it's still important to understand what we've done. With that in mind, let's review the code changes I hope you will now have in your documentation files in more detail.

Breaking Apart the Code Changes

Throughout this chapter, we've created a series of documentation files in Storybook for our components. We've covered all except SideBar – it's a shame we can't include it at the moment, but hopefully, that is just a temporary measure!

In the last exercise, we spent time updating the help content for each of the Navigation group of components. The process was the same for each, so to avoid repetition, we'll cover the method used for all three as a collective, not individually.

As before, we started first with deleting the contents of the original Markdown file we created earlier in the book – this we replaced with an import from Storybook's `addon-docs` plug-in and the relevant import for the affected component (such as Input). We then added the `Meta` tag entry, which we use to give the page a title, define the navigation in Storybook, and tell the story file which component we're using. At the same time, we also added an introduction and jump links to each variant for the component.

We then worked through adding the variants – in each example, we started with the Default (i.e., out-of-the-box) instance before adding anywhere between one and three different variants. Each variant consisted of a named anchor, title, introductory sentence, and a `Canvas` example of the variant (except for SideBar). In the Canvas example, we specified the story's ID, taken from the URL – Storybook then inserted an instance of that story into our documentation page. To finish off the page, we added an `ArgsTable` entry for the component before previewing the results in a browser.

The story ID links are case sensitive – they must match what is in the address bar, including the case. Otherwise, they will not operate correctly.

Okay – we have one final set of components to document: the ImageGrid component. Yes, you read it correctly: I did say one component name, but with good reason!

We saw in the previous chapter how we created a composite component from three different, smaller objects; in the same vein, we will update the documentation for this one component, and not as three separate items. The process will be very similar to the one we've just used, if not near identical – let's dive in and take a look.

Updating Documentation for Grid Components

This last category is something of an oddity. You may remember in Chapter 6 that we talked about creating Grid components, yet we only created one. Seems a bit odd, no?

Well, this is one of those occasions where we could have gone about this differently – we could have focused on creating three individual, fully fledged components and brought them together. Or – as we have done – create something that we were able to split into three subcomponents. Both methods have their merits, but it all depends on how you want to architect or develop your components in the future.

For this reason, you will see from the documentation that I initially called this group "Grid Components" but then reference a Table component, which in turn uses a Grid component and a Cell component, respectively.

The latter two are really dependencies of the Table component – after all, we can't have cells without a table, right? I admit that this can make things a little confusing regarding naming and structure. I'm hoping that, over time, we can add features and develop each component into something more standalone and reusable for other projects.

In the meantime, let's dive in and look at how we can update the documentation for our ImageGrid component in more detail.

DOCUMENTING THE IMAGEGRID COMPONENT

To update the documentation for our ImageGrid component, follow these steps:

1. First, crack open the `TableDocs.mdx` file from within the `\src\lib\storybook` folder – go ahead and replace the existing `@import` and `<Meta>` tags lines with this:

```
import { ArgsTable, Canvas, Meta, Story } from '@
storybook/addon-docs';
import Table from "../ImageGrid/Table.svelte";
```

2. Next, leave a line blank, then add this code – compared to other components, we don't have too much to add! We'll start as always with the shortcut links for the only variant:

```
# Grid

Grid is the primary component. It has two
possible states.

- [Default](#default)
- [Placeholder Images](#placeholder)
```

3. Next, miss a line, then add this code for the main (and only) variant:

```
<a id="default" />

## Default

This is the default version of the grid component.
<Canvas>
  <Story id="cobalt-ui-library-notification-components-
  grid--default-story" />
</Canvas>
```

4. Let's add the second variant, for Placeholder Images:

```
<a id="placeholder" />

## Placeholder Images

This variant disables the ImageGrid component.

<Canvas>
```

```
<Story id="cobalt-ui-library-grid-components-image-
grid--placeholder-images" />
</Canvas>
```

5. We'll finish off by adding the block that takes care of displaying the properties for our component:

```
## Properties of component
```

```
Below is a list of arguments available for this
component:
```

```
<ArgsTable of={Table} />
```

6. Save the file and close it. Once you run the demo in Storybook, if all is well, we should see the Tabs appear, as shown in Figure 8-10.

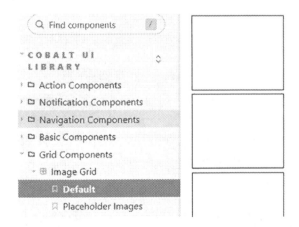

Figure 8-10. *The ImageGrid component on display in Storybook*

7. That last image teased a variant for this component – Figure 8-11 shows what it will look like in Storybook.

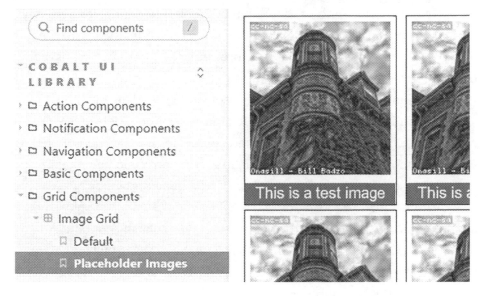

Figure 8-11. *The Placeholder Images variant of the ImageGrid component*

Phew – we have at last completed documentation for all of the components, at least those we can display in Storybook! I know it's been an epic undertaking, but it's one of those necessary evils we all must do at some point, particularly if we want others to use our code.

At this point, I would heartily recommend taking a breather – let what we've covered sink in, and then when you're ready, let's crack on with a review of what we've done. I'm sure you will notice some oddities around how we've created our documents, particularly in the last group; we'll dive in and explore the changes in more detail.

Understanding What Changed

This demo is one of those instances where you would be forgiven for being a little confused – did we create one composite component or three smaller ones?

In reality, we did both: it shows that with some planning, it's perfectly possible to create a working component based on others we add to the library. It does make naming a little more complex, but that's just part and parcel of developing composite components.

To document the ImageGrid component, we followed the same process as previous components. We first updated the imports and Meta tag before replacing the remaining content with new content from a copy of the Spinner documentation. This part was necessary to get the correct documentation format in place, such as the links, anchors, and arguments table.

We then added a Story block into the file: with that block in place, the last step was to work through the documentation, replacing content or labels where appropriate. We deliberately kept the same format for each component throughout to make it easier to search and replace automatically or manually, where applicable.

We can then preview the results in our browser to confirm that all the correct links are in place for our ImageGrid component.

A Final Tidy-Up

"And relax…" – or can we?

Truth be told, it's very tempting to sit back and rest on our laurels at this stage, but the reality is that we still have a few more tasks to do! We made many changes throughout this chapter, so it's worth spending a little time just to review the state of the library and perform a little tidying up if we can – it all helps keep things shipshape!

There are a couple of tasks that come to mind that we should do before we move on to testing our components in the next chapter:

- We can remove the (now redundant) example stories from Storybook; these are in the `\src\stories\` folder. Go ahead and delete this folder in its entirety.

- There may also be a `Counter.svelte` lurking in the `\src\lib\` folder – we can delete this, as it is a remnant from the example components added when we set up the structure.

These may only be small tasks, but every little one helps – the critical point here is to ensure our code is as tidy as possible and ready for the testing stage in the next chapter!

Summary

Phew – we've covered a lot over the last two chapters when it comes to documenting our components!

The reality is that it demonstrates how important it is to have good documentation – it need not all be present from the get-go, but it should at least be accurate. We've covered a lot of material in this chapter, so let's review what we have learned.

This chapter's focus was on updating each of the existing documentation files with the values provided in the text. We had worked through some of the pages in the previous chapter, so this time, it was reusing the same process but updating with different values where appropriate. We then rounded off with a quick note about tidying up some loose ends so that our site is as ready as it can be for the next stage of the development process.

Talking of the next stage – what is that, I wonder? We've written a lot of code, so it's time to test it! It's an essential part of the development process, but hopefully, not one that will be too testing for us (oops – sorry, another pun!). There's plenty more to do, so stay with me, and I will reveal it all in the next chapter – including a reference to Cyprus – and no, I don't mean the country!

CHAPTER 9

Testing Components

So far, we've spent time creating our masterpiece, ready for use, but – can we be sure it all works? What guarantee do we have that it won't suddenly collapse in a heap the first time someone tries to use it?

Before we release our library to the outside world, we need to test each component to ensure they all work as expected. In this chapter, we will go through the process of setting up unit testing for our library before exploring some examples of tests we can write, so end users can see how each component performs in a real-world capacity.

Setting Up the Testing Environment

Right – where do we start? Well, the first task is to choose our testing library. I know this might sound a little odd, given you might already have a preferred tool and assume that you can just use that, right?

Unfortunately, it would seem not: when testing Svelte web components, the options are somewhat limited. My original intention would have been to use my go-to suite: Cypress. However, it throws errors over using the `<svelte:options>` directive – pretty much killing any chance of us using the package!

Instead, I've elected to go with Svelte-Testing-Library, available from `https://github.com/testing-library/svelte-testing-library`; the core library is Testing-Library, and this version adapts it for use with Svelte. It's pretty straightforward to set up, so without further ado, let's dive in and get it installed and configured.

© Alex Libby 2023
A. Libby, *Developing Web Components with Svelte*,
https://doi.org/10.1007/978-1-4842-9039-2_9

SETTING UP THE ENVIRONMENT

To get the Svelte Testing Library set up within our project area, follow
these steps:

1. First, fire up a Node.js command prompt, then change the
    working folder to our project folder.

2. We need to install a host of dependencies – at the prompt, type
    this command and press Enter:

    ```
    npm install @babel/core @babel/preset-env jest babel-jest
    svelte-jester jest-environment-jsdom -D
    ```

3. Next, switch to your editor and add the following code to a new
    file, saving it as `babel.config.cjs`:

    ```
    module.exports = {
      presets: [
        [
          '@babel/preset-env',
          {
            targets: {
              node: 'current',
            },
          },
        ],
      ],
    }
    ```

4. We also need to set up a new configuration file for Jest – go
    ahead and add this code to a new file, saving it as `jest.`
    `config.cjs`:

    ```
    module.exports = {
      transform: {
    ```

```
    '^.+\\.svelte$': 'svelte-jester',
    '^.+\\.js$': 'babel-jest',
  },
  moduleFileExtensions: ['js', 'svelte'],
  testEnvironment: "jsdom",
}
```

5. We have one more package to install, which is testing-library/
    svelte itself – revert to your Node.js terminal session from
    earlier, then run this command:

    ```
    npm install @testing-library/svelte --D
    ```

6. Crack open package.json, and add this entry below the
    build-storybook entry:

    ```
    "build-storybook": "build-storybook",
    "test": "jest"
    },
    ```

Note the addition of the comma after the end of the build-
storybook line!

---

7. There is one last task to do, which is to create a folder for
    storing test files – go ahead and add a new folder at the root of
    the project area, and call it __test__.

We now have a Testing-Library ready for use – we will test to ensure
it works in the next exercise when we start to write tests for our library.
Before we do so, it's worth spending some time going through the setup –
there are some interesting points we should cover in more detail.

Breaking Apart the Code Changes

Testing our components is an essential part of the development process. Usually, we could pick any one of a range of testing suites to facilitate this, but as we're developing Svelte web components, our choice seems to be a little more limited. That said, Svelte Testing Library (STL) is a great choice – what did we need to do to get it set up?

We kicked off by installing a host of dependencies, such as babel(`core`, `preset-env`, and `babel-jest`) – it seems a lot, but they are all required by STL. Next, we then set up two configuration files: `babel.config.cjs`, and one for Jest, `jest.config.cjs`. Notice how we use the `.cjs` extension? The files are in CommonJS format, which we need when using Node and Svelte.

We use both files to configure Jest, providing settings such as processing test files based on their extensions (`*.svelte` using `svelte-jester` and `*.js` using `babel-jest`), as well as the test environment Jest should use (in this case, `jsdom`).

Note   If you've used Jest before, you might already be aware that Jest sets up the `jsdom` environment by default in versions before Jest version 28. Newer versions do not install `jsdom` by default, hence the extra dependency at the start of the exercise.

The next part is the critical bit where we installed Jest – we had to install the dependencies first. Otherwise, Jest might not install correctly if it can't find them during its installation! To round out the demo, we added an entry to the script block to allow us to run tests as a shortcut before creating a folder for sorting tests that we will write in upcoming exercises in this chapter.

Okay – let's crack on: with the testing suite up and running, it's time to test it to see if it works as expected. There is no better way to do this than by writing a test, so let's dive in and look at what is involved in more detail.

Testing the Components

So – what should we test? How in-depth should our tests be?

These are both great questions – we'd test absolutely everything in an ideal world to ensure we have covered all possible eventualities. However, that isn't always possible (or even practical) – you can bet that someone will find a way to use a component that wasn't in the manner we intended and so could claim it's not working as expected! This "use" opens up that proverbial back-and-forth can of worms about what should have/shouldn't be tested...you get the picture.

Leaving that aside (and for reasons of space), let's start creating the tests for our library; we'll focus on the Basic group of components but touch on the remaining tests at the end of this next demo.

Writing Tests for Our Library

For this book, we'll keep each set of tests reasonably simple to start with – at this stage, it's more important to ensure we have a good grounding in place and that we can develop the tests over time.

I know this means that there may be areas where we don't include tests, but it's important to remember that this isn't a book about testing but creating web components! It's an excellent excuse to revisit and iterate on what we create, to develop the tests into something more refined over time.

We have a lot to cover in this next exercise, but before we make a start, there are two changes we need to make to our component files.

PREPARATION FOR TESTING

The changes we need to make are as follows:

1. First, crack open `Checkbox.svelte` from within the `\src\`
   `lib\Checkbox` folder, and look for this line:

   ```
   type="checkbox"
   ```

2. Immediately below it, you should see a value beginning with
   `id=…` – change this to `data-testid="checkboxId"`.

3. Below this new entry, go ahead and add two more properties:

   ```
   name="checkbox-name"
   role="checkbox"
   ```

4. Save and close the file.

5. Next, open `Input.svelte` in your editor, then look for this line:

   ```
   id={fieldID}.
   ```

6. Add these two additional lines immediately below the line from
   the previous step:

   ```
   data-testid="inputId"
   role="textbox"
   ```

7. Save and close the file.

We've now completed two crucial changes to help facilitate testing – let's
move on and begin writing our tests.

WRITING TESTS

With our basic testing structure in place, we can begin to create our first tests – to do so, follow these steps:

1. In your editor, open a new file, and call it `Input.test.js` – save it into the `__test__` folder we created in the previous demo.

2. We have a fair chunk of code to add, so we will do it in sections – first, add these two imports and a describe statement:

```
import { render } from '@testing-library/svelte';
import Input from "../src/lib/Input/Input.svelte";

describe("Tests for Input", () => {

});
```

3. Next, immediately below the opening `describe` line, add this props block – this we will use to render an instance of our Input component:

```
const props = {
  id: "Input",
  class: "cobalt",
  disabled: false,
  placeholder: "example text",
};
```

4. Leave a line blank after the closing bracket from the props
   block, then add this assertion – this will check our component
   renders as expected:

```
it("should render properly", () => {
  const result = render(Input, props );
  expect(() => result).not.toThrow();
});
```

5. This next assertion checks to see if the placeholder text is as
   we have defined:

```
it("should show a textbox with correct placeholder
text", () => {
  const result = render(Input, props);
  const inputPlaceholder = screen.getByRole("textbox").
  placeholder;
  expect(inputPlaceholder).toEqual("example text");
})
```

6. This last assertion simply takes a snapshot of the component
   and checks to see if there are any differences visually:

```
it("get a snapshot of component", () => {
  const tree = render(Input, props);
  expect(tree).toMatchSnapshot();
})
```

7. Save the file and close it – that test is complete.

8. Next, create a new file and save it as Slider.spec.js in the
   same __test__ folder as before.

9. As we did before, we'll add the code block by block, beginning with three imports and the describe statement container:

```
import { render, screen } from '@testing-library/svelte';
import { fireEvent } from '@testing-library/dom';
import Slider from "../src/lib/Slider/Slider.svelte";

describe("Tests for Slider", () => {

});
```

10. Next, immediately below the opening describe statement, add this props block:

```
const props = {
  id: "Slider",
};
```

11. Leave a line blank, then add this assertion – this tests that our component renders as expected:

```
it("should render properly", () => {
  const result = render(Slider, { props });
  expect(() => result).not.toThrow();
});
```

12. These next two first check that the slider sets the correct value when moved, and then it takes a snapshot for visual checks:

```
it("should show a new value when slider handle moved",
async() => {
  render(Slider, props);
  const slider = screen.getByRole("slider");
  fireEvent.change(slider, {target: {value: '23'}});
  expect(slider.value).toBe('23');
})
```

```
it("get a snapshot of component", () => {
  const tree = render(Slider, props);
  expect(tree).toMatchSnapshot();
})
})
```

13. Save the file and close it – the changes for this test are complete.

14. Next, create a new file and save it as Checkbox.spec.js in the same __test__ folder as before.

15. As we did before, we'll add the code block by block, beginning with two imports and the describe statement container:

```
import { render, fireEvent, screen } from '@testing-library/svelte';
import Checkbox from "../src/lib/Checkbox/Checkbox.svelte";

describe("Tests for Checkbox", () => {
...insert here...

});
```

16. We need to add a props block in the same way as we've done before – go ahead and add this code immediately below the opening describe statement:

```
const mockText = "This is a checkbox";

const props = {
  id: "Checkbox",
  class: "cobalt",
  checked: false,
};
```

17. Leave a line blank, then add this assertion – this makes sure our component renders as expected:

```
it("should render properly", () => {
  const result = render(Checkbox, { props });
  expect(() => result).not.toThrow();
});
```

18. This next assertion adds a label as a new prop – we test to make sure this displays correctly:

```
it("show show a label with correct text", () => {
  const result = render(Checkbox, { ...props, label:
  mockText});
  expect(result).not.toBeNull();
})
```

19. These last two assertions test first that we show a check when we click the checkbox; the second takes a snapshot for visual checks:

```
it("should show a check when clicked", async() => {
  render(Checkbox, { ...props, label: mockText});
  const checkbox = screen.getByRole("checkbox");
  await fireEvent.click(checkbox);
  expect (checkbox.checked).toBe(true);
})

it("get a snapshot of component", () => {
  const tree = render(Checkbox, { ...props, label:
  mockText});
  expect(tree).toMatchSnapshot();
})
});
```

20. We have the remaining tests for our library to add in – these are all available in the code download accompanying this book. Go ahead and extract the contents of the remaining tests folder in the code download, then save the files to the __test__ folder.

21. Save this file and close it – switch to a Node.js terminal session, and make sure the prompt points to our project area.

22. At the prompt, enter npm run test and press Enter – if all is well, we should get a result similar to this:

```
PASS   __test__/Checkbox.spec.js
 PASS   __test__/Slider.spec.js
 PASS   __test__/Spinner.spec.js
 PASS   __test__/Dialog.spec.js
 PASS   __test__/Alert.spec.js
 PASS   __test__/Input.spec.js
 PASS   __test__/Accordion.spec.js
 PASS   __test__/Breadcrumbs.spec.js
    ...(rest trimmed for brevity)

Test Suites: 12 passed, 12 total
Tests:       27 passed, 27 total
Snapshots:   42 passed, 42 total
Time:        12.972 s
Ran all test suites.
```

Congratulations if you managed to get this far – I know we covered a lot of code in this last demo! This previous demo was undoubtedly a meaty exercise but an important one: we're starting to test our code so that others can have confidence that it works as expected in development. Let's pause and explore what we created in more detail.

Exploring the Changes in Detail

Most of the code is similar since we have a describe block for each test and a call to `matchSnapshot` for each test. So – in among all that, what did we do?

We started by creating the initial test for the Input component – we first set two imports: one for the testing library and the other for the component itself. Next up, we added a `props` block to pass in properties for our Input component before writing the first assertion to test that our component renders as expected. In the second assertion, we render the component again, but this time search for (and get a reference to) the placeholder text in the Input component. We then check to ensure it contains the correct text specified in the props block. To round out that test, we call the `toMatchSnapshot()` function to take a snapshot and check for any visual differences in our component.

In test two from step 8, we follow broadly the same format – we first create the describe block before setting up our props block. We then check to make sure that the component renders correctly before making sure that if we move the slider in the test, it correctly returns 23 as our chosen value. We finish that test with a call to the `toMatchSnapshot()` function to take a snapshot and check for any visual differences in our component.

In the third and final test (for now), we add the two imports for the testing library and the Checkbox component before setting up the initial `describe` block. We then set some mock text to a variable before adding a props block and the now-familiar test to ensure the component renders as expected. We then run a similar assertion, but this time add a new `label` property to ensure that it displays as expected. For the third test, we then get an instance of our component before clicking the box and testing to ascertain that this now correctly registers as checked in our test. We then round out this test with a final call to `toMatchSnapshot`, to perform a visual check on the code in our component.

Okay – a critical point before we move on: you will notice that I didn't go through all of the tests in this chapter in detail. Part of this is for space reasons, but also, this book isn't about testing. The critical factor is that we focus on getting components in place, then testing them. I've worked through a few examples to show you what's possible; the others use similar principles and cover the remaining components. On that note, let's begin with the next task: explore how we can bundle our components for use in our projects.

Bundling the Components

With the testing complete, we can move on to the next stage: bundling our components. Bundling, I hear you ask – what exactly is that I wonder? It is where we prepare the components to be released in a format that makes it easy to drop into projects – let me explain what I mean.

So far, we've created Svelte components with just standard CSS, HTML, and vanilla JavaScript – they work great (except SideBar) in environments such as Storybook.

However, one of the benefits of Svelte components is the ability to release them as web components that we can use in other environments, such as React. To do this, we need to bundle the code into files that we can consume outside of our development environment – in the same way, we might import a third-party library into our code. There are several ways to do this, depending on our requirements; before we explore them, let's first set up our library, ready to bundle our components.

Configuring the Build Process

To bundle our components isn't a complex process – we need to set up the main index file for our components and make sure we have a place to demo our components.

The latter might sound a little odd, as it's not something anyone consuming our components would need to use, but trust me: if that file is not present, Svelte will complain! With that thought in mind, let's dive in and look at what we need to do to get our library ready for bundling.

CONFIGURING THE BUILD PROCESS

To bundle our components ready for use, follow these steps:

1. First, we need to rename `index.html` and `main.js` to `index.old` and `main.old`, so we can create new versions of both files.

2. Next, go ahead and create a new file – add the following code:

```
/* Main components */
export * from './lib/Alert/Alert.svelte'
export * from './lib/Accordion/Accordion.svelte'
export * from './lib/Breadcrumbs/Breadcrumbs.svelte'
export * from './lib/Checkbox/Checkbox.svelte'
export * from './lib/Dialog/Dialog.svelte'
export * from './lib/ImageGrid/Table.svelte'
export * from './lib/Input/Input.svelte'
export * from './lib/SelectBox/SelectBox.svelte'
export * from './lib/Slider/Slider.svelte'
export * from './lib/Spinner/Spinner.svelte'
export * from './lib/Tabs/Tabs.svelte'
export * from './lib/Tooltip/Tooltip.svelte'

/* Ancillary components */
export * from './lib/Alert/Icon.svelte'
export * from './lib/Dialog/Close.svelte'
export * from './lib/ImageGrid/Cell.svelte'
export * from './lib/ImageGrid/Grid.svelte'
```

3. Save this as `main.js` at the root of the `\src` folder.

4. We also need to replace the `index.html` file – for this, create a new blank file and add this code. We'll do it in two parts, with the main boilerplate first:

```
<!DOCTYPE html>
<html lang="en">
  <head>
    <meta charset="UTF-8" />
    <link rel="icon" href="/favicon.ico" />
    <meta name="viewport" content="width=device-width,
    initial-scale=1.0" />
    <title>Svelte Web Components Demo</title>
  </head>
  <body>

  </body>
</html>
```

It might seem strange that we're not displaying anything between the `<body>` tags – there is a valid reason for this: I'll return to this shortly.

5. Save the file as `index.html` at the root of the project folder – you can close both `index.html` and `main.js` at this point.

6. We also need to add a new configuration file and update a second one – create a new file, saving it as `vite.lib.config.js` at the root of the project folder. Add this code:

```
import { defineConfig } from 'vite'
import { svelte } from '@sveltejs/vite-plugin-svelte'
```

```
// https://vitejs.dev/config/
export default defineConfig({
  build:{
    lib:{
      entry: './src/main.js',
      name: 'CobaltLibrary',
    }
  },
  plugins: [svelte({
    compilerOptions:{
      customElement: true
    }
  })]
})
```

7. Next, crack open `vite.config.js`, and modify the svelte
    object within, so it looks like this:

    ```
    svelte({
      compilerOptions: {
        customElement: true,
      },
    }),
    ```

8. Save and close both configuration files – the configuration part
    of the process is now complete.

Excellent – we're ready to bundle! It's at this point that we will have
some decisions to make. Do we release packages for each component
individually, in groups, or one that covers all components?

If we did the latter, does that mean people have to download the entire
library if they only want one component? That doesn't seem sensible, but
we need to balance that against maintenance and where package versions

might diverge if we update one and not the other. It's just a few questions we have to ask; before we do so, let's first explore the changes we've made in more detail.

Exploring the Changes in Detail

Throughout this book, we've created a set of functional components for our library and tested most (except for SideBar) in Storybook. This is all good, but most of these components wouldn't operate if we used them outside of a Svelte environment. Why? The reason lies in our configuration – if we didn't complete the steps we've just taken, we will likely have a space or empty page where our component should be.

To fix this, we first created a central `main.js` file – we had to discard the one we used for SideBar, but that can't be helped (Svelte won't accept any other files when it comes to exporting components for bundling).

Inside this file, we added exports to all the critical components – the core ones such as `Alert` and `Accordion` and some subcomponents used by a handful of the parent components.

Moving on, we then replaced the contents of the `index.html` file – Svelte also needs to see this file as part of the bundling process; without it, it will throw an error. Notice, though, that we didn't initially put anything in between the <body> tags because we need the number in the file names generated as part of the build process; we will not get these until we run the next demo.

The key to the bundling process is the changes we made to the Vite configuration. We first added a `vite.lib.config.js` file; inside this, we imported two functions from `svelte` and `vite` and then defined a setup for Vite to specify the name of the library and the main entry point for our components. At the same time, we also added the `customElement` property, which we set to `true` – this is what tells Svelte to make the component available to other frameworks. Without it, we will end up with a warning such as this one:

```
09:22:07 [vite-plugin-svelte] C:/cobalt/src/lib/Accordion/
Accordion.svelte:1:16 The 'tag' option is used when generating
a custom element. Did you forget the 'customElement: true'
compile option?
```

To round off the demo, we also modified the `vite.config.js` file too, to add in the same `customElement` property; the significance of this will become apparent in the next demo.

Right – let's crack on with running the build process. We have our configuration in place, so it should just be a matter of running a command, right? There's more to executing a single line of code – it all hangs around how we want to make our code available to others. To see what this means, let's dive in and look at the second part of this process in more detail.

Running the Build Process

Remember how we alluded to the fact that we can run this process in one of three ways? We could

- Bundle all components together – typically producing multiple files in the same process

- Generate a single file – larger but easier to move around for portability

- Generate single files for each component – it creates more files but keeps them smaller, with less redundant code to download

The first two options are straightforward – we can run the first now without any further configuration, and the second only requires changing the file we run during the process. The third option is a little more complex; let's dive in and look at all three to understand what this means for us in practice.

RUNNING THE BUILD PROCESS

With the build process set up and ready to go, we can now run it – to do so, follow these steps:

1. We'll start with the all option – fire up a Node.js terminal prompt, then enter this command and press Enter:

   ```
   npm run build
   ```

2. If all is well, we should see output similar to this:

   ```
   > cobalt@0.0.0 build
   > vite build

   vite v3.0.2 building for production...
   ✓ 28 modules transformed.
   dist/assets/arrow-forward-outline.1b223722.svg    0.25 KiB
   dist/index.html                                   0.46 KiB
   dist/assets/index.8ed12653.js                     51.18
   KiB / gzip: 15.49 KiB
   ```

3. This is good, but we might get more than one JavaScript file appearing, which is not ideal. We can use the build process to generate a single JavaScript file to get around it. At the Node.js terminal prompt, run this command:

   ```
   $ npm run build -- -c=vite.lib.config.js
   ```

4. If all is well, we should see output similar to this:

   ```
   > cobalt@0.0.0 build
   > vite build "-c=vite.lib.config.js"

   vite v3.0.2 building for production...
   ✓ 26 modules transformed.
   dist/cobalt.mjs    69.55 KiB / gzip: 17.05 KiB
   dist/cobalt.umd.js    50.89 KiB / gzip: 15.53 KiB
   ```

5. This is better – but what if we wanted to produce a package purely for specific components? To do this, we need to make a change to `vite.lib.config.js`. Crack this file open, then replace the contents of the build: option with this code:

```
export default defineConfig({
  build:{
      rollupOptions: {
        input: ['./src/lib/Accordion/Accordion.svelte',
        './src/lib/Spinner/Spinner.svelte'],
      }},
  ...
```

6. Switch to the Node.js terminal session from earlier in this demo; then at the prompt, enter this command and press Enter:

```
npm run build -- -c=vite.lib.config.js
```

7. If all is well, we should see output similar to this:

```
> cobalt@0.0.0 build
> vite build "-c=vite.lib.config.js"

vite v3.0.2 building for production...
✓ 7 modules transformed.
dist/assets/Accordion.3db6c480.js   4.55 KiB / gzip:
1.98 KiB
dist/assets/Spinner.8cd256b1.js     3.14 KiB / gzip:
1.38 KiB
dist/assets/index.d0d80846.js       6.41 KiB / gzip:
2.96 KiB
```

With the build process done, it's time to test it! We already have the demo in place (we created it as part of running the initial `npm run build` command). We need to make one change to it, though, to test the new file we've just built:

8. First, crack open the index.html from the `\src` folder in your editor. Change the src location for Spinner to this:

    ```
    src="/dist/assets/Spinner.8cd256b1.js"
    ```

Note   The `.XXXXXX.js` part of the file name will be whatever was displayed at the end of step 6 in this demo; if you missed it, check the Spinner file, which will be in the `\dist` folder.

---

9. Save the file and close it.

10. Next, switch to a second Node.js terminal session, then change the working folder to our project area.

11. At the prompt, enter npm run dev and press Enter.

12. If all is well, we should see an instance of the Spinner component running if we browse to `http://localhost:5173/index.html`, as shown in Figure 9-1.

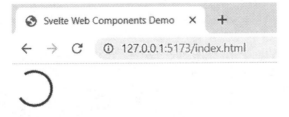

Figure 9-1. *The newly compiled Spinner component working in our demo*

This demo looks great, but how can we prove it's our new component and that it's coming from the newly built file? For the more adventurous, feel free to look at the compiled code from within a developer console. You should see something similar to that shown in Figure 9-2, where we reference the component <cobalt-spinner> and the newly generated distribution component file:

```
<!DOCTYPE html>
<html lang="en">
  ▶<head>…</head>
  ▼<body>
    ▼<cobalt-spinner color="#19247c" duration="0.75s" size="40"
      variant="circle">
      ▼#shadow-root (open)
        ▶<style>…</style>
        ▼<div class="cobalt"> flex
          ▼<div>
              <div class="circle" style="--size:40px; --color:#19247
              c; --duration:0.75s;"></div>
            </div>
          </div>
      </cobalt-spinner>
      <script type="module" src="/dist/assets/Spinner.8cd256b1.js">
      </script> == $0
  </body>
</html>
```

Figure 9-2. *Proof that we're using the newly compiled component*

We've covered quite a bit there, which has left us with plenty to think about going forward! There is no right or wrong answer as to which process we choose to use – it comes back to that age-old chestnut of "it depends."

In this instance, it's most likely to depend on what people consuming our components will ask for; we might start with something large and split off components over time as each one matures. Let's first review the changes we made in the last demo – it covers some exciting features worth learning about when bundling our components into releasable codeSpinner component .

Breaking Apart the Code

This is one of those occasions where writing code is arguably less important than the decisions behind it – in our case, what do we do? We could take this in several ways: we've proven that the demo works with individual components, but as a starting point, it (kind of) makes sense to have a single file and split it into smaller components once we develop them. All thoughts aside, it's still essential to understand how this part of the process works, so let's review the code we created in the previous demo.

We started by simply running the `npm run build` command without any further changes – this was possible as it uses the `vite.config.js` file to specify how the build should run. It gave us three files – an SVG, the `index.html` demo file, and a JavaScript asset file containing the components.

It's a good starting point, but what if we didn't want to download multiple files? To get around this, we switched to the alternative configuration, `vite.lib.config.js`, which we set up in the previous demo. This gives us two files – in both cases, it's all of the components bundled into one file but formatted for use as JavaScript modules (either UMD or MJS, depending on your preference).

Let's turn this on its head – if we wanted the best of both worlds (i.e., one component, one file), is there anything we can do? As it so happens, there is: we modified the `build:` options to use a `rollupOptions` property. Here, we can specify which components we want to include – in our example, we listed the files for Accordion and Spinner, but we could list them for any component in our library. It does mean that we could have multiple configuration files that group several components in the same way.

To round out the demo, we ran the final build option, which gave us the compiled files for Spinner and Accordion. Before running it under localhost, we used the latter to update the `index.html` demo to confirm that the package works as expected in a browser.

Note also that although we're referencing the `Spinner...js` file we created in step 7 of the last demo, we are using the compiled `Index...js` file – the `Spinner...js` file is referencing this.

Okay – let's continue: we've tested our components and bundled them into a format suitable for release. It's time to put these bundles to a proper test: let's add them to a demo to see how they perform.

Creating Demos in a Test Environment

When it comes to testing our component bundle files, there are several ways we can do this – my preference is to pull them into a CodeSandbox demo.

As it happens, we've already done part of the work required to facilitate this; the rest of the work will be around hooking the files into a CodeSandbox demo. Let's dive in and look at what is involved in more detail, using the Spinner component as a testbed for our next demo.

CREATING A SANDBOX DEMO

To create a CodeSandbox demo that uses our newly generated files, follow these steps:

1. First, go ahead and browse to `www.codesandbox.io`; then once you are there, click on Create Sandbox in the top right corner.

2. From the list of templates that appears, click on Vanilla, then wait for it to prepare a new demo.

3. Next, we need to upload two files: the `Spinner.XXXXX.js` and `Index.XXXXX.js` files from the `\dist` folder of your project area. Click on the arrow pointing upward in the Files section of the CodeSandbox demo to begin the upload process.

The XXXXX will be the number assigned to your files during the bundling process.

---

4. We now need to create our markup – in the CodeSandbox demo, click on `index.html` to select it.

5. Take a copy of the entire contents of the `index.html` file in our project folder, and paste it over the top of what is in the CodeSandbox demo.

6. As a final touch, we can upload a favicon file – it's not obligatory, but CodeSandbox will complain if one is not present, so if you want to fix it, upload the one I've prepared in the code download that accompanies this book.

If you want to create your own, you can use an online generator like the one at `https://favicon.io/favicon-generator`. I used the letter C (for cobalt) as the basis for our one.

---

7. We should have a file structure in our CodeSandbox demo that resembles the listing in Figure 9-3.

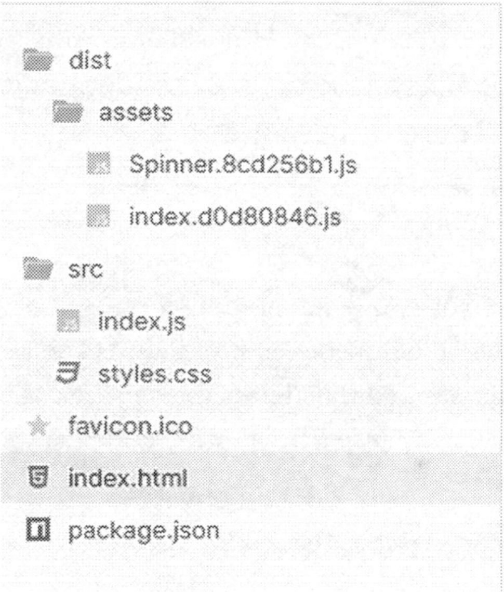

Figure 9-3. *The file listing for our CodeSandbox demo*

8. Hit the refresh button on the right in the CodeSandbox demo
    (it's next to the address bar) to refresh the page – if all is well,
    we should see our new component running on the right and the
    markup used on the left (as shown in Figure 9-4).

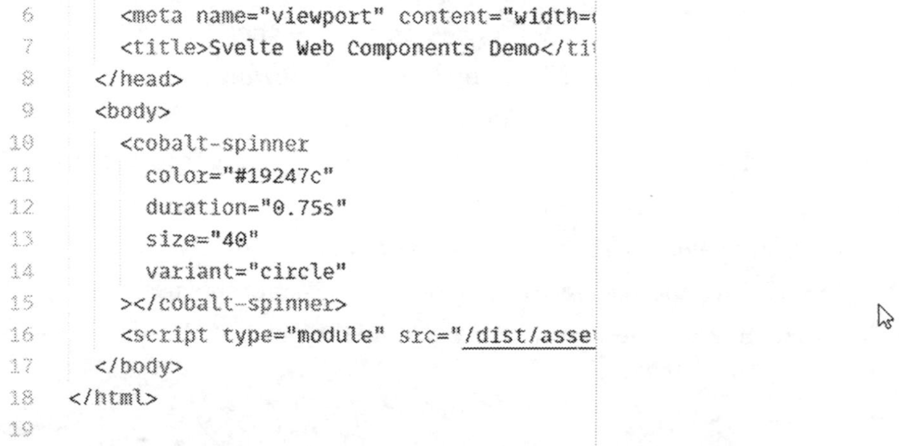

```
 6       <meta name="viewport" content="width=
 7       <title>Svelte Web Components Demo</ti
 8     </head>
 9     <body>
10       <cobalt-spinner
11         color="#19247c"
12         duration="0.75s"
13         size="40"
14         variant="circle"
15       ></cobalt-spinner>
16       <script type="module" src="/dist/asse
17     </body>
18   </html>
19
```

Figure 9-4. *The new component and its markup in CodeSandbox*

If you get stuck, feel free to look at my version, which you can see at `https://codesandbox.io/s/condescending-shtern-1eu87e?file=/index.html`.

Phew – that was a slight relief there: I was a little apprehensive about whether it would all work while researching for this book. However, my fears were unfounded: it has worked better than I expected!

Even though this was a simple demo, it nevertheless revealed a few interesting points, so let's pause to review the code in more detail.

Breaking Apart the Code

This is one of those occasions where we didn't have to do a great deal, as we'd done most of the hard work already! The main focus of this demo was to set up an example of one of our components to work in a CodeSandbox demo – we began first by uploading two files, `Spinner...js` and `Index....js`, into a new CodeSandbox window.

Next up, we copied over the markup from our existing HTML file and added a favicon – the latter wasn't obligatory, but CodeSandbox complains if one isn't present. At the same time, we confirmed that the file directory matched that shown in the illustration before previewing the results in the mini browser window within our demo.

Perfect – we've completed the initial test, but: the real test is yet to come! One of Svelte's features is that any web component we create should work in a non-Svelte environment, such as a React demo. After all, it is just plain CSS, HTML, and JavaScript, so why not? Let's put this to the test and explore what might happen if we were to consume one of our components in a React demo.

Testing with Other Frameworks

At this point, I must admit to a slight air of trepidation and doubt – I, like many of you, will be familiar with the fact that React components run in React demos, Angular ones in Angular, and so on, right? Svelte is an exception: it claims to run in any framework, so how can we test it?

There are a couple of ways to achieve this, but my preference would be to create a second CodeSandbox demo, this time using a React template. Thanks to its predefined template options, CodeSandbox makes this a cinch to complete, so let's dive in and take a look at an example using the Spinner component.

If you get stuck at any point, my version is available in a CodeSandbox at `https://codesandbox.io/s/loving-breeze-ir8c9w?file=/src/App.js`.

USING OUR COMPONENT IN A REACT DEMO

To set up the example, follow these steps:

1. Browse to `www.codesandbox.io`; then once you are there, click on Create Sandbox in the top right corner.

2. From the list of templates that appears, click on React, then wait for it to prepare a new demo.

3. Find the `App.js` file in the left-hand navigation and click on it to display it in the editor.

4. We need to add three files – for this, we need the `Spinner.XXXXX.js` and `Index.XXXXX.js` (where XXXXX is the number from earlier demos). First, create a folder called `dist` at the top level; then inside this, create one called `assets`.

5. Click on the upward arrow to select and upload the two files
    into the assets folder.

You might wonder why I've replicated the same folder structure
here when it isn't entirely necessary. It's purely to replicate what we
receive when we run the bundling process – keeping it similar helps
prove that the component works as expected outside of Svelte.

---

6. With the files imported, switch to App.js in the CodeSandbox
    editor. At the top of the file, add this import immediately below
    the existing one for styles.css:

    ```
    import "../dist/assets/Spinner.8cd256b1.js";
    ```

7. Next, find the line with the <h2> tag, and add this code
    immediately below it, as highlighted:

    ```
    <h2>Start editing to see some magic happen!</h2>
    <div className="layout">
        <cobalt-spinner
            color="#19247c"
            duration="0.75s"
            size="40"
            variant="circle"
        ></cobalt-spinner>
      </div>
    );
    }
    ```

8. Switch to the styles.css file in the left navigation, then add
    this rule below the one for .App. This will center the spinner on
    the page:

```
div.layout {
  margin: 0 auto;
  width: 100px;
}
```

9. To complete our code, we need to replace the existing src
    location in the script tag with this:

    ```
    <script type="module" src="/dist/assets/
    Spinner.8cd256b1.js"></script>
    ```

10. Click on File ➤ Save to save the demo – if all is well, we should
    see our spinner running, as shown in Figure 9-5.

Figure 9-5. *The Spinner component running inside a React app*

Yay – we finally have one of our web components working in a non-Svelte environment! It might have taken us a while to get there, but in the tradition of "best things come to those who wait," we finally got there.

This is one of the best things about Svelte: unlike other frameworks, we can create reusable components in any framework, including Svelte. On a more practical matter, there are a few interesting points of note in this demo, so let's take a moment to review the code in more detail.

Understanding What Happened

This last demo might seem to have a sense of déjà vu, but that is to be expected – most of the hard work in bundling our components we've already done, so all that remains is to add our component into a demo.

On this occasion, we ran through a similar procedure to the last CodeSandbox demo, but this time, we created it as a simple React demo based on one of the templates available in CodeSandbox. We first began by uploading two files, `Spinner...js` and `Index....js`, into a new CodeSandbox window while replicating the same folder structure generated during the bundling process.

Instead of copying over the existing markup as we did before, we added an import to the Spinner file before inserting the Spinner component into the React markup. We also updated the src location at the bottom of the demo to point to our Spinner file. Once done, we previewed the results in the mini browser window to confirm that the Spinner component worked as expected within our demo.

Notice that I used a different format to call the Spinner component this time? This change makes it a web component – we specify it in the `svelte:tag` options line in each component, and we have to use it when working in a non-Svelte environment such as React.

Summary

Testing is essential to creating any code, period – be it a simple one-liner, right through to a whole website! We need to ensure it works (to the best of our ability) and does what we expect. We've covered a lot of material about testing our library in this chapter, so let's review what we have learned.

We started by working through the steps needed to set up our testing environment – we chose to use Svelte Testing Library, as it's one of the few (if indeed the only?) options that I know supports Svelte web components. A lack of wide choice isn't ideal, but Svelte is still relatively new, so it should be a matter of time before other libraries offer similar support.

Next, we moved on to creating tests – for reasons of space, we focused on the components in the Basic group to get us started but were able to extract copies of other tests for the remaining components from the code download accompanying this book.

We then switched focus to exploring how we can bundle our components – this is essential to prepare them for use in a production environment, although we know they are not yet ready for that stage! This process came in two parts; the first was configuring the build process before we ran through the building in part 2.

In the last stage, we rounded off the chapter with a look at how to test our components in an environment outside our current project area. We began with creating a demo in CodeSandbox, using a Svelte template, before replicating something similar as a React demo. We saw how the component worked fine in both cases, proving that Svelte works in pretty much any environment we might use, unlike other frameworks!

Okay – we've come to the end of this chapter, but we have the most critical part left: release the library into production! The state of our library is such that we would have other things to do first, but – it's crucial to understand how the release process might look for our library. Stay with me, and I will reveal it all in the next chapter.

CHAPTER 10

Deploying to Production

This chapter is the most critical part: we've spent all this time creating our new library, but no one can use it unless released into production!

In this chapter, we will go through releasing our library into the wild and explore what documentation is required so that others can use the library for the first time. Let's start with a simple task: perform some final checks before we release our code into production.

Performing Final Checks

Throughout this book, we've done some great work in creating our component library – it would be a shame to release it out into the wild without at least making sure we've tidied up loose ends!

We should do this task by default, but I've encountered dozens of instances where developers haven't performed this task. For example, I've seen sites containing components without documentation (or minimal at best), spelling mistakes, or code that isn't formatted well. I've even seen the occasional spelling mistake too, which isn't great.

It is a symbolically important step too – we may not need to make any final changes, but doing the last check is also a way to say, "I'm happy with what is there and ready to sign off." Let us be realistic, though: I know our library still needs work, so we wouldn't do this until we're ready to release to a wider audience.

© Alex Libby 2023
A. Libby, *Developing Web Components with Svelte*,
https://doi.org/10.1007/978-1-4842-9039-2_10

Leaving that aside for a moment, let's consider what we might want to do at this point:

- Check each file in the repository: is it still needed, or is it one that is no longer required, and we can therefore remove it.

- Do all of the component files have a consistent layout? For example, I usually start each component with the `<script>` block, followed by the markup, and finish with the `<style>` block, but you may prefer to change it.

- Are all the file names correctly named (i.e., in title case), where appropriate?

- Have you pushed up any final changes in your local version?

- We created a SideBar component but, for various reasons, couldn't include it in Storybook: it might be wise to remove it for now and bring it back when we can get it working in Storybook.

- We added a `.gitignore` file earlier in the book: Is this up to date, or are there any other folders or files we need to exclude?

We might want to make more changes to tidy up, but this will depend on your circumstances. The critical point here is that we take the opportunity to make sure our library is as tidy as possible before we release it into the wild.

Okay – let's crack on: now that we've completed the final checks for our site, we should look at deploying our library. Getting our library out into the wild will require a few steps, such as pushing our code into a repository, releasing packages, ensuring documentation is good, and more. Before we get stuck into the various tasks, let's first take a quick look at what we need to do in more detail.

Understanding the Deployment Process

Throughout this chapter, we will transition our library from being a locally hosted project into something available for others to use (and hopefully help improve and develop too). From the outset, though, there is one thing we need to be mindful of.

Although we've done a lot to develop our library, I would not consider it production ready yet. There is plenty more we can add, such as more extensive testing, making CSS styles more consistent, getting the SideBar component working inside Storybook, maybe developing the RadioButton component (remember that one?), and more.

It's important to note, therefore, that while we will cover the process, tips, and hints on deployment, we should only do these at the appropriate moment, when **we deem our code to be production ready**.

Okay – enough of the doom and gloom: let's move on! We've mentioned that the process of deployment will include various tasks, which will include the following:

- GitHub: If we don't upload our code somewhere, nobody will be able to use it! I've chosen to use GitHub for convenience (primarily because I already have many repos on this platform). Feel free to change it to a different platform, such as GitLab, Azure, or even Bitbucket.

- We need to release our code in a format that's easy for others to use – we have several options:

    - We can release as one or more npm packages.

    - We also have an opportunity to bundle components as compiled JavaScript files.

    - We could even push code to a Content Delivery Network (or CDN).

- In addition to releasing code, we should also release
  our version of Storybook to a public hosting webspace,
  such as Netlify.

There's plenty to do! It might seem like such, but it's important to remember that much of this will be a one-off; once we complete steps such as setting up GitHub, we can switch to applying updates and new features throughout the lifetime of the component library.

With that in mind, let's begin the process by getting a GitHub site set up and ready for use.

Publishing to GitHub

Although publishing content on GitHub requires quite a few steps, we can split the process into two distinct parts – the first is to create the repository and get it ready for use, while the second is uploading our code.

Let's focus first on setting up the repository: if you've already used sites such as GitHub, then much of what you will see shortly will be familiar to you. Before we get stuck in, though, there are a couple of points we should be aware of as part of setting up our repository:

- Do not feel obliged to use GitHub if you already have
  an existing account with sites such as GitLab or Azure;
  this part is less about the specifics of the technology but
  more about the process of getting our code out into the
  wild. For this book, I will assume you are using GitHub
  and Netlify; please feel free to adapt where appropriate.

- The instructions over the next few pages are written
  for Windows, as this is the author's regular platform;
  please adapt if you use macOS or Linux.

Okay – with that in mind, let's dive in and start setting up the library's repository.

Setting Up a GitHub Pages Repository

At this point, things start to take shape – we are stepping ever closer to releasing our site into the wild.

The first task will be to set up a GitHub repository; I will use `cobalt` for the account name, so you can see how to configure your version, particularly if you use a different name. Setting up the repository uses the standard GitHub process – let's take a look.

SETTING UP THE REPOSITORY

To set up our GitHub Pages account, follow these steps:

1. The first step is to sign in to your GitHub account using the details you registered with before this demo; once done, browse to `https://github.com/new` to set up a new repository.

2. Once at the Create a new repository page, go ahead and enter your repository name (Figure 10-1).

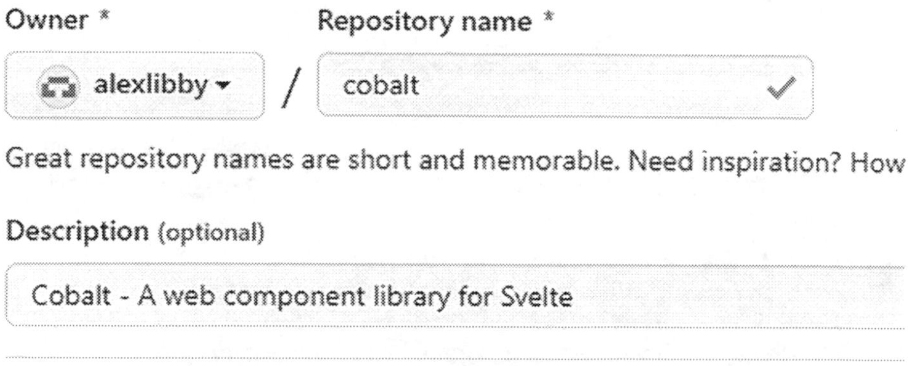

Owner *   Repository name *

[🐙 alexlibby ▾]   /   [cobalt   ✓]

Great repository names are short and memorable. Need inspiration? How

Description (optional)

[Cobalt - A web component library for Svelte   ]

Figure 10-1. *Creating the repository*

3. GitHub has already populated the Owner field – leave this unchanged.

4. Next, give it a description – it's optional, so you can skip past it if you like, and it won't affect how the demo works.

5. You should see two fields present: Public and Private – GitHub has preselected the former, as private repositories are not available on a free tier.

6. Next, set all three options under the Initialize this repository with… label – you should end up with a configuration similar to that shown in Figure 10-2.

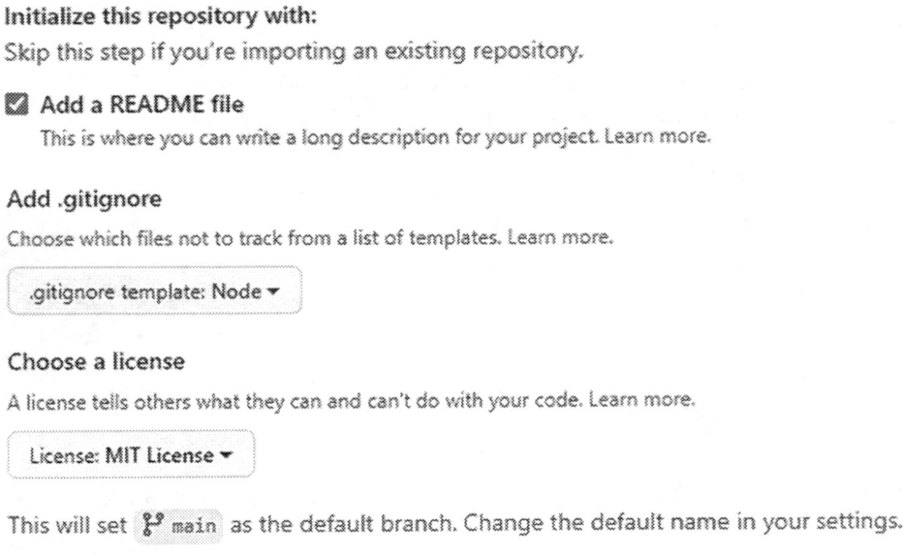

Initialize this repository with:
Skip this step if you're importing an existing repository.

☑ **Add a README file**
  This is where you can write a long description for your project. Learn more.

Add .gitignore
Choose which files not to track from a list of templates. Learn more.

  .gitignore template: Node ▾

Choose a license
A license tells others what they can and can't do with your code. Learn more.

  License: MIT License ▾

This will set ⑂ main as the default branch. Change the default name in your settings.

Figure 10-2. *Settings to use for the new repository*

7. Hit Create a repository to generate our new repository.

8. If all is well, we should end up with a new repository with a URL
    of `https://github.com/alexlibby/cobalt` – it should
    look something like that shown in Figure 10-3 (allowing for your
    username and repository name, if different).

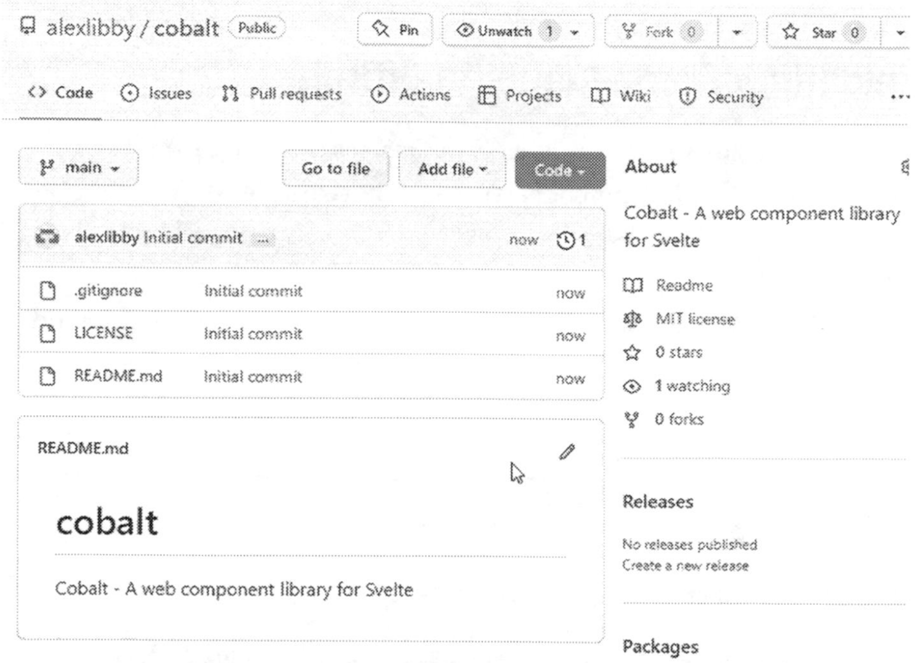

Figure 10-3.   *Screenshot of our GitHub repository, ready for use*

9. Our repository is ready for deployment.

Excellent – we now have a working repository ready to upload content
from our project area.

To achieve this, we worked through the standard process for creating a
GitHub repository, including setting appropriate values for entries such as
name or whether to include a license or `.gitignore` file.

With our repository in place, we can now move on to the next task, which is to upload our library code – fortunately, this is easy enough to do, using standard Git commands. I suspect some of this will be familiar to many of you already; for those new to Git, don't worry – let's dive in and take a closer look at what's involved.

Uploading Components to GitHub

With our repository set up and ready for use, it's time we turned our attention to uploading our code. We can achieve this in one of several ways: uploading directly from editors, Git GUI clients, or the Git command line.

For this next exercise, I will keep it simple and use the Git command line; feel free to adapt if you already have a process for uploading to GitHub. Let's make a start.

UPLOADING TO GITHUB

To upload our code to the repository, follow these steps:

1. We first need to rename the original `cobalt` folder to `cobalt-source` – this will allow the upload process to continue.

If you already have Git installed for your platform, please skip the next step, and proceed to step 3.

---

2. Next, we need to install Git – head over to `https://git-scm.com/downloads`, then download and install the version appropriate for your platform. When asked, please accept default settings – this should be sufficient for this exercise.

3. With Git installed, fire up a Git Bash session, then change the working folder to the same level as the `cobalt-source` folder we renamed in the previous step.

4. Next, we need to clone the empty repository down to your PC so that we can upload content – for this, enter this command at the prompt to pull down a copy of the repository:

```
Git clone https://github.com/XXXXX/cobalt.git
```

Please replace XXXXX with your account name – alternatively, you can get this URL from GitHub by visiting the Code tab, then clicking on Clone, and hitting the icon to the right of the URL to copy the address.

5. On pressing Enter, you should see something akin to this:

```
Cloning into 'cobalt'...
remote: Enumerating objects: 5, done.
remote: Counting objects: 100% (5/5), done.
remote: Compressing objects: 100% (5/5), done.
remote: Total 5 (delta 0), reused 0 (delta 0),
pack-reused 0
Receiving objects: 100% (5/5), done.
```

6. Switch to your file manager, then copy all of the files from `cobalt-source` to `cobalt`, **except for the following**:

```
index.old, node_modules, .vscode, dist
```

If prompted, overwrite existing files.

7. With the files copied over, revert to a Node.js terminal session, then change the working folder to the cobalt folder, and run this command at the prompt:

```
npm install
```

8. Once this is complete, we need to add the files together, ready to push up as a commit to our repository. Run this command at the prompt:

```
git add .
```

9. With the files ready, run this command to bundle the code into a commit:

```
git commit -m "Initial release"
```

…which will produce results akin to this:

```
[main 4d38b60] Initial release
 103 files changed, 52901 insertions(+), 106 deletions(-)
 rewrite .gitignore (94%)
 create mode 100644 .storybook/main.js
 create mode 100644 .storybook/preview-head.html
 create mode 100644 .storybook/preview.js
 rewrite README.md (100%)
 create mode 100644 __test__/Accordion.spec.js
 create mode 100644 __test__/Alert.spec.js
 create mode 100644 __test__/Breadcrumbs.spec.js
 create mode 100644 __test__/Checkbox.spec.js
```

10.   Before we can push up, we need to create a PAT
      (or Personal Access Token) – first, browse to this page:
      `https://github.com/settings/tokens`.

You can also get to this page by clicking on Profile ➤ settings ➤
developers setting ➤ personal access tokens. Don't be tempted to go
to the repository settings page – you must do this within your profile
settings page!

---

11.   Click on Generate a new token, log in if prompted, and enter the
      name Cobalt UI for the Note field.

12.   Set the expiration as high as you feel comfortable with, or is
      permitted in your environment, then click on workflow and repo
      as selected scopes. Make a copy of the token – **you will need
      it** – then at the bottom, hit Generate token.

13.   Switch to your desktop, then search for a Windows application
      named *Credential Manager*. Open it, then click on *Windows
      Credentials*.

Please complete either step 14 or step 15, depending on whether
you have an entry for github.com, but not both. Once done, please
continue from step 16.

---

14.   Look for an entry marked github.com – if it is there, then edit
      it to replace the password with the token you generated in
      GitHub. Hit Save and close the Manager.

15. If you do not have it, then hit Add a Windows credential and enter the details as follows:

Entry	Value
Internet or network address	github.com
Your username	The username you use to log into your GitHub account
Your password	Your PAT token created in step 12

16. Hit Save, then close the Manager.

17. Switch back to your Node.js terminal; then at the prompt, enter `git push`.

18. You will likely be prompted to log into GitHub – click on the Token open when prompted, paste in your PAT token, and then hit Enter.

It may appear as a small window, which might be hidden under others – check your taskbar to see if anything appears.

---

19. Assuming your login is successful, Git will continue to push items up; if all is well, you should see something akin to this:

```
Enumerating objects: 131, done.
Counting objects: 100% (131/131), done.
Delta compression using up to 8 threads
Compressing objects: 100% (118/118), done.
Writing objects: 100% (128/128), 429.01 KiB | 5.72
MiB/s, done.
Total 128 (delta 26), reused 0 (delta 0), pack-reused 0
remote: Resolving deltas: 100% (26/26), done.
To https://github.com/alexlibby/cobalt.git
    be80a29..4d38b60  main -> main
```

20. Switch to your GitHub repository and check the Code tab to
     confirm that all files are present and correct, as shown in the
     extract in Figure 10-4.

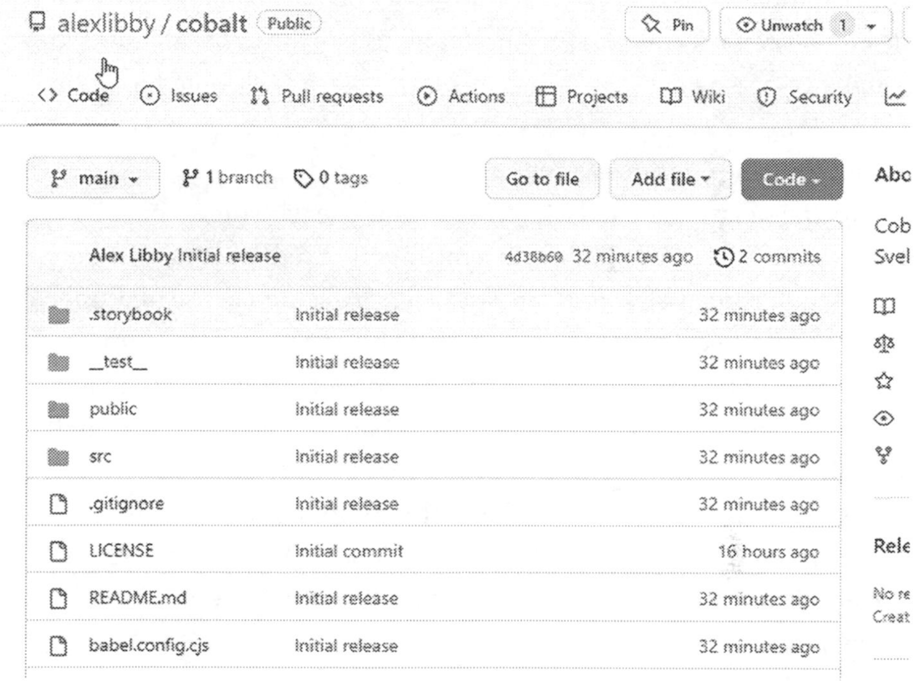

Figure 10-4. *Files uploaded to Git*

Phew – that was a mammoth exercise! However, we have now got all of
our content into GitHub, ready for release. It took a bit of doing, but much
of this last demo is a one-off, so we won't have to do it too often.

With the content available on GitHub, we can now take a breather –
the code is ready for us to start releasing as component packages on npm
or bundling into compiled files we can download and use in demos and
projects. Before we explore that, let's take a few moments to explore what
we covered in that last demo in more detail.

Exploring the Code in Detail

So what did we achieve in that monster demo?

We began this exercise with a small but essential step: rename the `cobalt` folder. It was necessary to allow us to clone the remote Git folder to our PC without Git complaining of a folder already present. In hindsight, though, we could have avoided the need for this, as we could have done the Git cloning step first; renaming it now means we have a backup copy just in case anything goes wrong!

Moving on, we installed Git (at least for those who didn't have it present already) before cloning the empty cobalt repository down to our PC. We then copied files from our original project area to the new one before creating a commit for our new repository. To push them up, we had to set up a PAT or Personal Access Token; once done, we completed the upload before checking they had successfully been committed to the repository.

Okay – let's crack on: we now have our component code in the repository, so we can release it for others to use! Other developers can access the code directly, but what about publishing a component or two to npm?

Releasing Components to npm

"Yikes – releasing a component…will it work?"

It's a perfectly valid question, and I'm sure you will feel a sense of trepidation as we take that leap into the unknown! But don't worry, though – while there may be a few steps involved in releasing our components, it is a straightforward process, and some of it we will only need to do for the first time. To understand what I mean, let's quickly summarize the steps involved:

- Update our component folder into a monorepo, or a sub-repository, ready for publishing.

- Set up a configuration file to tell Svelte how to release a compiled version of our component.

- Publish the component onto npm, ready for use.

The first two steps only need to be done once for each component – step 3 is the one we will repeat each time we publish a new version of our component(s) or library. Perfect: now that we know what is involved, let's get stuck in! Before we get to writing code, there are a few points of housekeeping we need to be aware of:

- Please make sure you log into `www.npmjs.org` with your account (including two-factor authentication, if you have it enabled) **before** you start this exercise.

If you don't have an account, you will need to create one, which you can do at `www.npmjs.com/signup` – there is plenty of documentation online if you need assistance.

- We should complete the upload to npm after uploading to GitHub and not before – the upload process relies on GitHub.

- We will use the Checkbox component as our example – please feel free to adapt if you want to try a different component.

- Please create a new folder called compiled at the root of the Checkbox component folder – this we will use to store a compiled version of the component.

We need to be mindful of another point before we get a little trigger-happy and create packages. We must remember that what we're building is **still a pre-production version**, and we will need to do more work before releasing a production version.

For this reason, I've marked the version in the upcoming exercise as alpha1, and it's still important to be aware of the release steps, ready for when we're good to release into production. With all that in mind, let's crack on with creating our package for upload to npm.

RELEASING TO NPM

To release a component from our library to npm, follow these steps:

1. First, we need to turn our chosen component into a "monorepo"; for this, fire up a Node.js terminal session, then change the prompt to the Checkbox component folder within our project area.

2. At the prompt, enter this command and press Enter:

```
npm init --y
```

Leave the session open but minimized throughout this exercise – we will use it a few times.

---

3. It creates a `package.json` file with a few fields prepopulated – go ahead and open it, then modify it, so it has these fields:

Note   Change XXXXX to your npm account name, where shown.

```
{
  "name": "@XXXXX/checkbox",
  "version": "1.0.0-alpha1",
  "description": "A simple checkbox component from the
  Cobalt library, for Svelte",
  "main": "index.js",
  "scripts": {
    "test": "echo \"Error: no test specified\" && exit 1"
  },
  "repository": {
    "type": "git",
    "url": "git+https://github.com/XXXXX/cobalt.git"
  },
  "keywords": [
    "svelte",
    "react",
    "custom elements",
    "web components"
  ],
  "author": "Alex Libby",
  "license": "MIT"
}
```

4. Next, switch to your editor, then create a new file and add
    this code:

```
import { defineConfig } from 'vite'
import { svelte } from '@sveltejs/vite-plugin-svelte'

// https://vitejs.dev/config/
export default defineConfig({
  build:{
    rollupOptions: {
      input: ['./src/lib/Checkbox/Checkbox.svelte'],
    }
```

```
    },
    plugins: [svelte({
      compilerOptions:{
        customElement: true
      }
    })]
  })
```

5. Save the file as `vite.checkbox.config.js` at the root of our project area.

6. Revert to your Node.js terminal session; then from the root of the project area, run this command:

    ```
    npm run build -- -c=vite.checkbox.config.js.
    ```

7. Replace `index.js` with `./compiled/Checkbox.XXXXXXXX.js`, where X is the number in the file name created during the build.

8. Once complete, look for the `\dist` folder at the root of your project.

9. Copy the `Checkbox.XXXXXXXX.js` into the compiled folder we created earlier, within the component folder.

10. We're almost there – just a few steps to go! The next task is to publish the component: Revert to your Node.js terminal session and set the working folder to the root of your project area.

11. At the prompt, enter this command and press Enter:

    ```
    npm publish -access=public
    ```

12. You should see something similar to this response appear,
     allowing, of course, for the change in account ID:

```
npm notice
npm notice 🎁  @alexlibby/checkbox@1.0.0-alpha-1
npm notice === Tarball Contents ===
npm notice 1.5kB Checkbox.svelte
npm notice 6.3kB compiled/Checkbox.25348327.js
npm notice 509B  package.json
npm notice === Tarball Details ===
npm notice name:           @alexlibby/checkbox
npm notice version:        1.0.0-alpha-1
npm notice filename:       @alexlibby/checkbox-1.0.0-
                           alpha-1.tgz
npm notice package size:   3.7 kB
npm notice unpacked size:  8.4 kB
npm notice shasum:         cd4fa8a5c8128c7d6688aea
                           e6fe095900d662133
npm notice integrity:      sha512-nbbiBPdJ/
kQL9[...]u8dLX5dVHY4Bg==
npm notice total files:    3
npm notice
npm notice Publishing to https://registry.npmjs.org/
+ @alexlibby/checkbox@1.0.0-alpha-1
```

13. At this point, the component is published! To check this is the
     case, navigate to www.npmjs.org, then search for @XXXXX/
     checkbox, where XXXXX is your account ID. If all is well, we
     should see something similar to that shown in Figure 10-5.

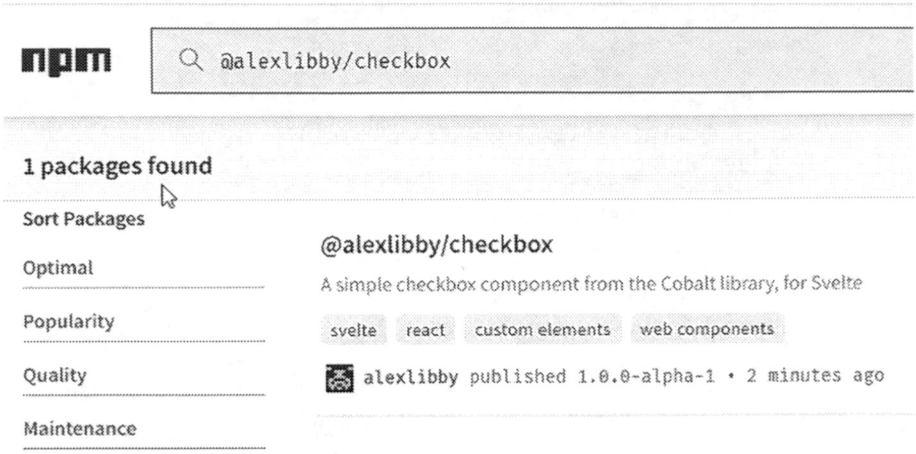

npm   Q @alexlibby/checkbox

1 packages found

Sort Packages

Optimal

Popularity

Quality

Maintenance

@alexlibby/checkbox

A simple checkbox component from the Cobalt library, for Svelte

svelte   react   custom elements   web components

alexlibby published 1.0.0-alpha-1 • 2 minutes ago

Figure 10-5. *Confirmation that our initial package has been published*

14.   You will also receive a confirmation email if you entered a valid email address!

Brilliant – we have published our first component! Granted, it's only an alpha version, and there is still more we can do to develop and improve on it, but it's a good step in the right direction.

Building a Demo

Of course, though, there is one thing we should do: How about testing if it works? We know it's now available on npm, but (as they say) the proof is in the pudding – we should test it in a demo.

This testing is easy enough to do, so let's dive in and look at what we need to do in more detail.

TESTING THE NEW COMPONENT

Testing our component is a quick job – to see how, follow these steps:

1. First, navigate to `www.codesandbox.io`, then create a new React site using their template.

2. Next, click inside the Add Dependency box on the left, and start typing the name of your component – in my case, `@alexlibby/checkbox`, but yours will be whatever name you decided to use.

3. You should see the component's name appear in a list after just a few characters – when you do, click on it to add it as a dependency.

4. CodeSandbox will install it automatically – this will take a moment or two, so be patient!

5. Once done, click on the `App.svelte` entry in the file list at the top of the page – add a reference to the Checkbox component as highlighted:

    ```
    <main>
      <h1>Hello CodeSandbox</h1>
      <h2>Start editing to see some magic happen!</h2>
      <cobalt-checkbox></cobalt-checkbox>
    </main>
    ```

6. Wait a few moments for CodeSandbox to save the change – if all is well, we should see something akin to that shown in Figure 10-6.

Figure 10-6. *The newly published component available from npm*

Yes – we have finally arrived! In the hope that this wasn't too premature, we now have a working component and have proven it works in a demo.

What is interesting to note is the use of this component's web component reference. We're not using it as `<Checkbox />` (which we would in a Svelte environment), but by using `<cobalt-checkbox></cobalt-checkbox>`. You will also notice that I've used the full name, not the shorthand; I've noticed instances where the latter doesn't work well. It is why you will see me using the longhand version when referencing components in a web component capacity.

Okay – let's move on: we covered a lot of practical steps in the previous demo, so now's a perfect opportunity to review the changes in more detail, understand how they all work, and what we need to do when it comes to releasing further changes.

Breaking Apart the Code Changes

Our last demo was a complex affair – who would know that publishing to npm could require so many steps? In reality, many of these steps will be a one-off – if not for the repo, at least for each component package we create and publish to npm.

The key to making this process work is compiling it into a file that other developers can use. To understand what I mean, let's take a look at the changes we made.

We began first by converting the Checkbox folder into its own monorepo – for the uninitiated, this is effectively a repository within a larger parent. To do this, we created a package.json, to which we added a host of fields required for publishing the component as a package.

Next came the addition of the vite.checkbox.config.js file – this tells Svelte how to compile the component into a format we can pull into future projects. A key point here is that we created this file purely around the Checkbox component, but we could equally have included other components too – we just need to add their names and sources to what will be a comma-delimited list in the input: field.

We then ran the build process, which resulted in a compiled file – this we copied from the \dist folder into a new compiled folder, ready for packaging. At this point, we ran the npm publish command, which created a package for us on npm. To finish this part of the process, we ran a quick check to confirm that our package had been published successfully on npm and that we got a confirmation email to boot!

By comparison, the second part of this process was a far more straightforward affair – we used CodeSandbox to create a basic React site using their template. To this, we added the newly published component – once CodeSandbox had saved the update, we saw the component appear in the preview window in our browser.

Now that we've published our component on npm, there are a couple of interesting points of note that we should be aware of:

- You will notice that when we check that the component exists in npm, we only see limited information if we click through to the package's page. All of this is provided by the package's README file, if one is available; I've gone ahead and pushed one up on my version of the Checkbox component in the library at https://github.com/alexlibby/cobalt/tree/main/src/lib/Checkbox.

- We have had to use the format @XXXXX/YYYYYY to publish the package, where X is your account name and Y is the package. This naming is known as a scoped package – there used to be a time when we didn't have to provide the name. Since GitHub took over npm, GitHub is now enforcing the use of scoped names – in the background, we are publishing to GitHub Packages, not npm. It means that we also had to provide the `-access=public` tag. Otherwise, the component won't publish on what is a free repository.

- An essential part of the publishing process is managing the version number – I've started with `1.0.0-alpha1` to clarify that this is a pre-production version and that we should assume the usual caveats around using it. I would recommend researching how to automate this manual process to get the correct version number applied for each release automatically. An excellent example is the semantic-release package available on npm at `www.npmjs.com/package/semantic-release`.

Okay – what's next? Now that we have our component on GitHub, it's time to make our component documentation available for others to view online. The easiest way to do this is by publishing a static version of our Storybook instance; let's dive in and look at how we can do this as part of our next demo.

Publishing Storybook to Netlify

Wow – I'm sure you'll agree with me when I say that the last few pages were a little intense! Nevertheless, the steps we covered were critical to getting our first component out; we still have work to do in this respect, but that will come with time.

In the meantime, we should move on to the next important step: making our documentation available for others. There are several ways we could do this, such as hosting on AWS, Vercel, Surge, or Now – I've chosen to use Netlify as I'm a big fan of this tool and have used it in the past.

Getting our content published is straightforward – Netlify links into GitHub seamlessly, so we need to complete a few steps, and our content will appear online. Let's take a look at what is involved in more detail.

At the time of writing, some of this is still in beta – the steps are solid, although some things may change by the time this book is in print!

PUBLISHING THE COMPONENT STORYBOOK

To publish our instance of Storybook, follow these steps:

1. We first need to export Storybook as a static application – for this, fire up a Node.js terminal, then change the working folder to our project area.

2. At the prompt, enter npm run storybook-build and press Enter.

It may or may not show warnings – we can deal with any later. The critical point is that it must not show any errors, indicating a failed build.

---

3. Let it churn through the process – it will finish with lines similar to this:

```
info => Manager built (1.03 min)
info => Output directory: C:\cobalt\storybook-static
```

4. Node will have created a few files and folders – we need to push these up to GitHub. At the prompt, enter these commands and press Enter after each:

```
git add .
git commit -m "Add exported version of Storybook"
git push
```

Assuming no errors appeared, we have our files ready for the next part of the process: publishing the content for other developers to view and use.

At this stage, we have our Storybook exported content ready for publication – people won't see it until we hook it into our hosting. As you have already noted, I've elected to use Netlify; feel free to use a different system if you prefer!

I recommend selecting one that hooks into GitHub to get the best from the next exercise.

Setting Up Netlify

Although Netlify has only been around since 2014, it has quickly become one of the most popular ways to host content. It's perfect for hosting our Jamstack-based site – all of the content is already on GitHub, so we need to link it to a Netlify account and let it publish the site onto the Internet. Let's take a look at what we need to do in more detail.

If you see a reference to XXXXX in the following demo, change it to your GitHub account name.

SETTING UP NETLIFY

To set up our site, follow these steps:

1. We first need to sign up – for this, browse to
    `https://app.netlify.com/signup`, then hit GitHub.

2. When prompted, click Yes to authorize Netlify to access your
    GitHub account.

3. Next, click on Add new site, then Import an existing project.

4. At this point, select GitHub, then Authorize Netlify.

5. When prompted, enter `cobalt` – it won't find it: don't worry,
    this is to be expected! It will prompt for an update that we need
    to do to permissions so Netlify can access your GitHub site.

6. Click on Configure Netlify on GitHub. Scroll down on the
    next window to Repository Access, then choose Only select
    repositories ➤ Select repositories ➤ XXXXX\cobalt. If all is well,
    you should have settings similar to those shown in Figure 10-7.

○ **All repositories**
This applies to all current *and* future repositories owned by the resource owner.
Also includes public repositories (read-only).

◉ **Only select repositories**
Select at least one repository.
Also includes public repositories (read-only).

🖥 **Select repositories ▾**

Selected 2 repositories.

🖥 alexlibby/cobalt   ✕

Figure 10-7.   The settings for updating permissions for Netlify

7.   Once done, hit Save.

8.   On the previous screen, click on XXXXX\cobalt; then in the Basic build settings, enter the values shown in Figure 10-8.

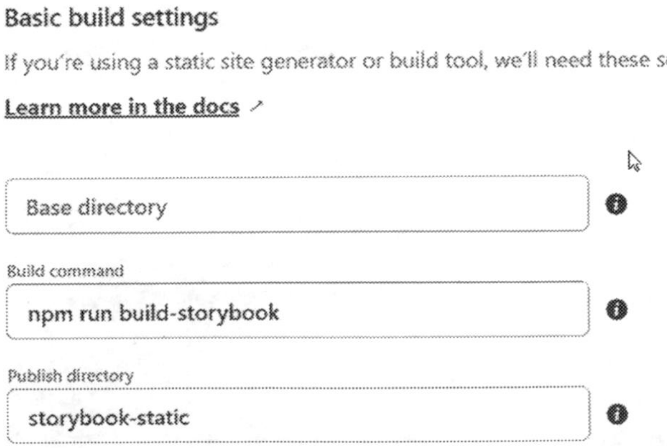

Basic build settings

If you're using a static site generator or build tool, we'll need these s

Learn more in the docs ↗

Base directory   ❶

Build command
npm run build-storybook   ❶

Publish directory
storybook-static   ❶

Figure 10-8.   Settings to trigger the build process

9. Once you've entered the values, click on "Deploy site." If
    everything goes well, you should be able to deploy and follow
    along with the build log – click on the Team Overview link at the
    top of the page, then on the name of the site, and the topmost
    entry under Production deploys.

10. Assuming no errors pop up and Netlify shows a Published in
    black text against the relevant build, you will be able to see
    your site if you click on Team Overview ➤ the name of your site
    (which will be on the left of the site preview image).

Yay – we have published our site! Publishing is only the start, as we will
need to update it as and when we make changes to our components. That
comes later, though; for now, let's review the code changes we made in
more detail to understand better how this fits into the broader picture.

Understanding the Changes Made

When it comes to releasing code onto a hosting site, dozens of different
providers are available – sometimes, it can be hard to decide which to
use! Of course, you might already use an existing system, which makes
choosing one a moot choice.

But I digress. I chose to use Netlify as it is one of the more popular
hosting systems: it also links to GitHub seamlessly and has an excellent
API for more custom development.

To get our Storybook instance set up, we first had to sign up – for this,
we used its GitHub authentication process and pointed it at our repository.
All that remained was to provide some values for the basic build process
and hit Deploy site! As the last step, we checked that Netlify published the
site successfully before viewing the final result in our browser.

Adding Polish to the Repository

Now that we've set up our Storybook installation, pushed our code up into GitHub, and released (albeit an experimental) version of our component, it's time to start adding polish to our library so that it looks the best it can be for people using our library.

We could do different things, such as adding more screenshots, better documentation, or creating templates for raising issues. Unfortunately, there's too much for us to do in the confines of this book, so I'm going to focus on two items:

- Adding a README for the Checkbox component file

- Installing a custom domain name for the Storybook installation

There are a few steps required for us to complete both tasks, which we will do over two separate exercises; let's dive in and take a look at the first, which will be adding a custom domain name.

Adding a Custom Domain Name

Before you all start worrying, I should point out from the outset that adding a custom domain name is not an essential part of running our site – the Storybook installation will run perfectly fine with the subdomain URL given to us by Netlify!

For me, though, adding a custom domain name makes it easier to access the site, as it is easier to remember; depending on what name you use, the cost isn't too expensive either! There are various ways to do this, depending on whether you want to use a custom subdomain or a top-level domain from Netlify or provide your own. For simplicity, I will assume that if you do this step, we will register that name directly through Netlify so that it can take care of provisioning the domain for us.

Before we start with the purchase and configuration process, there are a couple of assumptions we should be aware of:

- I'm assuming that the domain name you select is not already registered to anyone.

- We're purchasing directly from Netlify, so the DNS and domain will be held by Netlify.

If either of the aforementioned is different for you, then there will be other steps you need to follow, such as making sure your host points the DNS entries to Netlify.

Let's crack on with setting up our custom domain as part of the next exercise.

ADDING A CUSTOM DOMAIN

To add a custom domain, follow these steps:

1. From the site overview page, click on Domain settings.

2. Scroll down to and click the green Add custom domain button.

3. Go ahead and enter your chosen domain using the format shown in the text box.

4. Click on Add payment method; then in the modal, enter your payment details – note: this will auto-renew at a slightly higher price in year 2: this is to be expected.

5. Enter your address, then hit Save. Back on the previous screen, hit Register domain now for…, and wait for it to complete.

At this point, Netlify will likely state that an SSL/TLS certificate can't be provisioned to secure the site until the domain is validated. If you scroll up the page, you will see the primary DNS entry has changed and that it shows "Check DNS configuration" against it.

This process requires 24 hours for the newly created domain to propagate, so you will want to return later to complete the next part of this process.

Assuming you have waited 24 hours, follow these steps to complete the process:

1. Hit Verify DNS configuration. Assuming that it returns "DNS verification was successful," click on Provision certificate, twice.

2. Netlify will trigger a request to Let's Encrypt to provision the certificates. You may get a "missing certificate error" – if you do, cancel and return to the previous Settings page.

3. Keep refreshing the page – if Netlify has managed to provision the certificate, you will eventually see the "Check DNS configuration" entry replaced with something similar to that shown in Figure 10-9.

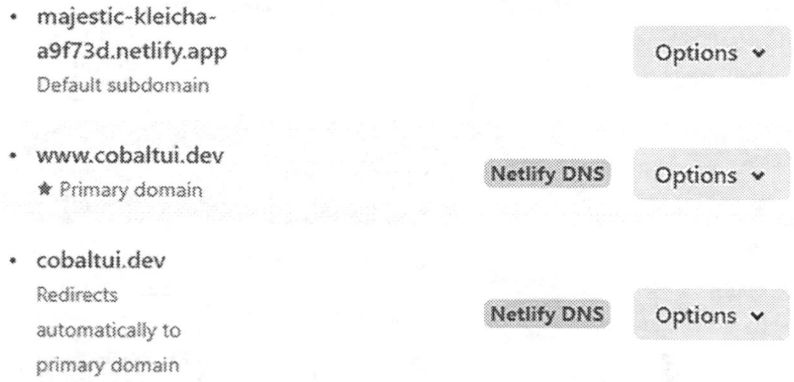

- majestic-kleicha-
  a9f73d.netlify.app   Options ∨
  Default subdomain

- www.cobaltui.dev
  ★ Primary domain   Netlify DNS   Options ∨

- cobaltui.dev
  Redirects
  automatically to   Netlify DNS   Options ∨
  primary domain

Figure 10-9. *Confirmation that DNS has been updated*

4. Take a quick look lower down on that page – you should also
    see that the SSL certificate has been successfully provisioned.

Please note this period can take up to 24 hours to complete; I was
able to view these details after about five to six hours, but it may be
longer for you.

---

5. The real test is to browse to the site – go ahead and browse
    to your new domain (in my case, `www.cobaltui.dev`). If
    all is well, we should see our Storybook appear, as shown in
    Figure 10-10.

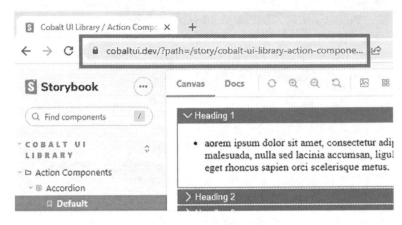

Figure 10-10. *The Storybook installation, under the new domain*

Perfect – we have a domain name that points to a working site! Although we could have stayed with the default name assigned by Netlify, I'm sure you will agree this one is a much nicer name to use.

Let's move on and take a look at the second exercise we'll complete as part of this process – adding a readme file with a version badge.

ADDING A README WITH VERSION BADGE

To update the documentation readme file for our component, follow these steps:

1. We will first begin with adding a version badge for our component – head over to `www.shields.io`, then click on Version at the bottom of the list.

2. On the next page, you will see a long list of license types – scroll down until you see the entry for npm (scoped). It's a long list, so you might want to use the search option in your browser!

3. Click on either the badge or the text to the right; then in the package name field, enter the name of your package (I will assume `cobalt`, but change it if you decide to use something different).

4. On the next page, enter your NPM account ID in the format of @XXXXX, then enter the name in the package name field.

5. If all is well, you should see a black and orange badge appear with the version number of your package – click on the Copy Badge URL drop-down and select Copy Markdown.

6. In your editor, create a new file as `README.md` (note the case), and save it to the root of the Checkbox folder in `\src\lib`.

7. Inside the file, add the following text – adjust the name of the package and the account ID to match your own:

```
![npm (scoped)](https://img.shields.io/npm/v/@alexlibby/
checkbox)
```

```
## Checkbox - a component from the Cobalt library
```

```
This is a test release of the Checkbox component from my
upcoming book, Creating Web Components with Svelte, to be
published by Apress.
```

```
To install, enter this command in a Node.js terminal
session:
```

```
`npm install @alexlibby/checkbox`
```

```
License: MIT
```

8. Save the file – we can always come back and add more later, but this will be enough to get us started.

9. We need to push this change up – fire up a Node.js terminal prompt, then change the working folder to the project area.

10.   At the prompt, enter git add . && git commit -m "Add README", then press Enter.

11.   Once done, enter git push to complete the upload.

12.   To confirm all is well, browse to your GitHub site, then navigate to the \src\lib\Checkbox folder – you should see something akin to that shown in Figure 10-11. I've gone a little further and added a temporary screenshot for the API, a screenshot of the component, and an extra badge for the license version.

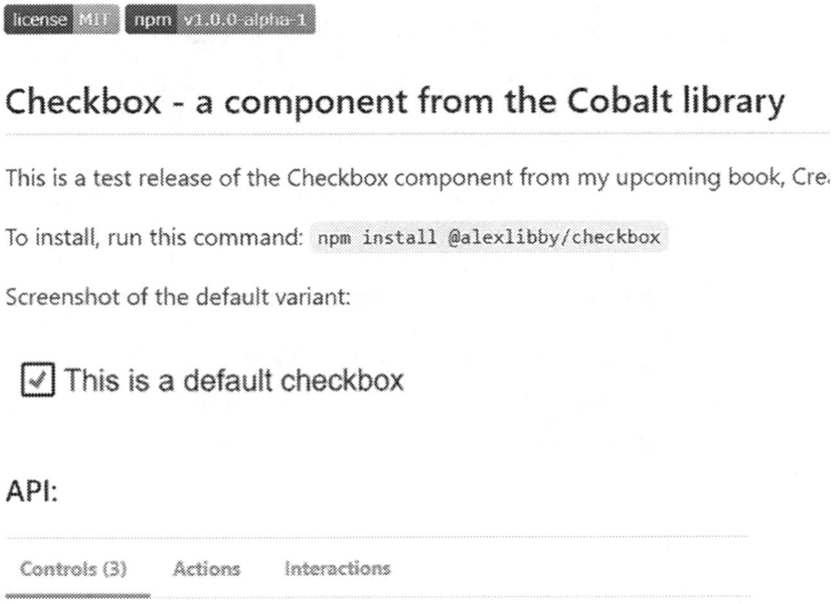

Figure 10-11. *The updated README for the Checkbox component*

Wow – we now have a working GitHub repository and Storybook site and released the first version of our component to our unsuspecting audience! Congratulations if you managed to get this far; it's been a lot of work, but hopefully an enjoyable and worthwhile experience.

However, it is just the start of our journey: there is more we can do! We'll touch on some of this in the next chapter, but before we do so, let's take a moment to review the changes we made in this demo to understand how they all hang together.

Breaking Apart the Code

For me, adding a custom domain is one way to add that extra touch – I know that many people might be happy with the default URL provided by services such as Netlify. Don't get me wrong – this is a perfectly valid option. However, going that extra distance means your library should make it a little more memorable and encourage people to return.

That only time will tell – for now, what did we do to get here? We started by working through Netlify's standard process for purchasing a domain name and initiating domain registration. We kicked off a request for Netlify to provision a certificate using the Let's Encrypt service; this initially failed me while researching for this book, but I believe it was just a matter of waiting for the service to kick in once the domain had replicated around the Internet.

The lesson here is that it does pay to be patient – I would strongly recommend making the payment at the end of the day so that you stand a chance of it being available the following morning! Once the request for the SSL certificate was provisioned, we ran a quick check to verify that the site had been updated and was now available via an HTTPS address.

In the second demo, we switched to creating our component's README file – we began first by visiting the Shields.io website to generate a badge with the appropriate version of the current package available on npm. We took a copy of the link for this badge as Markdown text before adding it to a new README file; once saved, we committed this to the repository before checking the results in our browser.

Summary

Phew – this might have been a long chapter, but we've finally reached the point where our Storybook site and the component library will now be live! We've covered a lot of content in this chapter, so let's relax for a moment and review what we have learned.

We began way back when (yes, it does feel like a while ago!) with a quick discussion around performing the final checks. Not only did we cover some areas to consider, but we also understood that this is a symbolic way of confirming that we are ready to sign off the results and release them into production.

Next up, we moved on to pushing our code into GitHub; we first walked through the process of setting up the repository before exploring the steps required to commit our code into our new library. We then switched to releasing a test component into the npm repository as a package – we covered the fact that this was an alpha package and a way to explore the process; we would do this for real once we were ready to release our code.

Moving on, we worked our way through publishing the Storybook instance to a hosting site, using Netlify as our preferred platform. We first set up the authorization between GitHub and Netlify before configuring Netlify to run the build step for Storybook and create our site. As a final touch, we explored creating a new README file with a version badge and the steps we would need to take to release our site through a custom domain for our customers.

And relax! We've done most of the hard work now – the library is available on GitHub, Storybook is hosted on Netlify, and we released our component's first instance as a package. There is still more to do, but the focus of our journey changes – it's time now to focus on how we can develop and expand our library. There's plenty we can do in this respect, so stay with me, and I'll reveal more details in the next chapter.

CHAPTER 11

Taking Things Further

We've almost reached the end of the book – there is one more question we should answer: What next? At times like this, I am reminded of the phrase "the world is our oyster."

It is up to us to decide where to go next…as well as maybe have a little fun too! To answer that question, we'll explore a range of topics, which might include the following:

- Now we've built our library – is there anything we want to change or improve?

- What's next – how about setting a road map?

- Converting components from other frameworks

- Revisiting some of what we've already done

- Can we optimize specific areas, such as CSS?

These are just some of the questions we should answer – I'm sure I can think of more! To get us started, let's first review what we've done so far, so we can see where we might have any gaps that we need to fill.

Reviewing the Site

Although we completed some of this task during the release process, I can almost guarantee that there will be things we want to add or change!

© Alex Libby 2023
A. Libby, *Developing Web Components with Svelte*,
https://doi.org/10.1007/978-1-4842-9039-2_11

I'm not talking about adding new components, although that will come. We must also consider areas such as tidying existing code, leveling the number of variants for each component, or improving test coverage. With that in mind, let's take a quick look at a few likely candidates for improvement in the immediate future:

- Improve test coverage.

- Implement a dependency update mechanism to keep the site secure and vulnerability-free (where possible).

- Add more detailed documentation.

- Finish RadioButton – get it working.

- Get SideBar working in Storybook.

- Expand the variants for each component, and level up to a minimum of three where possible.

- Augment the CSS Grid properties for ImageGrid.

- Release more component packages – individually and as a whole.

- Realign components into named group for npm – not under my name, but a collective name of cobaltui (or similar, depending on availability).

That's just a small selection of what we could do to improve the code base within the first three months of release – I'm sure there will be others! I prefer not to commit to many changes too early and to focus on our gaps before expanding with new components. (As you will see, I will break that "preference," but hey – rules are meant to be broken!) The critical point here is that we take note of what we need to do and create a plan for implementing the changes.

You can see a more extensive road map in the GitHub repository, in `roadmap.md`, at the root of the library.

The plan doesn't need to be complex – we could list everything we want to do and then put rough dates against each one (ideally quarters rather than months – it helps give yourself some flexibility). Remember that you will have to keep your promises in some form or another!

Taking the Next Steps – Setting a Road Map

Ouch – where does one start with setting a road map? The truth is that it will depend on one of two things:

- Where do you want to take the library?
- What features are others asking for?

Deciding on what to add can be a double-edged sword – there could be some no-brainer features that you just have to incorporate, or you might find you want to add something that others will hate!

In some cases, others will make the decision easy – you might find you want to add components that your colleagues could use in a corporate environment and that releasing to the outside world will be a bonus. However, we need to balance this against those instances where you are in control of what you add – we have to prepare for those who dislike what you might have in mind. Still, as long as you are transparent about it and go with the majority decision, you will at least maintain a good audience.

Keeping all of that in mind, let's pause for a moment to consider some examples of what we might want as future components in our library:

- Avatar
- Cards – such as for product information
- Progressbar

- Switch

- Tags

- HTML5 form field elements, such as email or telephone

- Popover

- ListBox

I'm sure there will be more, but as mentioned before – let's not get too ahead of ourselves! Most of our focus should be on leveling up existing components and strengthening what we've developed

Converting Our Next Component

Okay – enough talking: we need to get stuck into some coding.

For the first demo of this chapter, we're going to look at our next component: Avatar. Usually, I would work through creating one, adding it to Storybook, and so on…you know the drill by now!

However, that would mean us missing out on a helpful tip when creating Svelte components. If you're converting from an existing feature found on the Internet to Svelte, then forget the lift-and-shift approach. What do I mean by this? I hear you ask.

Well, it comes down to one simple principle: instead of focusing on the technical elements, look at the *functionality* offered by the component. Svelte requires a different mindset, which can be weird for developers using other frameworks. You can lift and shift values such as imports (if appropriate) or variables already declared in the React code, but that's probably as much as we can use.

To illustrate this, I've picked a React example of an Avatar component, this one created by the CoreUI team and which is available at `https://github.com/coreui/coreui-react/blob/main/packages/coreui-react/src/components/avatar/CAvatar.tsx`; it uses standard React/TypeScript to create a simple component. Now, let's dive in and look at how this component might look if we rebuilt it in Svelte.

CREATING THE AVATAR COMPONENT

To create our new Avatar component, follow these steps:

1. First, we need to avail ourselves of a suitable avatar image – for this, look online to see if any image libraries have one that takes your fancy! I recommend keeping the size as close to 128px square as possible for this exercise; the file format isn't critical. Please save the file as `avatar.png` – if you've changed the file format or name, then please adjust the code to suit.

2. Once you have a suitable image, drop it into the `\public` folder at the root of our project area.

3. We now need to create a new folder for our component – go ahead and add one called Avatar into the `\src\lib\` folder.

4. Next, crack open your editor and create a new file, saving it as `Avatar.svelte` in the newly created Avatar folder.

5. In the file, we need to add quite a bit of code – as before, we'll do it in sections, starting with the `svelte:options` tag and a handful of export statements:

```
<svelte:options tag="cobalt-avatar" />

<script>
  export let src = "";
  export let status = "available" || "busy" || "away" ||
"unavailable";
  export let statusSize = "small" || "medium" || "large";
```

6. Next, we need to add a reactive statement block to look after
    updating values if the size or status should change:

```
$: statusClasses = () => {
  let inputKlasses = [status, statusSize];
  inputKlasses = inputKlasses.filter((klass) =>
klass.length);
  return inputKlasses.join(" ");
};
</script>
```

7. The most important part comes next, which is the markup for
    our component:

```
<div class="cobalt-avatar">
  {#if src}
    <img {src} class="avatar-img" alt="avatar" />
  {/if}
  <slot />
  <span class={["base", statusClasses()].join(" ")} />
</div>
```

8. We can finish off the component with some styling – the first is
    the container for our component and a common style rule for
    the indicator:

```
<style>
  .cobalt-avatar {
    position: relative;
    display: inline-flex;
    align-items: center;
    justify-content: center;
    vertical-align: middle;
    border-radius: 800px;
    width: 32px;
```

```
  height: 32px;
  font-size: 12.8px;
}

.base {
  border-radius: 800px;
  position: absolute;
  border: 1px solid #373737;
}
```

9. Next up, we have two styles for size – small and medium:

```
.small {
  width: 8px;
  height: 8px;
  top: 25px;
  right: 0px;
}

.medium {
  width: 12px;
  height: 12px;
  top: 22px;
  right: -4px;
}

.large {
  width: 16px;
  height: 16px;
  top: 22px;
  right: -4px;
}
```

10. We also need some styling for availability – for this, we have four rules for available, danger, away, and unavailable:

```
.available { background-color: #00ff00; }
.danger { background-color: #ff0000; }
.away { background-color: #ffff00; }
.unavailable { background-color: #ffffff; border: 1px
solid #000000;}
```

11. This last style is for the avatar image:

```
.avatar-img { width: 100%; height: auto;
border-radius: 800px; }
</style>
```

12. Save and close the file – we are done with the changes for now, and we'll do the first test of our new component shortly when we link it into Storybook.

Perfect – we have a component ready to test; we'll do this shortly when we add it to Storybook. Although much of the code should be relatively familiar by now, there are some critical highlights I want to touch on – with that in mind, let's review the changes we made in the last demo in more detail.

Dissecting the Code

In our current age of social media, avatars are probably one of the most widely seen features you will see. It doesn't matter if they show letters or a fancy picture; the basic premise of identifying you as a person is still the same. We've taken the opportunity to create such a component for our library and base it on an original, built using React – let's take a moment to review the changes we made in more detail.

We began by looking for a suitable image online – we understood that it needed to be around 128px square where possible to ensure it works as expected in our component. Next, we created the component itself – we began setting the now-familiar `svelte:options` tag before creating three variables for export: `status`, `src`, and `statusSize`.

We then moved on to creating a reactive block, which uses the $ keyword in Svelte – as a reminder, this reacts (hence the name) to any changes in the current state or value in variables and updates them accordingly.

Next, we added the markup for our demo – this we kept simple for now, using an if block (`{#if}...{/if}`) to determine if we should display an image. Everything else will go in the `<slot />`, including text, markup, or other components we might use. We then finished this off with styling – we created `.cobalt-avatar` for the container, three styles to cover the size of the status indicator in our component, and status to cover most of the presence statuses we might want to use as developers.

There is one last point I want to cover from this component before we move on: the translation process from React to Svelte. While researching for this book, I found a great article on using Svelte for those who usually develop using React. It's by Sina Farhadi and available on the Plain English website at `https://javascript.plainenglish.io/svelte-for-react-developers-7edc099e03ed`. Suffice to say, Svelte requires a different mindset to React, which can be a challenge for some; if you get it (so to speak), it often means a cleaner code result and one that is frequently faster to boot!

Adding to Storybook

So far, we've explored how to create an equivalent Avatar component in Svelte and seen that it's not just a lift and shift of existing code but that it's better to focus on functionality rather than technical code.

We now need to test our component – as we've done previously, there are two ways we can test it: writing a test case for it using Svelte Testing Library and adding it to Storybook.

LINKING AVATAR INTO STORYBOOK AND ADDING A TEST

To set up our Avatar component in Storybook, follow these steps:

1. First, fire up your editor, then create a new file, saving it as
    `Avatar.stories.mdx` in the `\src\lib\storybook` folder.

2. We have a lot of code to add, so as usual, we'll break it
    into sections – we'll start with the imports and the usual
    `<Meta>` tag:

```
import Avatar from '../Avatar/Avatar.svelte';
import AvatarDocs from './AvatarDocs.mdx';
import { Meta, Story } from '@storybook/addon-docs';

<Meta
  title="Cobalt UI Library/New Components/Avatar"
  component={Avatar}
  parameters={{ page: null }}
/>
```

3. To display the component, we need a template to tell Storybook
    how to display it; for this, miss a line after the code from step 1,
    and add this block:

```
export const Template = (args) => ({
  Component: Avatar,
  props: args,
});
```

4. With the template in place, we can add stories for each variant
    we want to display. The first one is the default, which displays a
    green status to show that the person is available:

```
<Story
  name="Default"
  args={{
```

```
        status: "available",
        statusSize: "small",
        src: "/public/avatar.png"
      }}
      parameters={{
        docs: {
          page: AvatarDocs
        }
      }}>
      {Template.bind({})}
    </Story>
```

5. Next, miss a line, then add this next Story – this takes care of cases where the person is busy and displays a red status:

```
    <Story
      name="Busy"
      args={{
        status: "danger",
        statusSize: "small",
        src: "/public/avatar.png"
      }}
      parameters={{
        docs: {
          page: AvatarDocs
        }
      }}>
      {Template.bind({})}
    </Story>
```

6. For this next Story, we'll display the Unavailable status, which shows a white circle, but this time in a larger size:

```
    <Story
      name="Unavailable"
      args={{
```

```
      status: "unavailable",
      statusSize: "medium",
      src: "/avatar.png"
    }}
    parameters={{
      docs: {
        page: AvatarDocs
      }
    }}>
    {Template.bind({})}
  </Story>
```

7. For the last example, we'll display the Away symbol in a medium size – this is a yellow status:

```
  <Story
    name="Away"
    args={{
      status: "away",
      statusSize: "medium",
      src: "/public/avatar.png"
    }}
    parameters={{
      docs: {
        page: AvatarDocs
      }
    }}>
    {Template.bind({})}
  </Story>
```

8. Save and close the file.

9. We also need a copy of the `AvatarDocs.md` file as our documentation – this is available in the code download for this book, so extract a copy and put it into the `\src\lib\` storybook folder.

At this point, we should have a handful of files to push up to our repo – to get them committed, follow these steps:

1. Next, switch to a Node.js terminal session, and change the working folder to our project area.

2. We need to push up all of the changes we've made so far – at the prompt, enter `git add .` and press Enter to pull all of our files together, ready for committal.

3. Next, enter `git commit -m "Various changes"` to create a commit and press Enter.

4. Finally, enter `git push` to upload all of the changes to our repo – assuming you set up Netlify earlier, this will kick in and build the library.

5. If all is well, we should see updates appear on our Storybook pages, as shown in Figure 11-1.

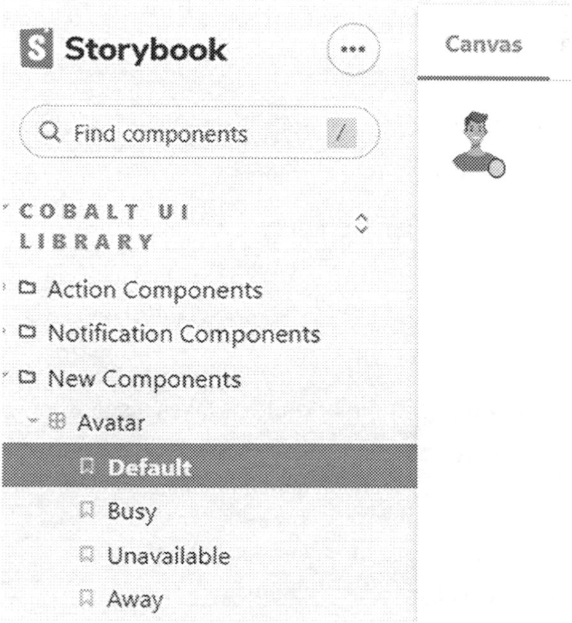

Figure 11-1. Storybook with the updated Avatar component on display

We have one last step to perform, which is to add a test – as this is only a status icon, we'll keep it simple and set it to run a snapshot for now. To do this, follow these steps:

1. Crack open a new file, saving it as `Avatar.spec.js` in the `__test__` folder at the root of the project folder.

2. Go ahead and add the following code into the file – we'll begin with the imports:

```
import { render, screen } from '@testing-library/svelte';
import Avatar from "../src/lib/Avatar/Avatar.svelte";
```

3. Next up, let's add the opening part of the test – this contains a props declaration for our component:

```
describe("Tests for Avatar", () => {
  const props = {
    src: "",
    status: "available",
    statusSize: "medium",
  };
```

4. We should test it renders correctly – for that, miss a line, then add this assertion:

```
it("should render properly", async() => {
  const result = render(Avatar, { props });
  expect(() => result).not.toThrow();
});
```

5. To close off the test, add this step – it takes a snapshot, which we can use for visual testing:

```
it("get a snapshot of component", () => {
  const tree = render(Avatar, props);
  expect(tree).toMatchSnapshot();
})
});
```

6.   Save and close the file. Switch to your Node.js terminal session, ensuring the working folder is still set to the project area.

7.   At the prompt, enter `npm run test` and press Enter – if all is well, we should see our tests pass without issue.

8.   Next, switch to a Node.js terminal session, and change the working folder to our project area.

9.   We need to push up all of the changes we've made so far – at the prompt, enter `git add .` and press Enter to pull all of our files together, ready for committal.

10.   Next, enter `git commit -m "Addition of test and storybook changes"` to create a commit and press Enter.

11.   Finally, enter `git push` to upload all of the changes to our repo – assuming you set up Netlify earlier, this will kick in and build the library.

Excellent – assuming all went as planned, we now have a new Avatar component that we've written based on the original created in React and that we've plumbed into our Storybook instance.

By now, most of what you've seen will seem somewhat familiar, particularly as we've created over 12 components for our library! That said, it's still good to review what we've created, so let's pause and dig into the code in more detail.

Understanding the Changes Made

Although the last exercise was quite lengthy, most of it covers steps that we've seen before – it may have been for different components, but that doesn't matter: reusing the same principles makes life much easier! So what did we achieve in this latest addition to our library?

We began by creating a story for our instance of Storybook – we imported a set of functions from Storybook, along with the documentation file and our component. At the same time, we added the now-familiar `<Meta>` tag to tell Storybook where to place the new component in our setup. You will notice that I've used the New Components location; this is purely to keep any new additions separate from the original components, at least for now!

Next up, we moved to add various stories to our Story file – all four follow the same format as others – we call the component and pass in different values for the `src`, `status`, and `statusSize` arguments. We then finished the first part of this demo by committing all of the changes thus far into our repository before previewing the changes on the Netlify site.

We're not quite finished yet, though – there is still one more addition: a test! We need to add a test file to our existing collection to show we have at least basic test coverage for this component.

Adding this test was straightforward – we first created a test spec file before importing the Svelte Testing Library (as we did for other components) and the Avatar component. We then added the describe block, starting with setting some prop values to pass to our component, before creating the first assertion to test that the component renders without issue.

We then added a second assertion to get a visual snapshot; once the test was saved, we ran it to confirm a successful pass before uploading all changes to our GitHub repository. Before we move on, though, I want to call out one small but important point: the location of our Avatar image. You will notice that we put it into the `public` folder at the top, but there is no reference in the URL path within our component. What gives?

Well, this is down to the power of Svelte – it is clever enough to know that the public folder is really for static images, so we will treat this as if it were the root of any website. It means that even though we used / in the URL path for our avatar image, it translates to the public folder – Svelte links to it during the build process.

If we had used a relative URL to this folder, as one might have expected to do so, then you would get this warning in the console log: `...files in the public directory are served at the root path. Instead of /public/avatar.png, use / avatar.png.`

Okay – let's crack on. By now, I'm sure you will have thought that we've added all of the components we set out to create, right?

Well, perhaps not. All of these changes, exploring possibilities and generally figuring out what we can do, got me thinking – what if we were to revisit one particular component for the last time as a kind of encore?

Remember That RadioButton Component?

Yes, indeed, we did struggle to get our original version of the RadioButton working – with a bit of time and effort, I've managed to fix the problems, so it now works as expected! Granted, it required a bit of a rewrite, and I've decided to use different styling, but hey – it is now a functional component. Let's dive into the code as part of the following exercise to see what has changed and how I managed to get our version working.

REWRITING THE RADIOBUTTON COMPONENT

To build our replacement RadioButton component, follow these steps:

1. First, we need to rename the original RadioButton folder – change its name to `OLDRadioButton`. The name isn't critical as long as we have a backup copy of it for safekeeping.

2. Next, crack open your editor, and create a new folder, saving it as `RadioButton` in the `src\lib` folder.

3. We need a new file for our rewritten component – create a
    new file inside the new `RadioButton` folder, saving it as
    `RadionButton.svelte`.

4. We have a lot of code to add, so let's begin with the `<script>`
    block, which contains a bunch of variable declarations:

```
<script>
  export let id;
  export let options = [];
  export let checkedOptions = [];
  export let type = "radio";
  export let legendLabel = "Radio buttons";
</script>
```

5. Next up, we can add in our markup – for this, leave a line blank,
    then add this code:

```
<fieldset>
  <legend class="legend">{legendLabel}</legend>
  {#each options as { name, value, label }, index}
    <label class="radio-label-wrap">
      <input
        class="radioClasses"
        id="{id}-{name}-{index}"
        {type}
        {name}
        {value}
        checked={checkedOptions.includes(value)}
        on:blur
        on:input
        on:click
        on:focus
        {...$$restProps}
      />
```

```
    <span class="radio-label-copy">{label}</span>
  </label>
 {/each}
</fieldset>
```

6. Last but by no means least – we need to add some styling! For this, skip a line, then add this code, starting with some generic rules for the document, fieldset element, and radio group:

```
<style>
  *,
  *:before,
  *:after {
    box-sizing: border-box;
  }

  fieldset {
    display: flex;
    flex-direction: column;
    line-height: 1.4;
  }

  .radio-group {
    font-family: Arial, Helvetica, sans-serif;
  }
```

7. Next comes the main rule for our radio button:

```
  input[type="radio"] { position: relative;
margin: 0; cursor: pointer; vertical-align: text-top;}
```

8. We have a handful of rules that take care of some pseudo-selectors used in our component:

```
  input[type="radio"]:before {
    transition: transform 0.4s cubic-bezier(0.45, 1.8,
0.5, 0.75);
```

```
      transform: scale(0, 0);
      content: "";
      position: absolute;
      top: 0.14rem;
      left: 0.1rem;
      z-index: 1;
      width: 0.55rem;
      height: 0.55rem;
      background: #16a085;
      border-radius: 50%;
    }
    input[type="radio"]:checked:before {
      transform: scale(1, 1);
    }
    input[type="radio"]:after {
      content: "";
      position: absolute;
      top: -0.1rem;
      left: -0.125rem;
      width: 1rem;
      height: 1rem;
      background: #fff;
      border: 2px solid #e2e2e2;
      border-radius: 50%;
    }
  </style>
```

9. Save and close the file.

Great – we now have our rewritten RadioButton component, which
hopefully works better than the original version! We're still using a
standard HTML element as the basis for rendering radio buttons, but this
time, the markup is more complete than the original.

It's worth taking a look at the changes we made this time, but before we do so, let's focus first on adding our component to Storybook, so we can test if it works as expected.

Adding to Storybook

REWRITING THE RADIOBUTTON COMPONENT

To set up our Avatar component in Storybook, follow these steps:

1. First, fire up your editor, then create a new file, saving it as `Avatar.stories.js` in the `\src\lib\storybook` folder.

2. We have a lot of code to add, so as usual, we'll break it into sections — we'll start with the two imports and declare an object for event handling:

```
import RadioButton from "../RadioButton/RadioButton.
svelte";
import { action } from "@storybook/addon-actions";

const actionsData = {
  click: action("click"),
  blur: action("blur"),
  change: action("change"),
  input: action("input"),
  focus: action("focus"),
};
```

3. Next up, we need to set up the data for our radio button group — miss a line below the end of the previous step, then add this code:

```
const reusableOptions = [
```

```
    {
      name: "frequency",
      value: "daily",
      label: "Daily",
    },
    {
      name: "frequency",
      value: "weekly",
      label: "Weekly",
    },
    {
      name: "frequency",
      value: "monthly",
      label: "Monthly",
    },
  ];
```

4. As with previous components, we need to add a Meta tag – this time, as we're using a different format of the Story block, we need to add this export statement instead:

```
export default {
  title: "Cobalt UI Library/New Components/RadioButton",
  component: RadioButton,
};
```

5. Next up comes the template – this will be similar to previous examples we've created earlier in the book:

```
const Template = ({ ...args }) => ({
  Component: RadioButton,
  props: args,
  on: {
    ...actionsData,
  },
});
```

6. For it to all work, we need to bind that template to a story – this takes a slightly different format to the usual <Story> tag we've used in previous examples:

```
export const Default = Template.bind({});
Default.args = {
  id: "r1",
  type: "radio",
  options: reusableOptions,
  legendLabel: "Radio legend",
};
```

7. Save and close the file. Next, switch to a Node.js terminal session, and change the working folder to our project area.

8. We need to push up all of the changes we've made so far – at the prompt, enter `git add .` and press Enter to pull all of our files together, ready for committal.

9. Next, enter `git commit -m "Addition of test and storybook changes"` to create a commit and press Enter.

10. Finally, enter `git push` to upload all of the changes to our repo – assuming you set up Netlify earlier, this will kick in and rebuild the library. If all is well, we should see our component appear when browsing to the Netlify site, as shown in Figure 11-2.

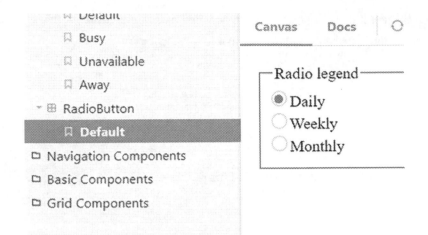

Figure 11-2. *The rebuilt RadioButton component in Storybook*

And we can relax…! That was sadly the last component, at least for the book – we've covered some great tips throughout these pages and created some useful features along the way. There will be more to come – but for that, check out my website at `www.cobaltui.dev`. (It's a shameless plug, but I hope you will visit…!)

That aside, you will notice that this time around, we've used a different format to host our Storybook page for RadioButton. There are some similarities to what we've done before, but they are equally diverse enough that we should take a moment to digest the changes made in that demo, in more detail.

Breaking Apart the Code

When I first wrote the original version of this component, I couldn't help but think we should revisit it. After all, it would be a shame to spend time on it and not get it into a format we can use in Storybook. With some relief, we've managed to achieve something; there are still things to do, such as writing tests, but we can at least say goodbye to the original!

The flip side to this is that we've had to use a different format for Storybook – this is one of several changes I've implanted in this component. We began with the usual steps of creating a folder and placeholder component file before adding a script block that contains a handful of exported variables, such as id and options.

Next up came the most significant part – the markup. It may look complex, but we base the markup on a standard HTML5 fieldset, with a label and input for each entry in our list. We use an {#each...} block to iterate through each entry – into the <input> element, we pass values such as type, name, and checked, along with the Svelte on: event handlers. We round off the first part by applying some simple styling – this takes care of positioning each element, hiding the original radio, and creating the replacements styled for our library.

Phew! It might not look like it, but most of that first part contains a lot of similarities to previous components – the format, exported variables, use of keywords such as {#each...}, and Svelte event handlers.

This next part is where things get interesting – adding our component to Storybook. It's a different format from what we've been used to, but the only way we'll get our RadioButton component to work is to apply data. So – how does it all hang together?

We began by creating a story for our instance of Storybook – we imported the action function from Storybook and our component. We also created the event and data blocks that we will use to manage events triggered by our RadioButton components and provide data for the labels on the screen.

Next up, we added the equivalent of the Meta tag – this time, we use a default export, which looks different but performs the same task as the Meta tags we've used earlier in the book. You will notice that I've used the New Components location as we did with the Avatar component; this is purely to keep any new additions separate from the original components, at least for now!

Next up, we moved to add the template and default story to our Story file – both follow a different format but use the same principles. The Template tells Svelte to use the RadioButton component (as before). It also passes in the `args` value and details of events triggered by the user interacting with our component. With the template in place, we bind to it a story – this we call Default – and use the `Template.bind()` function to pair it with our story.

To finish off, we committed all of the changes to GitHub and reviewed them in the browser once Netlify had rebuilt the site.

Summary

"All good things must come to an end sometime…"

Although I can't proclaim to know who said these wise words, their meaning is very true – yes, sadly, we have indeed come to the end of our adventure with Svelte web components! We've covered a lot over the last few pages of this book, so let's take a moment to review what we have learned.

We began this chapter with a look at reviewing the site – we learned that it's essential to have that final check over our content to ensure we don't let any (at least apparent) mistakes fall through into production. At the same time, we understood that this step acts as a way to sign off the content – we can treat it as confirmation that development has finished and we're ready to move our code into production.

Next up, we then talked about setting a road map – I highlighted the importance of basing this around two critical decisions of what you want to see in it as the library author or what it might be used for if working in a corporate environment. We then started converting what will be our next component – this time, we based it on one originally written in React, while learning that understanding the component's functionality is a better way to translate it into an equivalent in Svelte.

We then finished off by revisiting the RadioButton component – this was effectively a last "hurrah," but it also highlighted that we shouldn't just focus on new stuff but also get the existing code up to an acceptable level before committing it to our library.

Phew – we really have come to the end of our adventure! I've had a great time building and writing this book – it's had its ups and downs while highlighting that Svelte is still a relatively new technology with a few quirks. But hey – all frameworks create their own little quirks over time; it's just a case of learning how to get around them to achieve your desired result. I hope you've enjoyed the content and found something helpful, as much as I have, and that you can put it to good use in your future projects.

Index

A

Accordion component
  AccordionItem atom, 78
  AccordionItem
    component, 78, 79
  code
    documentation, 82
    files, 83
    <Meta> tag, 82
    Story block, 83
  composite component, 77
  creation, 74, 75, 77
  data, 77
  data format, 78
  designers display, 74
  folder creation, 78
  import data, 78
  information, 74
  markup, 78, 79
  Storybook, 79–82
  unitary components, 78
Action components, 7
  Accordion component
    (*see* Accordions component)
  SelectBox component
    (*see* SelectBox component)

spinner component
    (*see* Spinner component)
Alert component, 121–123
  building the component, 123–128
  in Storybook, 130–133
  SVG icons, 122
  warning variant, 133–135
AlertDocs.mdx, 131, 213
Alert.stories.mdx, 131
Angular, 2, 23, 106, 265
ArgsTable entry, 196, 206, 219, 229
Atomic Design principles, 78
Autogeneration, 177
Avatar component, 311–313,
    316–318, 321, 323, 324,
    329, 333

B

badgesConfig object, 182
Basic components, 7
  checkbox component
    (*see* Checkbox component)
  input field component
    (*see* Input field component)
  slider component (*see* Slider
    component)

© Alex Libby 2023
A. Libby, *Developing Web Components with Svelte*,
https://doi.org/10.1007/978-1-4842-9039-2

Breadcrumb component, 119
   benefits, 90
   code, exploring, 95
   conditional blocks, 89
   creation, 86, 88, 89
   custom image, 89, 94
   data checks, 89, 90
   divider, 90, 93
   folder creation, 89
   HTML, 86
   links/menu, 86
   Storybook, 91–93
   Svelte, 94
   SVG icons, 86, 94
   text label, 90
   variables, 90
   website, 86
Bundling, 250
   build process, 250, 251, 253, 254
   compiled component, 259
   running build process, 255–258
   Spinner component, 258
   Vite configuration, 254
   writing code, 260

C

Cards, 311
Checkbox component, 51
   assumptions, 19
   code
      CheckboxDocs.mdx file, 39
      folder, 34
      HTML markup, 35

      <Meta...> tag, 39
      <Story> tags, 39
      naming convention, 35
      on, 35
      Storybook, 35
   creation, 31, 32, 34
   radio buttons
      creation, 41
      HTML markup, 40
      Storybook, 40, 42
   slugify constant, 41
   variations, 35–38
CloseIcon file, 139
CloseIcon.svelte file, 137
Cobalt UI library, 68
   components, 7
   e-commerce, 7
CodeSandbox, 261, 263–266, 268,
      269, 291, 293
columnCount, 160
CSS Flexbox layout, 158
CSS Grid, 158, 163, 173
customElement property, 254, 255

D

Deployment process
   GitHub, 273, 274
Developers, 2, 9, 17, 95, 271
Dialog component, 136
   CloseIcon file, 139
   showDialog, 139
   steps, building, 136
   in Storybook, 139–142

Documentation
final checks, 272
spelling, 271
Documentation files
Accordion component, 199
action component, 196, 197
Alert component, 215
Breadcrumb
component, 220–224
Checkbox component, 185–188
components, 184
Dialog component, 210, 212,
213, 216
Grid components, 230
ImageGrid component, 230–233
Input component, 188, 190–192
Navigation components, 220
SelectBox component, 200–202
SideBar component, 227, 228
Slider component, 192–195
Spinner component, 203–205
Tabs component, 225, 226
Tooltip component, 218
updating, 184
variants, 206, 219

E

e-commerce websites, 7, 43, 53, 158

F

Functionality, 100, 111, 312,
317, 335

G

GitHub, publishing, 274
explore code, 284
repository for use, 277
setting repository, 275, 276
upload files, 283
uploading
components, 278–282
GitHub repository, 311, 324, 334
.gitignore file, 272, 277
Grid components, 7
Cell component,
constructing, 164–166
and Cell components, 160, 161
coding, 163, 164
ImageGrid component, 166, 170
placeholderImages, 166
steps, constructing, 161–163
to Storybook, 167–169
variants, 171–173

H

HTML5, 19, 53, 61, 122, 129, 143,
312, 333

I

Icon.svelte, 128, 129
iconType, 129
ImageGrid component, 157–159,
163, 166, 167, 169, 170, 173,
229, 230, 232–234
imgHolder, 166

Input field component, 51
   assumptions, 19
   code
      adding markup, 22
      core component, 22
      folder structure, 22
      Input.svelte, 22
      on, 23
      {...$$props} operator, 23
   creation, 20–22
   documentation file, 28
   ID, 29
   InputDocs.mdx
      file, 28
   JavaScript, 23, 28
   links/H2 tag, 28
   <Preview> tag, 28
   Markdown, 28, 29
   parameters, 24
   Storybook, 23
      Markdown, 24, 26
      set up, 24–27
      Svelte, 23
   Svelte, 28, 29
   text box, 20
   variants, 29–31
Ionicons library, 122

J, K

JSON.parse, 166

L

ListBox, 312
LoremFlickr service, 166, 173

M

MVP approach, 8, 19, 61

N, O

Native CSS standards, 158
Navigation, 50, 65, 80, 85, 119, 133,
      196, 206, 209, 220
Navigation components, 7
   breadcrumb component (*see*
      Breadcrumb component)
   sideBar component (*see* SideBar
      component)
   tab component (*see* Tab
      component)
Netlify, 295
   changes, 299
   code, 307
   setting trigger, 298
   setting up, 296–298
Notification components, 7
npm
   building demo, 290
   code changes, 292–294
   initial package, 290
   new published component, 292

releasing component, 284, 286

testing component, 291

writing code, 285, 286

npm install command, 14, 181

P, Q

page:null change, 177

Phew, 174, 233, 235, 264, 283, 308, 333, 335

Placeholder documentation, 95, 112, 133, 151, 176

placeholderImages, 166, 171, 173

Popover, 312

Progressbar, 311

R

RadioButton component, 273, 325, 326, 328, 332–335

React app, 267

React components, 2, 265

React framework, 1, 3, 14

rollupOptions property, 260

rowCount, 160

S

SelectBox component

adding markup, 56

benefits, 57

code

files, 60

HTML5, 61

<Meta> tag, 60

Story block, 60

versions, 61

creation, 54, 55

displayText function, 56

folder, 56

importing, 60

HTML <select> element, 53

reusability, 57

Storybook

borders, 60

set up, 57–59

style rules, 56

showDialog, 139

SideBar component, 119, 226, 273

animation, 100

cobalt-hamburger component, 100

core functionality, 100

CSS styling, 99

demoing, 102–104

divider, 104

<div> tags, 106

dummy markup, 106

elements, 100

Hamburger icon, 96, 97, 100

HTML markup, 98, 99

links, 105

main.js, 106

on: click event handler, 100

reusability, 101

sidebar, 96, 98, 99

Storybook, 101

style library, 101

Slider component, 51
  assumptions, 19
  code, exploring, 50, 51
  creation, 43–46
  Storybook, 47, 49, 50
Spinner component
  adding markup, 64
  code
    documentation, 68
    files, 68
    <Meta> tag, 68
    Story block, 68
  creation, 62, 63
  data, 62
  exports, 64
  rotateCircle, 64
  SelectBox, 67
  Storybook, 65–67
  variants
    animation-delay style, 73
    core markup, 72
    creation, 69–72
    CSS styles, 73
    </div> tag, 71
    markup, 73
    rotateCircle, 73
    SelectBox, 69
    splash effect, 72
    variables, 73
Status badges, 178–180
Storybook, 130, 132, 133, 139, 140,
    147, 148, 151, 154
  Accordion component, 79–82
  add-on badge, 180

addon-docs plug-in, 196
BETA label, 183
Breadcrumb component, 90–94
Checkbox component, 35–38
Checkbox documentation, 188
consistency, 176
CSS styles, 182
custom domain name, 300–302
Docs tab, 175
downloading, 14
EXPERIMENTAL label, 182
input field component, 23,
    24, 26, 27
new domain, 304
npm install command, 181
page:null change, 177
plug-in, 181
publish, 295
readme file, 304–307
SelectBox component, 57–59
set up, 15–17
SideBar, 209
SideBar component, 101–105
Slider component, 47, 48, 50
Spinner component, 65–67
Tabs component, 111–113
updated DNS, 303
Svelte, 324
  approach/strategy, 8, 9, 18
  architecture, 1, 3
  automation, 17
  components, 312
  demo component, 6
  dependencies, 3, 14

error message, 17
files, 6
GitHub, 4
installation, 11–13
interoperability, 3
Node commands, 5
npx sb init command, 17
package.json, 6, 17
server, 14
src folder, 5, 6
Storybook, 14, 17, 18
tools, 10
version, 4
Vite, 14
weather-app folder, 5
weather component demo, 4, 5
website, 18
SvelteKit, 23
svelte:options tag, 96, 100, 110,
    159–161, 163, 166, 237,
    313, 317
Svelte syntax, 128
Svelte Testing Library (STL),
    237–239, 317, 324, 335
  preparation for testing, 242
  testing components, 241
  web components, 240, 241
  writing tests, 241, 243, 245,
    247, 248
Svelte web components, 78, 158,
    163, 237, 240, 268, 334
Switch, 26, 37, 49, 59, 67, 93, 113,
    129, 132, 141, 150, 153, 257,
    266, 281, 283, 312, 331

T, U, V

TableDocs.mdx file, 168,
    170, 230
Table.stories.mdx, 168, 171
Tabs component
  accessibility, 111
  adding call, 115
  adding variation, 114
  code, exploring, 110
  creation, 107–109
  <div> tags, 107, 118
  <Meta> tag, 115
  markup block, 119
  Story block, 115
  Storybook, 111–113
  variants, 115–118
Tags, 312
Tailwind, 101
Test coverage, 310, 324
toMatchSnapshot()
    function, 249
Tooltip component
  code changes, 151
  steps, building, 143–147
  in Storybook, 148–151
  values, 147
  variants, 152–154

W, X, Y, Z

Warning message, 133, 134
Web components, 2, 3, 100, 110,
    157, 250, 267

Printed in the United States
by Baker & Taylor Publisher Services